Clear Big Pictures—Full Room Vision on this Crosley Family Theatre Screen

ORDINARY VIEWING | CROSLEY VIEWING

CROSLEY *Full Room Vision*
puts every seat on the 50-yard line!

17-inch All-Entertainment Console Model 11-444 (Rectangular Tube) includes superb tone-engineered radio, 3-speed record player, is one of the 20 magnificent new models for 1951.

Brings you every play in clear, sharp big pictures . . . from the widest viewing angle

When you watch football on the new Crosley, let the players do the huddling! There'll be no more scrambling for position, no crowding of chairs "out front" at your house—because Crosley Family Theatre Television gives you *Full Room Vision.*

Contoured like the proscenium arch of a stage, the exclusive Family Theatre Screen*has a wider viewing angle . . . is tilted slightly forward to absorb stray light, and give you clear, crisp big pictures!

Then, Crosley's new Super-Powered Circuit provides the plus-power you need for big 16-inch, 17-inch, and 19-inch picture tubes.

With Crosley's new Precision Contrast Control you can adjust the intensity of the picture's "whites" and "greys," without weakening the "blacks." And with Crosley's improved Unituner you enjoy quick, sharp tuning without inter-channel interference.

And you get Crosley's patented—and exclusive—Built-in Automatic Dual Antenna, that is fully directional and requires no manual adjustment. Actually two aerials in one, it is designed for peak performance on all channels.

All this and pace-setting styling, too . . . for Crosley leads with twenty new 1951 models with big 16-, 17-, and 19-inch picture tubes . . . consoles and table models . . . traditional and modern . . . in mahogany, walnut, and blond wood veneers. See them today at your Crosley Dealer's!

*Pat. Pending

CROSLEY
Family Theatre Television

Crosley Division
Cincinnati 25, Ohio   (AVCO)   **Better Products for Happier Living**
Shelvador® Refrigerators .. Freezers ... Sinks ... Garbage Disposers .:. Radios .:. Electric Ranges.:. Electric Water Heaters ... Steel Kitchen Cabinets ... Television

THE PACE-SETTING DESIGNS ARE COMING FROM CROSLEY!

"There are some things which are impossible to know. But it is impossible to know these things."

— *Louis Jaffe*

"The hardest thing to know is what to do next."

— *Ira Schneider*

"The hardest thing to know is when to stop."

— *Dean Evenson*

Guerrilla
Television

Holt, Rinehart and Winston
New York • Chicago • San Francisco

Library of Congress Catalog Card Number: 75-160464

Published November, 1971
Third Printing, March, 1972

Designer: Ant Farm

ISBN: (Hardbound): 0-03-086714-2
ISBN: (Paperback): 0-03-086735-5

Printed in the United States of America

Acknowledgment is made for use of: Pages from "Closed-Circuit Television Handbook"; © 1964 by Howard W. Sams & Co., Inc.; Indianapolis, Indiana. Excerpts from The FCC and CATV: Overkill (prepared in response to the FCC's proposed rules of December 13, 1968) by permission of the National Cable Television Association, Inc.

ACKNOWLEDGMENT

The words in this book are solely my own, but the ideas are not. Wherever I have used specific phrases or articulations of concepts taken from someone else I have given credit in the text. Otherwise, the experience recounted here is the result of working with and feeding back to various people over the last two years and **Guerrilla Television** is thus a collective energy.

Special mention must go to Paul Ryan, Frank Gillette, Ira Schneider, Louis Jaffe, and Megan Williams, who were, and in some cases still are, the core people in my working relationships.

Other people with whom I work at Raindance and who have been particularly helpful are Beryl Korot; Dean and Dudley Evenson; and Jeff Casdin and Art Anderson, of Source Associates.

I'd also like to mention Gerald Moore, of **Life** magazine, who, although he is not involved in **Guerrilla Television** or its concepts, gave me both encouragement and opportunities to develop whatever marketable skills I have as a writer. (See Process Notes.)

Finally, the ideas listed here are not proprietary to Raindance. Working with other people from different video groups over the last two years has meant an environment where we all could thrive and help each other.

Knowing and being around the following people has been particularly helpful: The Videofreex: Nancy Cain, Skip Blumberg, David Cort, Bart Friedman, Davidson Gigliotti, Chuck Kennedy, Curtis Ratcliff, Parry Teasdale, Carol Vontobel, and Ann Woodward. Ken Marsh and Elliott Glass of People's Video Theater; and my friend Allen Rucker and his partners, Pat Crowley, Richard Kletter, and Shelly Surpin of Media Access Center.

CONTENTS
I. META-MANUAL
II. MANUAL

Fig. 137b. Video death-ray at California test site,1952. [USAF]

PROCESS NOTES

The term "guerrilla" in conjunction with media was first used, as far as I know, by Paul Ryan several years ago when he coined the phrase "cybernetic guerrilla warfare."

It was then picked up in a lame article on alternate television by **New York Magazine** entitled "The Alternate Media Guerrillas," and subsequently was used straight "Guerrilla Television," as the heading on an equally distorting **Newsweek** article.

After finishing the total text I discovered a book by Abbie Hoffman called **Steal This Book**, with a small subsection, "Guerrilla Television," but, typically, it deals only with one fringe use of the medium (breaking into broadcast-TV signals with your own transmitter) and offers no suggestions on how people can build their own support system instead of ripping off others'.

People reading this book with a similar frame of mind will be disappointed because it does not deal with clandestine, physical subversion at all, but instead suggests open and non-physical, or process, information tools.

The use of the word "guerrilla" is a sort of bridge between an old and a new consciousness. The name of our publication, **Radical Software,** performs a similar function. Most people think of something "radical" as being political, but we are not. We do, however, believe in post-political solutions to cultural problems which are *radical* in their discontinuity with the past. Thus, our use of the adjective acts to lure people from an old context (the political) into our own.

There are also other publishing facts which you should know. The first is that Holt, Rinehart and Winston is owned by CBS whom I have criticized strongly in the text. Rather than have some reviewer gleefully point out this irony, I do it for you.

That Holt, Rinehart and Winston is owned by CBS was a secondary consideration in how I felt about it as a potential publisher. I am not particularly concerned about generating profits for CBS, because it is more to their credit than to their detriment that they will support critical viewpoints (after all, that's what everyone asks them to do on TV).

Secondly, Holt, Rinehart and Winston was able to meet our specifications that the book be published as quickly as possible and that it sell for as little as possible. We did not have the wherewithal to publish the book ourselves, nor the necessary distribution.

Finally, all the book money — advance and potential royalties — is going to Raindance, not to me personally.

Meta-Manual

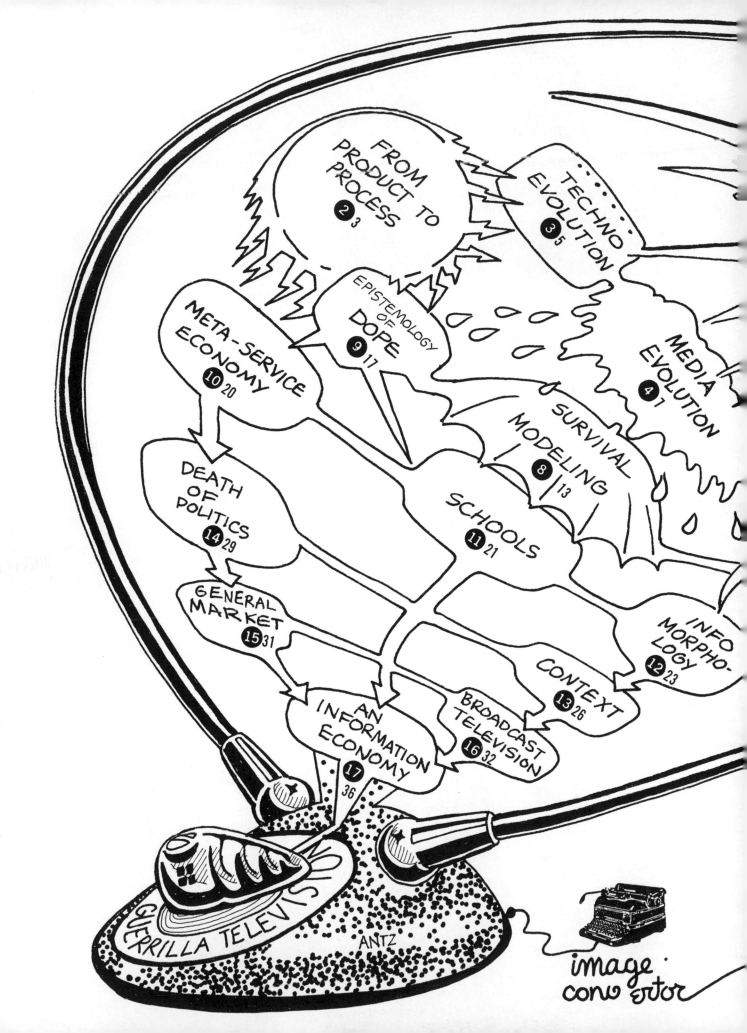

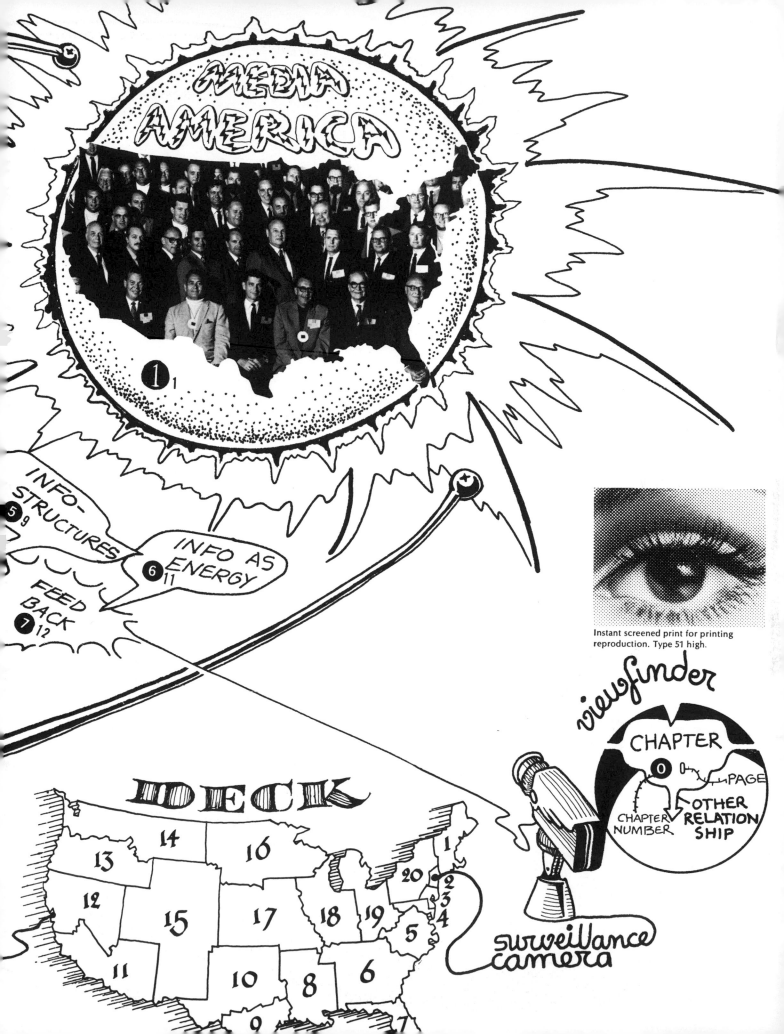

Americans are information junkies.

Almost every American home has a television set which is turned on an average of five-and-a-half hours a day as part of the environment, regardless of what's playing.

"All-news-all-the-time" radio stations re-cycle information every fifteen minutes but nonetheless captivate people for hours as a sort of information-Muzak background to any activity.

Homes and apartments are decorated with magazines like dentists' offices because they feel strangely sterile without them. Some people can't even handle the solitude of sitting on a toilet unless they have a toke of print to keep themselves occupied.

Instamatic and Polaroid cameras are travelers' tools because people know places as photographs and photograph them so they'll seem real. Home movies are a kind of surrogate sperm which ensure biological continuity on an information level. Taking pictures, regardless of content, has become an end in itself.

Organisms have always needed a minimum of information or novelty to stay alive and alert and ever-evolving, but Media-America has made that minimum a staple right behind food, clothing, and housing. Electronic media have become looped-in to our neural networks. We need a minimum of information flow not only for physical survival, but also for psychological balance because electronic media are as omnipresent as light.

My own addiction began when I was five, the year my family got its first TV set. As somebody later calculated for those of us of the first television generation, we spent more time with TV than we did with our parents.

I believe this dependency represents human evolution: to the degree to which it stimulates us, it enhances our survival. When it numbs us, it threatens our ability to adapt. In either case, the information environment is an inexorable part of our ecology.

But just as the consequences of disturbing natural ecology were ignored until we were surrounded by omni-pollution; so too is a media-ecology an alien sensibility to the people who control change in America.

The 1960s were a Pearl Harbor of the senses. Whole new technologies conditioned us from birth to relate to a world which was not that of our parents' childhood. It came as a sneak attack because print-man, impervious to his own bias, was unable to perceive that any time there is a radical shift in the dominant communications medium of a culture, there's going to be a radical shift in that culture.

What perils us now is that in electronic environments consequence is simultaneous with action. About the longest lag between us and ecological suicide is fifteen minutes, the time it takes the missiles to get to Moscow. Yet, there is no sanctioned study and understanding of media-ecology.

This is especially reflected in our schools and universities which, as I got older (I am now twenty-seven), wasted more and more of my time. As a media freak, *my* "homework" usually consisted of watching TV and when that was forbidden because I had to "study," I holed up in my room reading any and all magazines I could get my hands on.

Slowly, cumulatively, I came to realize that the school environment was wildly out-of-sync with an electronic environment it refused to acknowledge. It wasn't until I graduated from a so-called college, however, that I developed confidence in my intuition that *I* was right, and *they* were wrong. My information processing modes, conditioned by electronic media, were better reality models than theirs, which were and still are based on print.

In short, I had to learn how to survive in Media-America despite the very institutions whose job it is to teach survival. And that's heavy. Because a culture with sanctioned education processes which are out-of-phase with the life-process can't last very long. It's just such a culture that fears and even hates the most perceptive of its children.

For the demand of media-children that schooling be relevant is not, as the print-men mistakenly believe, a philosophical plea to be debated with print-based modes of perception called "rationality." Rather, it is an intuitive biological response.

Most of the sanctioned information models in Media-America are irrelevant *biologically*. They will not allow us to survive and adapt.

Unfortunately it's not just pre-Media-Americans who don't track what's going on. Ironically, many children of the first and subsequent television generations who have no choice but to rebel against the way Media-America is being managed nonetheless refuse to see that using the media as tools in-and-of themselves (not for political propaganda) can lever enormous social change. I have talked to college students who seriously wanted to blow up their school's computer instead of demanding access to it. Where's that at?

The same people who might be naturals with new information tools precisely because they're dissatisfied with the uses to which old tools are being put are still trapped in anachronistic political models.

The media have their own bias, just like guns. You shoot a gun and you kill somebody. Their being dead is a consequence of technology, not ideology. But not all technologies have the same consequences. Some enhance life more than others. If we can understand how to orchestrate these technologies, we can work directly on the level where Media-America is shaped.

This is the software or design level. How many political decisions of twenty-five years ago, for example, have as much influence today as do those criteria which went into the technological structuring of broadcast-TV? Aren't more American communities a reflection of highway design than of political philosophy? Would our culture be so rigid today if early school designers had been hip to living spaces like domes and inflatables?

While you can argue forever that the latter are reflections of political bias, in Media-America real power is generated by information tools, not by opinion. The information environment is inherently post-political.

This Meta-Manual is here to lay out why the information environment is a good and verifiable reality model; why we must perceive media structures biologically (media-ecology); and why video-tape, particularly portable video systems, can enhance survival and generate power in Media-America.

FROM PRODUCT TO PROCESS ②

The moon landing killed technology. Far from being the ultimate technological act, it demonstrated on a rather elegant scale that our hardware can do anything we want once we figure out the software. In fact, no major hardware breakthrough was needed to get us to the moon. The Chinese were on to rockets a few thousand years ago and computers are about as exceptional as automobiles. Super-software in control of super-complex hardware put us on the moon.

We learned that it's only a matter of time before developments will come about once we've scheduled them as software, which is why NASA* can blandly tell us when men will be on Mars and other planets. Similarly precise predictions made only a few decades ago were treated as science fiction, at best.

The death of hardware is the ultimate transformation of America to Media-America. It embodies our total shift from a product- to a process-based culture. It's much like the difference between renting a car and owning one: you pay for the service of using it (process), not for the value of ownership (product).

Not for nothing are the people who are hung-up on preserving products as a measure of worth the same ones who are most bewildered and alienated by Media-America. (Reagan called the National Guard to clear People's Park in Berkeley because it was private property, not because he objected to the way it was being used.) And not for nothing are property freaks called "reactionary." Because what they object to is essentially human evolution.

The dominant technology of a culture determines its character. Agricultural societies, for example, were spawned by breakthroughs in farming technology. Farming overloaded into trade and generated the great ship-building/ocean-going societies whose ultimate act was to get the Pilgrims to America.

Over the next couple of hundred years America got itself together, laid out a government, and prepared for "take-off" in the nineteenth century. Then the great patriarchal fortunes (which still haunt us, especially in New York) were scored in basic tool-up and energy industries like railroads, coal, steel, and so on.

They overloaded into mass production and the automobile, which has had more effect on life in America than all the native philosophy we learned about in our high school "civics" classes.

The savvy gained from automobile production, essentially the orchestration of the production line, got us through the so-called "Second World War."

Computer technology, the next step of man, was developed almost as a by-product of World War II by Cybernetic Superstars like Norbert Wiener and John Von Neumann (how many of you learned *those* names in school?) who were doing weaponry research for the military.

The commerical synergy of that stream culminated in the first real computer, Eckert and Mauchly's ENIAC, at the Moore School of Electrical Engineering in Philadelphia in 1948. At that time, broadcast television was just a few years old.

None of the technologies which are dominant today and make America Media-America were in the public space until after World War II. (Yet World War II still dominates accepted political and cultural thinking.)

All of the post-war corporate successes, however, have to do with radical new technologies; technologies which do not produce things but which *process* information: the IBMs, Xeroxes, and Polaroids, their suppliers and competitors.

Now, less than fifteen years after they got going, these industries are practically public utilities and the real entrepreneurs are scoring in software and leasing companies which have no vested equity in any particular hardware system.

Meanwhile, production lines are automated and controlled by processing lines of blue-collar information workers like clerks and secretaries and computer-programmers, none of whom work anywhere near the actual manufacturing plant. Instead, they and their supervisors — executives who spend their time having meetings and managing memos and computer print-outs — work in urban office buildings which are like huge, on-line filing cabinets.

Concomitant with this is the ascendance of the super-psychological marketplace where psychic benefits replace physical ones and we're exhorted to buy moods and services, or processes instead of objects.

You just can't track what's going down in Media-America with product models. Communica-

*It's ironic that NASA, probably the greatest government agency produced by America, has killed patriotism. National boundaries are simply not a motivating image when we have photos of the Whole Earth.

tions and computers are our central shaping technologies, and they have absolutely no object value. (What good is a TV set that won't turn on?) Only as process are they worth anything to us.

Now the upshot of all this is that history is practically worthless as a survival model. Not only is there no precedent for television and radio and airplane travel and so on prior to this century at the outside, but even those phenomena are evolving within a fraction of a lifetime.

I got my first transistor radio when I was twelve. It cost $75. Now you can play with them in your crib and they cost less than $7.50. When they break down you throw them away. Similarly, the carcasses of television sets are common sights in city garbage cans. Twenty-five years ago they were high technology. And jet travel, which to me was a big deal, is no more phenomenal to a kid growing up in Media-America than the existence of the sky itself.

It's not just that history lacks any of the forces operating today which makes it a burnt-out medium. It is also useless because it is product-based. Historical evidence like books, buildings, painting, and sculpture, is what's survived time, not necessarily what was crucial about being alive in the past.

The closest we can come to decoding the process of a past culture (outside of re-creating it through historical movies or flaky Walt Disney pageantry) is by reading about it. That means a print-grid has been laid on our entire past. When the schools try to interface that bias with kids who have been electronically imprinted, the results range from boredom to hostility.

After all, we read mostly for entertainment, not survival, and we throw away our (paperback) books instead of keeping them under glass like Gutenberg Bibles; buildings aren't built to last; and

art ranges from pure process to artifacts like Warhol silkscreens and Rauschenberg lithographs which are an enhancement of process.

The new art media are mechanical processes capable of an infinite number of copies. Only the object-value mentality of scarcity economics keeps us from mass-producing art. The result is an artificially supported seller's market which has grossly inflated the prices of "one-of-a-kind" paintings simply because there aren't that many more to go around. Even fairly recent paintings are going for up to $100,000 apiece.*

Nonetheless, the most far-out art object of our time — a box with an electronic canvas capable of monitoring this whole planet and others, i.e., TV — is readily available to everyone. High art is a myth promulgated by pre-Media-America.

There simply are no process artifacts from time past which can compete with even the worst television show as a kinetic experience. What will pass as historical artifacts from our culture are storage media like computer tape and videotape which are essentially process retrieval systems.

---

*A truer use of past artwork which is process-based is what David Smith calls "image ecology," or the re-cycling of images. Similarly, Ant Farm keeps an "image bank" of old photos and drawings clipped from back issues of magazines. Interspersed throughout Ant Farm's graphics, these images of how we saw technology (especially television) in the Forties, Fifties, and Sixties gives context to our current visions and makes them seem more transient, less immutable.

Indeed, history will only survive as a medium if it is generally re-cyclable. Studies of ancient civilizations which have no connect to current contexts will be yawned off. However, where information from the past has contemporary application then it has contemporary value.

Warren Brodey suggests that we research the past for forgotten skills (e.g., alchemy) which were lost when mechanization took command but which are needed again now as we revert to ecologically-valid life styles.

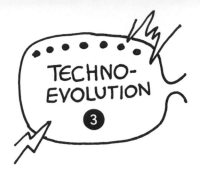

TECHNO-EVOLUTION

3

Evolution is parlay, or we'd still be back in the sea. If cells just combined one-on-one, organisms would be larger but not necessarily more complex. The best we could hope for would be a race of giant amoebas. Instead, we are enormously complex creatures relative to our size and development time.

As some scientist once charted out, if we take all of known evolution and equate it to one hour, then man comes in around fifty-seven minutes on the clock of life. In other words, the most complex organism to come along so far took but a fraction of the evolutionary process to emerge, which is a characteristic of parlayed complexity.

There is clearly some sort of velocity of evolution which is accelerating and parlaying back into itself so that the rate of acceleration is itself accelerating. Changes which used to take place over generations now must be accommodated in fractions of a lifetime. Nothing is extraordinary if it happened before you were born. Television and heart transplants and space travel are all *a priori* experiences to children whose parents still consider them phenomenal. Even the age at which girls first begin to menstruate has dropped over the last few decades, according to **The New York Times.**

But our bodies cannot keep up with what evolution via our minds would have us do. So we are evolving through our technology.

Computers come in generations, just like people. The moon landing module was a collective foetus given birth by a synergy of mind which could not propel its physical body alone into space. We send men into space instead of machines because the state-of-the-art of human beings is more advanced than that of our extensions. By the year 2000, however, computers may be pound-for-pound dollar-for-dollar more advanced. Then we'll start sending them.

This acceleration of succession simply can't be accommodated by the old model which calls it "change" and then generates distress because "change" is disorienting. Just because Richard Nixon's President doesn't mean that all of the 1970s are the 50s in drag, a sort of amphetamine replay of everything that's happened since World War II. "Future shock" is a condition of trying to lay yesterday on today. It's a bias of generations. Nobody who's hip to Media-America suffers from it.

Instead of being in the advanced stages of an old culture we are on the threshold of a new one. Human evolution has done a flip-flop. Like the lines on a logarithm graph which bunch together and then space out again we have crossed over from super-swift technology to the crude, nascent stages of controlling our own evolution. Already we can countermand nature's aging with biological engineering like heart pacemakers, synthetic arteries, transplants, and so on. Next, genetic engineering will enable us to control human development from conception on.

The consequence of this crossover is that we can no longer differentiate between man and machine. The ecology of America is its technology.

We can best understand and manage technology in a biological context. (For example, consider automobiles as a species which has simply overrun its niche. Indeed, all technologies evolve like organisms; towards doing more with less. Machines get smaller, cheaper, and easier to use. Compare transistor radios to antique crystal sets; portable videotape units to television studios, or desk-top mini-computers to room-filling units.)

This realization is only now being selected-in to our survival grids even though it was summed up twenty-five years ago in the subtitle of Norbert Wiener's book, **Cybernetics**, *i.e.*, **Control and Communication in the Animal and Machine.** What Wiener passed off as an elegant scientific breakthrough is also a major conceptual re-structuring.

Before then man and machine were similar only when human beings were pictured as mechanical extensions of the assembly line. In the early part of this century studies were actually done to see how man could better mimic mechanical motion. Wiener reversed all that. His studies showed that machines could be understood in the context of animal or biological processes, not vice-versa.

Technologies are embodiments of mind. Or, as Buckminster Fuller says, anything nature will let us do is natural. Technology is thus neither all good nor all bad because nature itself is not such a binary system. Forms on their way up co-exist with ones on their way down — which enhances the diversity essential to evolution. Once dinosaurs made it. Now they would be out of place, to say the least. And so on.

There is no possible realm which has an independent technology on one side and us on the other. While Luddites may have a comprehensive program, they are ultimately spiting themselves.

Nor can we run back to Walden Pond; it has to share its oxygen with the Con Ed plants in New York City.

Yet destroying technology or running away from it are our only accepted technological strategies other than unchecked growth, and they are especially prevalent among my contemporaries who should know better.

A better answer is to stay around and begin to structure and relate to technology. It should be remembered that pollution is not a product of man in general, but of men who are already into killing other men.

MEDIA EVOLUTION 4

Media and man evolve together. The bias of each new medium is that it seems more congruent with mental process than the one it supplanted. This happens in two stages.

First a new medium seems fabulously "real" and excites people no end. Perspective painting, for example, was once such a turn-on. Today you can still find people who think that film is a mainline into the brain.

But after a while a medium seems so natural that its effects are taken for granted and its bias is given the status of "objectivity." This is what happened with print, which put its hooks into thought process for five hundred years. Out of that experience came all sorts of biases, like the Cartesian mind-body dichotomy, which couldn't have made more sense at the time.

In videospace it's impossible to know where your insides end and your outsides begin. However, print-people in television think they are being "objective" by using TV as a radio with a screen. In other words, they wrap "subjective" images in objective words.

But kids who have never known a world without television don't make the value judgment that personal contact is real and TV is unreal.

My own experience straddles print and television. TV is "where the action is," but when I want to cool out I read a while because it slows me down. Print is television's Thorazine. Reading is an experience I select to fit my mood, not a natural process which transcends any mood.

Like techno-evolution, media evolution is accelerating. Within less than a century man has developed three major media: radio, film, and television. Each is an overload of a previous one, and was used first to do a better job than an old medium. Film first imitated theater. Television combined both film and theater. Or offset printing, for example, which was a natural response to an overload on the letterpress system, now has its own indigenous forms: paperback books and the underground press.

Then, the information diversity generated by offset printing overloaded into the Xerox machine which was initially a system for individual control of existing information. Now it is a new publishing medium. It can be used as a vanity press or to make every man his own anthologizer. In either case it completely destroys the notion of information as property to be copyrighted. Like videotape, which can be duplicated the same way as audiotape, the Xerox system is biased toward a process rather than a product use of information.*

High information density within a medium will also generate new soft media, or software patterns. For example, the great breakthroughs in biological research over the past decade have all come as a result of its being a high information field which demanded that the process of information-use itself be understood before discoveries could be made.

Information comes together and diversifies exactly like the evolution of organisms. In fact, it's impossible to draw a line between the evolution of man and that of his media. They feed each other. The more sophisticated an organism's media are, the more complex the organism.

Ants, for example, are limited in what they can pass on from generation to generation because they have no external storage media. Because man does, he can mutate himself within a generation or less. Instinct is but one of man's many media. But it's all an ant's got.

Man's media processes are cultural DNA; the assimilation of them we call education. For a medium to function like DNA, its genetic analogue, it must have three modes: record, storage, and playback.

Print meets those criteria. We record with writing, store on paper, and play back through reading. Film has never supplanted print because its three modes are expensive and demand an intolerable lag time for processing. Moreover, film technology, especially in playback, demands a fetishist's attention to equipment and environment, which is why film is a cult medium.

Film is the evolutionary link between print and videotape. Like reading, seeing a movie is essentially a solitary experience. Unlike print, film is highly kinetic.

Media also exist in symbiotic or hybrid forms. Film and TV combine into movies on television. The symbiosis of radio and TV is Walter Cronkite. And so on.

---

*Information can be owned only if it is in product form. Thus, copying technologies like Xerox, audio and videotape recorders destroy the notion of copyright because they allow for unrestricted processing of information. The upshot will be that markets will develop not for product information, as such, but access to tailored assemblages of information which reflect the user's taste and needs.

But each medium also demands its own context. Until the development of videotape it was possible to view TV as a hybrid. With videotape, however, television becomes a total system and succeeds print as our cultural DNA. Recording on videotape is analagous to writing, the tape itself is equivalent to paper, and playback through a TV set is video read-out. Only by pushing film to its limit can it match the ease of operation at which videotape begins. Videotape as a process medium frees film to become an art form.

A failure to understand which medium is cultural DNA at any point in time is counter-evolutionary. Because American education, which is only now getting into *film*, refuses to verify the assimilation of video literacy it has become anti-survival. In that context, rebellion is a biological response.

Evolution is essentially a process of information storage and retrieval. That's what genes are all about. Resisting the neurophysiological congruence of television and brain is schizophrenic. It may be that there will be no clear-cut new medium to suc-

ceed television, only symbioses of video, lasers, computers, and beyond. But cultural DNA is sure to ascend to new hybrid forms. Already people find holograms phenomenally "real."

Just as techno-evolution is gradually phasing out our bodies with increasingly sophisticated support technologies like heart machines, synthetic arteries, and so on, so too is media evolution transforming us into whatever technology can best record and retrieve information.

Some scientists for example are using a computer transfer system where one keys in his latest theory for feedback by others. The result, coupled with the amazing amplification of thought process that the computer already offers, is a whole new process of mind, which supplants "human" relationships.

Right now, the human brain in symbiosis with computers is the best thing going. But if some fabulous computer can process intelligence better than man all by itself, then at that point the computer may be man.

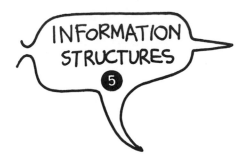

INFORMATION STRUCTURES ⑤

A system is defined by the character of its information flow. Totalitarian societies, for example, are maintained from a centralized source which tolerates little feedback. Democracies, on the other hand, respect two-way information channels which have many sources.

When a culture has only crude communications technology information flow is reflected in social ritual. But in an electronic culture like Media-America the communications systems themselves, not philosophy, are what shape social structure. Similarly, it is the structure of bureaucracy, not the decisions which are pumped through it, that determines government policy.

Because we are in an information environment, no social change can take place without new designs in information architecture. Re-design at any sublevel will only generate frustration. Many of Media-America's problems can be understood as a clash of information structures.

Print information, for example, is biased toward hierarchy and control because it fosters linearity and detachment. Electronic media are the opposite. They are everywhere all-at-once. Schools, which are based on print and centralized control of information, can no longer contain students who can be their own authorities simply by turning on a TV or a transistor radio. It's the very structure of TV that undermines the nature of school administrations, regardless of what the programming is.

But the structure of broadcast television contains its own schizophrenic contradictions. We get too much news to accept authority based on restriction of information flow. Yet pre-Media-Americans are conditioned to trust authority because "the President knows more than we do." Nonetheless our video sense of death in Vietnam is no less vivid than the President's.

Agnew's attacks on television are successful with pre-Media-Americans who are anxious because they know too much and yet believe that authority is based on someone knowing more than they do. While Media-Americans ask the government to get in sync with the information environment, Agnew demands the opposite.

Agnew is right about broadcast television being a system which minimizes diversity (although he makes it sound as if he wants his viewpoint in place of others, not alongside them). This is inherent in the technology which has no capacity for feedback.

Television sets, for example, are also called "receivers," a one-way term for a system which conditions passivity. So on the one hand we're given information to respond to; on the other there are no sanctioned channels of response. This results in spontaneous attempts at feedback like the pro-war construction workers who stormed around on Wall Street and then rushed home to see themselves on the evening TV news shows.

It may be that unless we re-design our television structure our own capacity to survive as a species may be diminished. For if the character of our culture is defined by its dominant communications medium, and that medium is an overly-centralized, low-variety system, then we will succumb to those biologically unviable characteristics. Fortunately techno-evolution has spawned new video modes like portable videotape, cable television, and videocassettes which promise to restore a media-ecological balance to TV.

And we're going to need similar technologies to save our cities. Modern urban design is largely a function of homogeneous information-processing structures. The result is an ahuman "international" style of curtain-wall architecture coming from hack construction company designers as well as from fashionable architects like Philip Johnson.

Instead of buildings which stress their structural elements and give a sense of tactility, print-men give us visual masterpieces which are to be looked at but not experienced. Where there used to be diversity of ground level shops, we now get homogeneous forty-foot-high granite slabs studded with elevator doors.

Park Avenue in New York, the quintessence of all that, has absolutely no human scale. Similarly they're killing off the Avenue of the Americas with buildings which are designed to expedite, not engage, pedestrian traffic. The only exception is the Saarinen-designed CBS building with its triangular columns which shift their perspective as you walk by. Everything else is unresponsive hard cybernetic technology which controls you and not vice-versa. Except perhaps for self-service elevators. But they're linear.

Corporations, which are still structured around centralized information flow, demand that their subsidiaries be responsible to a "home" office rather than to the cities which house them. Urban centers thus function as support systems for meta-national corporations which do not feed back to any local community.

Executives are either transferred frequently or use their offices as locker rooms for when they're not traveling. Travel itself is reduced to a problem in information processing. Either computers shuffle planes and passengers around or you can stay at home and teleport yourself with telephones and telefax.

Most of the men who control our cultural decision processes live in suburbs which bleed off deteriorating cities* while offering none of the diversity of a total country or a total urban environment. Suburbs may be ideal rest areas for executives who can feed on the variety of a city during the day, but as full-time whole environments they rob kids of any survival experience. Not for nothing can dope be found in almost every American high school.

Only the most powerless urban classes have a vested interest in the livability of cities, and they are informationally indigent.

---

*This is largely because taxation is product based, *i.e.*, you are taxed where you physically live instead of for the services which also sustain life. Thus, executives use the municipal services of cities, which are subsidized by the less affluent who live there, and then retreat to the suburbs.

Similarly, the American political process does not reflect the global context in which the American government must operate. As U.S. citizens we had no say in the central issue of the 1960's, the Vietnam war, because participatory democracy represents only hard territory.

We do not elect officials who deal with foreign policy even though their decisions affect us enormously. This was tenable before an electronic world of simultaneous cause and effect when the media were unable to tell us what was happening, and the cost of fighting a foreign war was offset by economic exploitation.

Now, however, we are all global citizens. And while we should not have the right to force our decisions upon alien cultures, we must be able to control our government in its global actions.

Congress had no voice on the Vietnam war because its constituency is local. This creates a dangerous imbalance wherein voters are expected to surrender collective decisions to the Executive branch of government, which for the most part is non-elective, and at best asks us to trust them.

It would have been unthinkable, much less a gross political liability, for Nixon to have tried to suppress a classified government report on domestic events as he did with the New York Times' publication of the Pentagon's study of the Vietnam War.

Even more chilling was the response of Maxwell Taylor, a former general and Ambassador to Saigon, to a question about whether people are entitled to know about those kind of decisions:

"I don't believe in that as a general principle . . . What is a citizen going to do after reading these documents that he wouldn't have done otherwise? A citizen should know those things he needs to know to be a good citizen and discharge his function." (In other words, to be a good citizen there are things we must not know!)

That we are asked to sacrifice elective control over global affairs is, at best, to have a government which is a benign dictatorship. We need to elect executives like Secretary of State, Defense Secretary and so on, or the power of the executive will be awesomely imbalanced when we begin to settle on other planets.

Man has this planet by the balls not just because he knows more than other organisms, but because he knows that he knows. (I think that I think, therefore I am.) This process of perception of perception is called apperception, and it's a measure of our evolutionary complexity.

Because we are apperceptive creatures we're not preoccupied with stimulus and response, but with the mechanisms of stimulus and response; or not with action, but with the meta-levels which control action. Not until this century, however, has that understanding been embodied in technology.

The first Industrial Revolution was essentially in technologies which imitated the work of the human body, only faster and better. The radical technologies of the Cybernetic Revolution mechanize control systems and thus extend the brain, which is exclusively a control system. The image of the brain trying to do its own physical labor — beating your head against the wall — symbolizes futility.

Information is the energy of control systems. Just as electricity magnifies physical action, information amplifies control processes. With the information output of just one finger, for example, I can control a multi-billion dollar network and relay information anywhere on earth. That's called "making a phone call."

Information, like other forms of energy, also has its basic unit, which is called a "bit." One bit of information is the least amount needed to make a binary, yes-or-no response. Combinations of binary decisions generate more complex controls. Only five brain cells or computer circuits, for example, can generate thirty-two different combinations. As the actual capacities of both brain and computer technologies range from millions to billions of circuits, their potentials are immense.

But the concept of a bit is essentially a sop to the product mentality. (Computers are sold or rented for prices which relate to their bit capacity.) For unlike other forms of energy, information has no product or potential mode. It is inherently process, which is why it's the energy of evolution.

We can calculate how much of other types of energy is available energy, like knowing the life of a battery. Thus they have value in a money/product economy. But information simply is not information unless it's applied, or processed.

The more process-oriented an information medium is, the sillier it seems as a product. That's why we approve of book collecting, indulge people

who collect old magazines, and lock up people who hoard old newspapers.

An unapplied bit is at best a fact. In context, it can become information. Here's an example: It is a fact that there is a chair in my room. When that chair is out of the way or I have no use for it, it remains a fact, a piece of data. But if I need the chair or it's in my way as I move around the room, then it enters into a feedback loop and becomes information.

Very little of what we experience is information, although everything is data. As you read this page only the words and paper are being processed, yet your eyes are also taking in the book binding, maybe the table it's resting on, and so on. Not to mention what your other senses are doing. Meanwhile inside your head previously assimilated data may be flipping into new contexts and thus becoming information independent of any external input.

Try this. Imagine the difference between yelling "fire" in the proverbial crowded theater and in your bathroom. Clearly the value of the information can be measured only in process. Information out-of-context is merely data or if particularly misplaced: dada.

Gregory Bateson thus defines information as "a difference that makes a difference." And Norbert Wiener has pointed out that clichés, because they are so familiar, have practically no information value. In other words, information is not information unless it reveals something new.

This means that unlike other forms of energy, which can ultimately be neither created nor lost, only re-distributed, information is inherently regenerative, or negentropic. (Negentropy is the reverse of entropy. Both words are from the lexicon of cybernetics. I acquired these elegant tools of thought only after I completed my formal education. Unless maybe you were a physics or an engineering student they were probably left out of your education too.)

Unless information regenerates from a past state there are no differences to transform. This book is a synergy of books I've read and experiences I've had. If everyone who reads it thinks it's a lot of crap then the transforms will remain personal. But if it makes sense to others then its range of regeneration will be greater and its function will become one of expanded consciousness, which is the drift of evolution.

7 FEED BACK

Feedback is the key concept of the Cybernetic Revolution for without it there would be no control technologies; only machines which run willy-nilly onward until they burn out or are stopped externally.

When Wiener discovered that control and communication in the animal and machine are the same, he meant that both respond to feedback process. The initial application of feedback concepts was in gunnery where to target a missile it was necessary to consider each successive state as stemming from the last rather than assuming an even velocity over the range of firing.

Before feedback came along people believed that the universe was a big machine wherein each action was initiated independent of the preceding one. And God was the mechanic who kept the thing running.

That was groovy for a long time because with a seemingly inexhaustible supply of resources we didn't have to worry about consequences. That's how pollution happened. Pollution is empirical evidence of feedback.

Evolution proceeds through feedback. Nature selects-in those creatures which are going to make it by the environment feeding back to animals and vice-versa. When the two are congruent, as with say an aardvark's long nose and enough ants to go around, then survival is enhanced. When the characteristics of an organism deviate from what the environment can feed back, then it perishes. Without feedback a creature exists in a vacuum and that's impossible.

Man, thinker that he is, experiences not just physical feedback, but psychological as well. In fact, feedback is a prerequisite for the verification of experience. People who get no feedback or who refuse it become autistic or catatonic.

In Media-America, our information structures are so designed as to minimize feedback. There is no feeding back to broadcast television; you can call up a radio talk show but the announcer usually works you over; and there's only so many times you can write a "letter-to-the-editor."

This makes for incredible cultural tension because on the one hand people cannot ignore media evolution, while on the other they require feedback for psychological balance. The result was the 1960s: every conceivable special interest group, which was informationally disenfranchised, indulged in a sort of "mass media therapy" where they created events to get coverage, and then rushed home to see the verification of their experience on TV.

Mass media therapy, however, is at best an *ad hoc* remedy for social problems because it demands abnormal behavior which cannot be integrated into normal living patterns.

The now legendary 1968 Democratic convention was energizing for people who were on the streets of Chicago because it was extraordinary in a superficial way that life is not: demonstrations and combat, staying up all night listening to music and smoking dope, a clear-cut enemy, and so on. That's exhilarating stuff, but totally unapplicable to an ongoing life style. The streets may belong to the people, but they're a crummy place to live.

But if our information structures are so designed as to minimize feedback and verify only what is essentially abnormal behavior, the psychological survival of Media-America is threatened. And mass media therapy will continue.

Moreover, if people are unable to believe that their collective will has a collective effect on the physical environment, they retreat from their feelings of impotency into conspiracy theories of social action.

Such a lack of feedback is exactly the opposite of democracy in America as de Tocqueville saw it: decentralized, self-governing units of people who could see that their decisions were being carried out.

It's nostalgia to think that that type of balance can be restored politically when politics are a function of Media-America, not vice-versa. Only through a radical re-design of its information structures to incorporate two-way, decentralized inputs can Media-America optimize the feedback it needs to come back to its senses.

SURVIVAL MODELING

Media-America is on information overload. The proliferation of information technology from techno-evolution and media evolution has revealed a sort of Parkinson's Law of Media: "Information expands so as to fill the channels available for its dissemination."

The result is that everyone feels they have to know more, instead of knowing differently. Thus people sign up for speed reading courses but refuse to try smoking dope. Or they subscribe to news-magazines which haven't changed their formats very much in the last thirty years instead of finding re-organized print resources like the **Whole Earth Catalog.**

But no system can survive continual overload unless it's re-structured. When electrical systems keep burning out or dams break we don't re-design them the same way. Similarly, the way to respond to "all-information-all-the-time" isn't to try to pump more into the same old head, but to treat it as a new medium, and expand your head.

It's unlikely there will be a significant, discrete new medium beyond television. Instead we're going to have symbioses of media. Things like Xerox machines giving a print-out of a televised copy of the daily newspaper; three media in one; or model testing by community groups using computer terminals to cure problems. (All electronic information can be transmitted as the same type of binary pulse. Thus the cable in cable television can supply any type of end-terminal from TV to computers to holographic chambers.)

"All-information-all-the-time" is thus an amalgam of media which transcends any specific hardware configuration. It is in essence a soft medium and requires new software patterns instead of beefing-up the old models. (It is also verification of the ultimate ascension of media evolution to a purely process condition in which mind will succeed mind independent of gross matter.)

Only reasonably adequate criteria of perceptual relevance permit a species to survive. If output — behavorial, genetic, or otherwise — doesn't sensibly correspond to input the species courts extinction. Almost any model can, of course, be verified by the user if he tries hard enough (that's what paranoia's all about), but some enhance survival more than others.

If I believed, for example, that there are no automobiles on city streets during rush hours, unless I modified that model very quickly, I'd be wiped out.

The breakdown of old models and the inability of authority to legitimize new ones by understanding that Media-America is discontinuous with the past is central to the crisis in our culture.

A recent study discovered that kids who think their parents are sources of useful information are the ones who get along best with mom and dad.

Formal education, *i.e.,* school, is exclusively a survival process. Creativity is a high form of survival because it optimizes flexibility. Kids who rebel at the inflexibility of schools are merely responding biologically to being subjected to an anti-survival mode.

The main problem is that in an age of process, authority is still using product models, things that you can see. Yet, as Buckminster Fuller points out, we went off the visual standard fifty years ago: from wire to wireless, track to trackless, and so on.

Nonetheless, the news media, because they have been unable to develop a process vocabulary, zoom after visually-oriented or product information every chance they get.

Each front page of **The New York Daily News** exploits some visual event as a headline (rape, murder, explosions, labor stoppages instead of wage negotiations, and so on) atop a huge photograph which is really a mini-TV screen. Often the picture has nothing to do with anything else; it just looks good, like a shot of two paraplegic sisters tearfully embracing after not having seen each other for fifty years when one was mistaken for a cow when they landed on Ellis Island, that sort of thing.

In such a context, resentment against the young is embodied in a visual symbol: long hair.

(Of course the other extreme is the baroque sophistication of a paper like **The New York Times,** especially the Sunday edition, fully half of whose content is information· about information: studies, reports, policy discussions, with headlines like "Wider Study on Humans Urged," as Peter De Vries once wrote.)

But all the old anthropomorphic models have been destroyed by techno-evolution. Our machines do things which are in no way representative of physical extensions. A moon landing module, for example, has absolutely no traditional, visual aerodynamic characteristics. And computers, even if they extend our brains, have no human analogue because you simply can't "see" the brain think.

"Reality" is now represented by information media like brain wave monitors or computer print-outs which are not visual reproductions but whole languages other than sight. The upshot is that man must now self-reference in an information space which has no product markers, only process.

The final supplanting by information territory of visual space came with the space program, ironically. Rockets are launched one place, controlled another, tracked in foreign countries, and retrieved in the ocean. Those flag decals which read "Good old USA, first on the moon," are reactionary precisely because they're so nostalgic.

The nostalgia is for a product-based view of social change which sees what's going on as the content of stable institutions, rather than realizing that the very nature of the institutions themselves is re-configured through events. (Governments always build their offices to last and be seen. The bias of architecture and construction in general is toward tearing down whole structures and re-building them in waves instead of incorporating time into their design. It's as if cities trade in their old buildings for new models every fifty years with no adaptation in between. Thus transition is discontinuous and disorienting. There is no respect for the diversity offered by old buildings co-existing alongside new ones. Nor do landlords budget space for expansion and play, or use materials which can be changed.)

The result is a discontinuity between the powerless who have to experience an institution as process (cops really do beat you over the head when you live in a ghetto) and those who have no personal contact with it and thus still buy the government product.

The ultimate shortcoming of the product mentality is that it makes for palliative rather than remedial solutions. We are forever treating problems after they become visible rather than re-designing whole systems. We're always reacting instead of acting. The result is that government is geared towards crisis management, not anticipatory response. (In fact, it's almost as if the government doesn't know what to do unless there's a crisis or something stridently visible to manage. It's not just because he needed a catchy title that the one book Nixon ever wrote was called **Six Crises**. His whole style of governing is one which demands visual confrontations which are "resolved" by his going on television so he can be seen doing his agonizing.

The ultimate result of crisis government is a de-moralized citizenry, however, because people are misled into thinking that things are out of their control and that only authority knows better.)

Cars, for example, are products; something you can see. And each American is hyped-up to buy at least one of his own instead of demanding a more collective form of transportation. (Cars are essentially tools of the mythology of the individual generated by a book culture. Media-Americans favor buses because they are communal.)

The result of all that, around New York City at least, is that the normal state of "expressways" during daytime hours is a traffic jam: row after row of automobiles with a capacity of up to six carrying but one or two people.

The real problem, of course, is one of transportation, which is a process word.* Nonetheless, the history of American transportation is one of our subservience to the production line. Each step always seemed a better palliative and no comprehensive remedy or symbiotic plan was developed. The government funded the Interstate highway system which ultimately undercut the railroads. Then when Penn Central goes bankrupt the government is asked to bail it out. Resuscitating the railroads means undercutting the airlines. And so on.

The reason the automakers are all of a sudden being such good citizens and vowing to clean up their cars is because that keeps us from seeing that the real problem is mass transportation in general and none is imaginative enough to undertake the necessary re-tooling.

The ultimate worth of a survival model depends on whether or not it is ecologically enhancing. There is an inherent consciousness in media evolution which thrusts forward survival models into the information environment when they are needed. For example, the image of man as a meta-ecological super-creature has been selected-out by the ascendance of information models, or "best-sellers," like the ape books by Desmond Morris, René Dubos, and Robert Ardrey which portray us as just smart apes who are not immune to ecological laws.

Concomitant with this is a feeling that there is an information territorial imperative that we

*Bucky Fuller says **I Seem To Be a Verb** because that's a process state, one of becoming. A media-background vocabulary stresses similar process words like "happening" and "trashing."

respond to media ecologically. That's why people don't like the fact that data banks possess them by infiltrating their privacy with often erroneous credit and surveillance information.

Consumerism is a similar response to information pollution. Savvy customers, rather than demanding fragmentary data about all the wonderful things a product will do for them, are now demanding useful information about what it will do to them.

This generates an overload on our basic financial modeling system. Money costs used to be the only constituents of financial models. But that wasted our environment. So now social costs are being figured in. In other words, basic survival re-adjustment must take place at the software level before the operation of hardware can be re-channeled.

This means we need a continual understanding of technology, as a model in the public space. But the only on-line models we get are political or financial, like stock market tables and analysis, and political columnists. There isn't one newspaper or TV station which has a daily technology or media column.

We're just now understanding the consequences of hardware, but nobody's anywhere near publicizing potential software fall-out. Twenty-five years too late people are concerned about the effects of broadcast-TV. But no one is looking into the potential of the technologies which will replace it. How are kids going to respond to cable television and videocassettes? Nobody asks, and as a result bad design decisions are being made.

CBS, for example, has developed a videocassette system called EVR. Its dominant characteristic is that it has no record mode. To do that CBS had to design a technologically reactionary piece of hardware. Rather than use videotape, which is indigenous to television, CBS chose a film medium because it won't allow you to do your own recording.

That was a deliberate design decision. It was probably motivated by men who think of information as property and thus wanted to minimize copying. The software ramifications are that people can't generate their own information with the system.

Now CBS is pushing very hard to sell EVR to school systems. That means that educational re-tooling money for those schools which buy EVR will be tied up for years in a system which mini-mizes student participation, other than to let them choose from a pre-recorded library over which they have no control. Interaction will be minimized when most educators agree that that's precisely the opposite of what is needed. Yet, because they have no sense of software they're going to frustrate their own wishes.

Software fall-out is a consequence of the media's failure to develop a grammar of process. Other than to anthropomorphize it, the popular press has developed no language to personalize the effects of technology. We do not learn about scientists and technologists in the same colorful way we learn about politicians or even athletes.

Yet the bias of technology, not ideology, is where the real power lies in Media-America. Our having no on-line technological analysis is an anti-survival mode.

In that context, Nixon can get away with indignation at the vote against more funds for the SST with the stated reasoning: 1. we've already put lots of money into it, and 2. without it we'll become a "second-rate power."

An overload of attention was paid to the political consequences of his logic, but no one called his bluff on the real, technological importance, the perpetuation of old myth-models: 1. if you've spent money on something, that validates it, so spend more, and 2. technology is basically a power tool.

We have no myth-modeling system for using the future (feedforward). Thus we can't adjust feedback models to attain desirable future states. Without a mythology of the future, "future shock" prevails.

Future shock is nothing more than the experience of product man lost in an age of process because he expects the future to be just a bigger past, not different. When it's not the same as they remember, people get upset.

Automation was one of the great triumphs of the future shock myth. Everyone mistakenly assumed that an age of automation would be exactly the same as it was, only some people would be put out of work by machines. What really happened was that automation created a new industrial climate and with it new, but different jobs. Anyone who's into systems could have told you that when you change a variable, you change the system.

Take a similar example of something that's not

yet here but is coming, teleportation, or the physical beaming of matter, which is a potential of the future. When it happens, product man will be amazed. Yet teleportation as process is already here, the future is in the present: I can get my physical body from, say, New York to California in only six hours in teleportation chambers which are within the state-of-the-art, *i.e.*, airplanes. Actual teleportation may take place at the speed of light, and that too is available now via telephone and television and telefax, which can transmit fac-similes of documents over phone wires.

Our lack of feedforward estranges us from our-selves. Important new materials, for example, are produced in a rear-view mirror: soybean food supplements are made to taste and *feel* like chicken or beef; plastic formica is given wood-grain patterns rather than an enhancement of its own material qualities; naugahyde replaces leather but looks the same (have you ever seen a live nauga?); and television sets are sold in French Provincial cabinets, which is very very heavy.

By embodying a nostalgia for the past in new materials we retard an acceptance of the present and by extension, the future, because the future is in the present. Instead we use the future as a place to re-*produce* the present, at best without its fuck-ups.

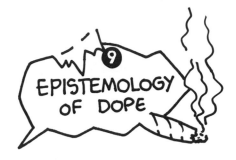

EPISTEMOLOGY OF DOPE

Media-America is a vast psychological environment. In it, most of our central experiences are information or process ones. For example, I have been to two professional football games in my life, but have seen perhaps a hundred or more on TV.

A "real" ballpark seems surreal to me, unfamiliar. At home I have a better seat than in the stadium. And the way I experience the game at home is indigenous to the information, not the physical environment. It would take strong LSD indeed to be able to see a game in a football stadium which had instant replay and slow-motion.

Yet we don't consider these experiences unreal. Similarly, most people who have never been to Vietnam nonetheless have strong, sometimes visceral, feelings about the war; the notion of "crime-in-the-streets" stimulates us although the percentage of people who have actually experienced it in person is very small.

In short, most of what we experience is information or process, not product events. Even our whole consumer product economy is essentially the marketing of moods. Advertising always stresses psychological benefits before physical ones when it exhorts you to buy a product. (And food is merchandised for taste qualities, even though much of it is nutritionally worthless. When I was a kid we were hyped-up about white bread which had, and still has, practically no nutritional value. I remember one year when the breadmakers announced a new process designed to eliminate big air bubbles and provide a completely homogeneous texture, loaf after loaf, as if that were some sort of ideal, although it contributed nothing to bread's health qualities.

(Similarly, people get upset when canned foods do not taste exactly the same from purchase to purchase. This requires taste formulas which add detrimental ingredients to packaged food. True organic food enhances nature not only because it has no harmful ingredients, but because it varies from serving to serving and is an extension of natural process, not an advertised product.)

There are then two ways to respond to the psychological environment. We can try to shut it out. Or we can search out channels of feedback which allow us to manipulate our information intake.

But our information structures are precisely designed to deny feedback. Thus any mechanisms which try to disrupt that imbalance are ruled il-

legal. Demonstrations are attempts at physical feedback. Mind drugs are the unsanctioned response to psychological pressure, and in a culture that supposedly prizes personal freedom their use is made illegal because psychic individuality is feared as subversive.

But you just can't tell people who've never known a mental or physical state other than Media-America that "history" says dope is bad for you. Yet that's what Agnew said once in a speech which concluded that alcohol's all right because "Western Civilization" has sanctioned its use for a few thousand years but has always frowned on dope. That's like telling somebody who's horny to take a cold shower and not think about it.

Dope is software in the information environment. For better or worse, it's perhaps the best psychological software we'll have until the electronic media are made more accessible. Kids have no aversion to dope because they have no history.

Adults, on the other hand, are trapped between the myth of history and Media-America. That mythology is one of the Protestant Ethic, which is product-based: you work hard and you get tangible, physical rewards (because God likes you). Such a schema has no option for process. Its response to overload is to shut it out.

Thus adults respond to process pressures with their drugs, which give the illusion of falling within the parameters of the Protestant Ethic. Dope, like alcohol, tranquilizers, sleeping pills, and even speed, is hyped for its physical effects as if it left the mind alone. Speed, for example, is called "diet pills." Mind drugs are somehow thought of as "fatuous" because everybody knows that hard work only needs "elbow grease."

But it's no longer possible to draw a line between work and play. Information stimuli bombard you both in and out of institutions like schools and businesses. The result is a total involvement in process, or life style, without the sharp line between vocation and avocation.

Pre-Media-Americans misunderstand this. They think that demanding total involvement and enhancement from a job, and refusing one if it doesn't offer them, is somehow decadent because work is something to be endured, not enjoyed.

Adults who remember "the depression" also refuse to forget it. Children of a post-scarcity economy, while they don't necessarily want to give up what products they have because there's no reason why they should, nonetheless want to go beyond them into process modes of sensitivity.

As long as the software of Western religions remains product-based, then the alternative survival response will be the selecting-in of Eastern, process software like the **I Ching** and astrology. Or medieval tools like the Tarot which were once shut out for being too "mystical." We owe the revitalization of those modes to dopers.

What's really heavy is the refusal of pre-Media-Americans to recognize that dope is a tool, and thus, like any tool, it has both uses and mis-uses. The result is an all-or-nothing attitude on both sides. There are few reliable places to get information on how to discriminate between good or bad drugs, or on what are reasonable and excessive doses.

Instead, people who have never had the experience themselves, or just those who couldn't handle it (*i.e.*, ex-junkies), are the authorities. The *a priori* assumption is that dope is bad but may, perhaps in a very rare case, have some benefits. That's exactly the opposite of how alcohol is put over on us.

The ultimate result is that people who know dope can be all right are psychologically, much less physically, repressed by a culture which refuses to verify their experience. Thus dope smokers seek each other out to legitimize their scan on Media-America.

And what's really twisted is that the same advertisers who prepare anti-dope ads are the ones who help create the need for it with their advertising. It's cheaper and easier to turn-on to get it off than paying five grand for an automobile. And nobody has the money, much less the time, to apply every form of body deodorant and grooming which they try to intimidate us into buying. It's a downer, as the kids say, but dope is a quicker, easier way to self-confidence than the cosmetics industry.

Moreover, the same "creative" people who prepare the anti-dope ads probably use it themselves. One of the weirdest things to come out of the whole mix is a six-foot subway poster captioned: "Did You Ever Wonder Why They Call It Dope?" which has the best pictures I have ever seen of every imaginable drug and names listed underneath. What is meant as a scare against dope is actually an education about it, especially for the subway riders who've never even seen the stuff. The result is practically the opposite of the one intended; it's an advertisement for dope.

Or consider the Coca-Cola slogan: "It's the real thing." In other words, just because you're stoned, don't forget to drink Coke.

Like consumerism, dope is an information survival response. Its ultimate context may be the quest for an information language.

So-called "all-information-all-the-time" is a hype unless we can get to it. Without an access modeling system information remains inert data. For it will be the accessing system itself, not the mere availability of information, that expands the possibility of information use.

In other words, storing every page of every book that ever was on microfilm is worthless unless we can retrieve it, which means knowing what we want to retrieve.

And when the contours of our culture shift, then we want to retrieve in a different way. The old retrieval models become obsolete. But the data is still there.

The interdisciplinary approach in scientific and social problem-solving is such an attempt at re-modeling information access.

But access models tend to break down when the information needed trends toward less finite categories. At M.I.T., for example, only the solid-state physics library has been computerized because its components are so discrete.

What we really need is a fluid information language to access data in ways congruent with mental process, rather than with print contours, which is what systems like the Dewey Decimal are all about.

When we develop super-sophisticated access models we'll be able to re-cycle all of man's past data to fit useful, contemporary contexts. At that point, the ability to re-cycle information, we'll have a true information ecology.

But those access models won't merely be beefed-up versions of current ones. We will have to learn, instead, to access information via whole new modes of knowing. It will be a media-evolutionary synergy of media, rather than a super-duplication of current categories.

That's where dope comes in. As with sophisticated uses of videotape and computers, it gives access to radically different ways of knowing. In his book, **Stranger In a Strange Land,** Robert Heinlein coined the word "grok." When you say you grok something that means you understand it fully: verbally, subverbally, and meta-verbally.

Marijuana, for example, can be a medium for grokking things. Under its influence one word can lay out a whole context, or even one look, or look at. You don't have to say anything to have a perception and apperception enhanced.

Without words it's possible to access your psychological self-structure: how you see others perceiving you, how they perceive themselves, and so on. When that leads to paranoia you work through that too. And the first thing you learn is that you can no longer make the value judgment between what is real and what is not. Just like with TV.

In short, the medium of marijuana was generated by media evolution to fill a software need. Of course it has its limitations. Like any tool it can be mis-used. Trusting it to navigate certain physical and psychological contours can be dangerous.*

But for dealing with psychological forms it is a genuine aid to sorting out input. Moreover, it's quite common to remember dope software patterns when you're not stoned. In fact, it's practical-

*That American universities did not pioneer in offering useful information about the effects of dope betrays their *a priori* commitment to maintaining existing life styles.

ly impossible to remember not remembering them.

The synergy of dope is that in less than a decade media evolution has radically altered collective perception. People aren't just getting different experiences, they're experiencing differently.

Nor is this phenomenon limited just to college students or just to those who chose to serve in the Vietnam War (where some of the best marijuana comes from. But also, unfortunately, some of the best heroin.

(That so many soldiers are tragically strung-out on heroin reflects a discontinuity between the actual military experience and the media-mythology of Second World War John Wayne-type heroism which they grew up with on TV and which their parents, and probably the military hierarchy, still cherish.

(It may be that in that context heroin is a sensible thing to do and rather than convince junkies otherwise, the whole context should be changed, *i.e.*, the war should be ended. Indeed, all a junkie-GI has to do is confess to his addiction and the war is over, for him).

America will simply have to realize and sanction the notion that the widespread experimentation with drugs is not a symptom of decadence but, on the contrary, one of adaptation.

META-SERVICE ECONOMY
10

Dope dealers get righteous at the suggestion that what they're doing is immoral. They know they're just servicing a demand, not creating one. After all, giving people services they'll pay for is well within even pre-Media-American tradition.

But dope is more than a first level service. What is called the service economy is essentially having other people manage products for you: leasing instead of buying, catered meals or restaurants in place of cooking your own food, secretaries and janitors, travel agencies, day-care centers, and so on.

A service environment means being able to buy a process to interface between yourself and products. The **Whole Earth Catalog** is a perfect example of this. If you're not familiar with the publication, it is a catalog of books, products, and services dealing with facets of total survival systems. Behind the **Whole Earth Catalog** is a mail order service which allows you to order what's listed. In other words, where you used to have to access different mail order services separately, **Whole Earth** does it for you. Thus, it is a service service.

Because it represents what Buckminster Fuller calls "ephemeralization," an evolutionary process of doing more with less, the service sector is the fastest growing part of the American economy. Over the past decade, according to the last census, the number employed in a service or non-physical job increased by approximately fourteen million people, while the job force as a whole increased only ten million.

The selling of services is a function of advertising which increasingly plays down the product value of an item anyway, and vends moods, not goods. The result is almost a pure process marketplace.

And that's where dope comes in along with a whole range of therapy services from psychiatrists to encounter groups down even to computer dating agencies. They are the nascent stages of a meta-service economy. Indeed, it's even been said that encounter groups are a growth industry of the 1970s.

The meta-service economy is an adaptive outgrowth of a process-based culture. It is a level completely removed from products. Whereas the service economy is a process relating to products, the meta-service economy is a process which interfaces purely with process.

The Media-American dream is having a kid who knows he doesn't have to go to college.

American education is still based on books. It embodies a print structure which is virtually antithetical to the realities of a process culture.

But education in this country is overwhelmingly biased toward a product mentality. The most ambitious programs and widespread spending are lavished on students in college because they are closest to becoming producers.

Yet psychologists believe that students learn the most during the first six years of life. At that age, however, education is pure process because little kids are the grooviest processors there are.

Nonetheless, because it's hard to conceive of six-year-olds as producers, education spends on early schooling one-sixth of what it does on college students. That's an anti-survival mode. It led John Culkin, who's very hip to media, to coin the slogan: "Support lower education. Give to the kindergarten of your choice."

The schools just seem to have too much tied up in old media, both emotionally and physically, to be useful. Educational companies which undertake contract teaching are supplanting the schools because their methods are based on new media, like computer assisted instruction (C.A.I.).

When television succeeded print as cultural DNA it killed American schools. School libraries are simply no longer our cultural data banks. Nor are professors who write books any longer our primary source of new knowledge.

Media-America de-legitimized the schools as the reservoir of survival information. Print structures are worthless in an electronic culture. Print morphologies are a secondary way to acquire information.

It's not just that the power structure of education is predominantly pre-Media-American, but the bias of educational education also reflects pre-electronic information patterns. Thus teachers who are hip enough to want to change things find themselves trapped not only in bureaucracy, but also by the actual physical design of the buildings themselves, which are an embodiment of the structure of print.

Print facilitates centralized control. Neither reading nor writing are collective activities. Rather, students are expected to sit next to each other in rows and interact mainly with a teacher, who commands visual space.

Most American secondary schools are thus a series of surveillance cells (*i.e.,* classrooms) strung along hallways. The hallways themselves are the students' only common room, but their function is to keep people moving and minimize interaction. Access to the hallways is further limited to five minutes at a time and otherwise requires a permit.

Teachers who can't penetrate their own print bias completely misunderstand media. They try to subject all other media, especially electronic ones, to a print information structure.

Educators love film, for example, because it generates the same type of control that print does. It's centrally controlled and individually experienced. (Remember the old textbook storage rooms?)

The reception of TV and radio is exactly the opposite. You can get their signals anywhere and listening to radio or watching TV is best in a group. And most important, unlike books, teachers can't control them.

The power structure of American schools is exclusively based on control of information. Teachers mis-use electronic media because they try to lay a control grid on it. Thus, the only radio permitted in schools is piped in from the principal's office. And television in the classroom is used as a surrogate teacher where everyone has to sit in rows and face a TV set at a pre-determined time. Moreover, the only time kids are allowed to make their own TV is when it's in the context of vocational training.

Educational television is probably the biggest hype that educators have ever put over on American kids. Even though TV has replaced print, I know of no school where the kids are encouraged to make their own TV as a primary mode of expression. Yet at home the kids are gobbling up TV. The result is that growing up in America on television is like learning how to read but being denied the chance to write.

A lot of that has to do with the morphology or form of print information. Print is basically a taxonomic medium. In other words, its mode of access is via classification. In a print school, those who can remember the most taxonomies are considered the smartest, even though that knowledge may have no relationship to life experience.

Teachers won't give up taxonomy because their own authority is based on it. They are certified Ph.D.s, M.A.s, and so on. The result is that they don't want to jeopardize their time and money investment by turning kids on to the notion that they can be their own authorities.

When I was a kid we used to go on "field trips." That meant we'd hop in a yellow school bus, drive fifty miles, and then be allowed to consider our environment as information. At all other times the teacher wouldn't label the outside environment so we wouldn't go out and learn from our friends or learn to observe our parents.

Video equipment is subversive of all that because it allows students to generate their own knowledge. Portable video equipment extends to the whole environment and thus invalidates the school itself as a place of learning.

Now it's hard to control a lot of kids who are turned-on to taping everything everywhere. So when television equipment is installed in schools it is usually as centralized and heavy as possible so the kids can't get at it without an "instructor" to monitor them.

At the Television School of San Francisco State College, considered one of the "best equipped" in the country, students are taught skills in studios where no smoking, eating, or drinking are permitted because the equipment is "too expensive" to take chances.

But try to imagine a true life situation without those activities. In other words, students there are being taught skills solely for non-life situations, ones which only have market value in the scarcity job market of broadcast-TV (which many of them say they dislike). And not only are there not enough jobs to go around now, there will be fewer in the future. Thus the school automatically prepares them for non-survival.

One student told me that the Television School refused to buy flexible portable video cameras because it had too much tied up in heavy, immobile, studio equipment and was actually saving all its money to buy more in a few years.

When video equipment is more flexible, teachers lock it in a closet because they're not sure what to do with it. Almost every teacher I've met says their school's video equipment, when they have it, goes unused. None have thought just to let the kids experiment with it independent of any pre-structured activity. My own experience with kids and TV is that when they know they're guaranteed access they'll think up a thousand things to do by themselves and start to get pissed off because the equipment can't make all the effects they want.

Electronic information is a psychic space which doesn't leave your head just because you're in a classroom. When teachers let their students decorate classroom walls, the first thing they do is slap up posters. I've been in school rooms with up to thirty posters on the wall. But they still couldn't compete with TV. There's more potential action in a short-term television access model, i.e., **TV Guide,** than all the Dewey Decimal System.

Electronic information is everywhere all-at-once. But school administrations are hierarchal. Without a legitimate information base, American secondary schools are exposed as behavioral control systems. They're not any more preoccupied with discipline than before, it's just that they have no substance to base authority on. The result is an awesome loss of energy.

Innocuous phenomena like long hair or black pride demonstrations have become major causes of suspension or even expulsion. (Print is an homogenizing medium. Print people like everybody to look and act the same. Check out an old-style "variety" show on TV, like Lawrence Welk, and you'll find that most of the entertainment consists of people dressed alike and singing or dancing in unison.) What should be routine decisions about student conduct become policy decisions which have to be decided at the top of the hierarchy by the local board of education. Systems that inflexible are entropic. It's the kids who *don't* rebel under those conditions whom we should worry about.

INFO-
MORPHOLOGY
⑫

Information morphology is the referencing form through which data is transformed into information in any particular medium. An information structure is the hardware or software pattern generated by its morphological contours. A taxonomic use of information, for example, is indigenous to print morphology. While structure and morphology are inseparable, they're not indistinguishable.

The breakdown of American secondary schools, whose concern has always been the actual physical control of students, is a manifestation of shifting information structures. Universities, on the other hand, tend to minimize behavioral control (class attendance is usually optional, dress can be individual), so that their falling apart is a result of adhering to anachronistic morphologies.

The university way is simply no longer the best one to model information in. It primarily reflects the morphology of print which separates cause from effect. Thus, at the university level you learn things in anticipation of using your knowledge later.

But students conditioned by electronic information have an intuitive, often post-articulate sense of process. They know that unapplied information is really moribund data and knowledge is not knowledge without a context of application.

The demand that learning have a context of immediate application is misread by book-men as a loss of some mythical "objectivity." But Media-Americans are intuitively hip to Heisenberg. Growing up in Media-America engenders an innate sense of system and the post-objective truth that just being is being involved.

This translates into an understanding that even the actual physical presence of a university in relation to its surrounding community is a value judgment. That's why students at Columbia got pissed off when the university wanted to build a gym which would have denied entrance to kids living in the neighborhood. Or why it's easy to see that even so-called "pure" science, or non-directed research, done for the military is a value judgment because it reinforces the context of the Defense Department, not the context of science.

Learning how to learn has always been the ultimate function of schools. Because electronic information has no lag time, the only legitimate function of a Media-America university is really that of a sophisticated vocational school, i.e.,

becoming involved in social problems as the learning process itself.

Old-line professors find that subversive because of their morphological bias, which is hierarchal. Electronic information is heterarchal because it's everywhere all-at-once.

Businesses now find that because middle managers (a hierarchal term) can have as much access to information as a company president via computer print-outs, they can no longer withhold responsibility and hope to hold good employees.

Decentralized management means that information managers aren't interested in ascending a hierarchy if it's not stimulating along the way. "Gold watch and pension" loyalty is dying. Within his first five years out of college, the average young executive changes jobs two or three times. While salary parity is a prerequisite, job involvement, not money, is the usual inducement.

Tenure is the university version of hierarchy. Older professors zap young ones they don't like by denying them tenure. Often the reason is the incredible book bias that they haven't published enough.

But hip professors know it's "process or perish," not "publish or perish." Nonetheless, young teachers who tend toward the most involvement, i.e., applied learning, usually end up being denied tenure.

A most recent case was at Georgetown University in Washington, D.C., where a law professor who had organized consumer groups which won actual legal victories was not given tenure. His methods were too flamboyant for his colleagues who prefer their knowledge in vitro.

Media-America's best young students are simply no longer in the universities, however. Some are on communes, others are setting up free schools, and so on. The only function left to the universities is that of professional certification like in medical and law schools. And even they are out-of-sync with the new information morphologies.

American medicine, for example, is heavily print-oriented. As a result, the bias of doctors is that knowledge can be applied only after something has gone wrong. Rather than going to a doctor to find out how to avoid getting ill, what foods to eat and hygiene procedures to follow, etc., we see doctors only when we've developed an illness. The result is a complete lack of anticipatory medicine, and a perpetual guarantee of business for doctors.

The standard form of institutional learning is the lecture of discourse in which a course is a progression of information and if you miss an installment you "fall behind."

An indigenous electronic morphology is the "rap." Rapping is a meandering interplay which renders nothing irrelevant and maximizes feedback options. It's also a self-defining word.

But generally, rapping is the antithesis of a developmental structure. You can come in anywhere, leave anywhere, and still come away with something. Significantly, two men whose literary style parallels rapping, Marshall McLuhan and Buckminster Fuller, are given no legitimacy in university curricula. If you've ever heard Fuller in person you know he can always do his rap to fit your context.

Yet McLuhan and Fuller are among those who make the most sense in Media-America. Compare the **Whole Earth Catalog,** which was inspired by Fuller, to a college catalog sometime. The latter is a lifeless file of course descriptions, while the **Whole Earth** method catalogs useful experience-based information and is itself an information tool.

The success of the **Whole Earth Catalog** is that it uses print but nonetheless embodies an electronic morphology: random access. Moreover, it is exclusively process information because people write about and recommend books and methods they've used themselves.

Print is still a viable mode of communication if you don't confuse form with format, hard or soft. It's cheap and quick. But its hard formats, books and newspapers, are rapidly becoming obsolete. They will be replaced by computer print-outs and alpha-numeric displays on cathode ray tubes (TV screens), which are essentially process media.

The conventional press never fails to get it off when they find electronic media people using print. They find it "ironic." It's because they confuse form with format that they have no sense of how to use print.

The soft formats of news magazines like **Time** and **Newsweek,** for example, have become a form of hardware. All the information they process must conform to their formats so that even if you had a group whose aim was to destroy news magazines, when they wrote an article about you it would re-confirm their context, not yours.

When I worked at **Life** we wrote stories essentially by parodying **Life** style. Whereas **Life** and **Time's** formats once seemed real and had the ability to amaze and inform, they are now tired weekly replays which homogenize information.

Because the way we model information conditions the way in which we respond to it, old formats have no surprise value and are thus entropic. They make new issues sound like more of the same old bullshit. Ecology, for example, had a half-life of six months.

But pollution certainly hasn't gone away. When our media only confirm their own product and don't move us to action, or at least pass on survival information, they are no longer ecologically valid.

A comparison of **Time, Newsweek,** and **Rolling Stone** points up the problem. When Henry Luce and Briton Hadden started **Time** in 1923 they felt this was going to be the American century and **Time** was to be, in effect, its house organ.

That was their vision because they felt a part of it. For example, both were gung-ho Yalies who got pissed off when they enlisted as pilots during World War I because since the war was almost over by the time they got there, they didn't "see any action."

The translation of that bias was that **Time** was once *of* American culture, not just merely *about* it. The magazine probably reached its peak when Kennedy was President because he was the one giving shape to American culture, and **Time** correspondents tend toward a Kennedy liberalism.

But the culture has since passed **Time** by. Its sense of cultural contours, reflected in (product) section headings like "Show Business" or "The Press," is practically nostalgic.

Newsweek, on the other hand, has a better sense of where the culture is and is going and reflects it in more interdisciplinary sections like "Media," which has done several articles, for better or worse, on Guerrilla Television.

Nonetheless, exposure in neither is a particular help. Both **Time** and **Newsweek** have unconsciously assimilated the time bias of broadcast-TV. Thus, stories about minor figures end with dreamy prophesies of how "they just might change the world someday," or casual events are puffed up as strident confrontations. Each week is a big deal. But re-read them six months later and they seem ludicrous.

Rolling Stone began several years ago to fill the vacuum generated by **Time** and **Newsweek,** on one side, and the underground press on the other. Unlike the newsweeklies, **Rolling Stone** wrote about the hip subculture subjectively, in the first, not the third person, and thus made it central, not peripheral, to American life; and unlike the straight underground papers, **Rolling Stone** avoided strident political journalism which propagandizes rather than informs.

Rolling Stone centered on rock music and dope, which had the advantage of appealing to all the subculture, without the disadvantage of anyone's having to stake out a political position. Moreover, the dope/rock scene is a total microcosm of the "straight" world with good guys, bad guys, burning issues, and especially myths. Thus, it is almost like a Tolkien trilogy, a whole alternate escape environment which, in **Rolling Stone**'s case, also had the advantage of still being part of America.

In place of nuance and subtlety in Presidential press conferences, **Rolling Stone** readers could get it off on what Mick Jagger did at his last performance, or whom Joni Mitchell was making it with this time.

The problem is that the **Rolling Stone** consciousness was transitional. Drawn out to its conclusion it could not lead to a true alternate culture, as it claimed to champion, but only to one supported by record companies owned by conglomerates which commodify culture for their stockholders.

Rather than give readers useful information about what they themselves can do, **Rolling Stone** degenerated into a gossip sheet about what others were doing which led fairly quickly to pure product information: a repeatable formula which sells advertising but does not inform. The *a priori* assumption of **Rolling Stone** reporting is that people should sit back and have something done to them, not do it themselves. This is a result of an alternate myth system which conditions passivity by publicizing superstars and one-way events.

The antithesis of that style is true process journalism which informs not just about events or even the process of covering events, but also the process of the publication itself, and how readers can follow through.

"Editor's notes" have always been the most intriguing part of most publications, because people like to be let in on process. It's like being fascinated by factory machinery which stamps out familiar products. That's why bottling plants often leave their machines in the window.

But not until the **Whole Earth Catalog** was it realized that process information could have high use value. Thus, **Whole Earth** tells you not only about how others say they've used things, but also how the publication itself is doing, what its printing costs are, how much money each issue costs to put out, and so on. In a way, that's information by-product with use value in itself.

Rolling Stone has no such follow through information. It does not tell its readers about its own distribution experience (which could be of critical importance to a true alternate culture). Its profit and loss statement is never a matter of public record. The identities of the people who do **Rolling Stone** are never explored the way superstars are. All process information is glossed over in the finished product which now has a chilling sameness to it, issue after issue.

Rolling Stone's ultimate fall from grace into a lust for legitimacy in the "straight" world is embodied in its advertising for itself.

It seems that **Time** takes a small ad in the business section of each Monday's **New York Times** which shows just a reproduction of the new week's cover. About a year after **Time** began that practice, **Newsweek** followed suit with its cover ad just below **Time**'s.

And you guessed it. Now **Rolling Stone** buys an ad to put its cover in each Monday's **New York Times** business section next to **Time**'s and **Newsweek**'s. And it certainly doesn't tell its readers about it.

But I digress.

The contours of rapping are predominantly my own bias. The structure of this book reflects that. While there is an order to the chapters, all can be accessed from different points. Moreover, the morphology of the information is such that no one section can completely contain a topic. Thus, my riff about schools falls into a whole string of chapters from the beginning "Media-America" through "Media Evolution" all the way to the last rap on "An Information Economy." And television itself is mentioned in practically every chapter. The only reason for any particular order is that getting some things out of the way first allows me to use terms later on without exposition, "Media-America," for example.

CONTEXT **13**

"Media-America" is my own phrase. Other terms in this Meta-Manual, like "scan" and "tracking" and "out-of-sync," are descriptive words from videotape technology which seem to be analogous to thought processes. Still others, like "junkie" and "heavy" and "hip," are taken from the dope/rock subculture. And finally, I have appropriated "feedback" and "software" and "parameter" and other words from the vocabulary of cybernetics and systems theory.

An idea whose time has come creates its own context. One of the first stages in the amplification of a cultural phenomenon is the creation of a new lexicon. Political movements, for example, have their own catchwords and slogans. That's why Eldridge Cleaver always refers to what he calls "Babylon" instead of America.

On the other side, conservatives are the ones who get most upset by changes in language, because they amplify new contexts. S.I. Hayakawa, one of our foremost semanticists, is also a right-wing hero who has written newspaper columns deploring the use of new words.

But new lexicons reflect and generate cultural change. The 1960s, for example, were given their character partly by the widespread use of psychoanalytic terminology to describe practically anything. Already new terminologies are competing for the direction of the 70s.

Some people, for example, see videotape as being merely a kind of "Polaroid home movies." Those of us working in the medium believe its significance is much greater than that of a mere improvement on an old medium, that rather videotape can be a powerful cultural tool, and so we want videotape to be accepted on its own terms. That means it has to have its own terms.

Moreover, because videotape is part of a whole way of viewing and using technology, and because technology has up until now been the province of scientists and government, by mixing technological jargon and slang we can make technological design responsible to a whole alternate cultural view.

Unfortunately, most people of the alternate culture don't understand the dynamics of information. They think that it's possible to use the message system of another context to put across your own. But contexts are co-opting, particularly in the nascent stages of a movement when, as Paul Ryan says, "overexposure means underdevelopment."

There is an economy of information which demands its own time frame as a value structure. If everyone swarms over your idea before you've fully developed it, it becomes just another buzz word with a short life.

Each magazine or TV show needs a fix of your information to feed its own format. Yet one of the first tenets of classical information theory is that redundant information, because it is so probable, has little surprise or "news" value.

When Walter Cronkite tells us the news each night the meta-message is that no matter what the event, he remains cool, calm, and well-groomed. If instead he went on the air with his shirt torn open, sweat on his brow, and said: "All shit has broken loose out there"; then we'd be surprised.

But Walter Cronkite lacks the power to surprise us. He's really just re-inforcing a format, and that's non-information, or no news. And "no news is good news." Avuncular Walter Cronkite makes people feel secure about world events precisely because he lacks the capacity to alarm.

One of the first gimmicks that the news media use in working you over is putting a label on you: "student activist," "ex- Georgia restaurateur," and so on. As McLuhan points out, when a cop stops you for speeding the first thing he does is take your name so he can control you. That's what labeling is all about.

Any time you're trying to interface with an entrenched context you'll be labeled because that's how they can track you. What they're really asking is that your process be a product in re-inforcing theirs. This is particularly prevalent with foundations and the grant scene.

They love to have you write and re-write proposals to fit their framework, not to express your own. And then they classify you. If you are poor they call you "an artist."

What happens next is that because you're "an artist" you need a broker to shepherd your idea. The broker is usually someone on the staff of the foundation who has become an authority through brokerage, not experience. Many people on foundation staffs are there because they were frustrated at whatever it is they're supposed to be experts at. Some harbor self-resentment that they couldn't make it outside the foundation.

My own experience was almost an overload on the whole process. Our video group scored a large grant to set up a project. Because the granting agency was government-funded and other groups felt they were unfairly being left out, not without justification, the grant was subject to political pressure.

What happened was that rather than try to enhance the context in which the grant was supposed to have been given, the foundation staff took its own vested interest in it. Instead of being impartial mediators they became power-brokers for their own context.

During the hassle one staff member told us he knew a lot about videotape because he'd produced educational TV shows "fifteen years ago" (before even the first commercial videotape machine was marketed). Another one told us that we couldn't know very much about it (portable video) because the technology was only a few years old. Thus, he concluded: "I probably know as much about it as you do," which he set out to prove by getting an $8,000 grant from the foundation to do *one* of his own productions. Then when a committee was set up to sort out the claims and counter-claims, this same cultural bureaucrat demanded representation for himself independent of his status as a staff member. (Meanwhile, the old educational TV producer was secretly setting up a video company with one of the competing groups.) The staff members who were honest and had no vested interest were of course the most powerless.

What happened next was that the culture-brokers, after reading everyone's proposals and counter-proposals, set themselves up as experts and began consulting other foundations and agencies about our speciality. Some even had the nerve to ask to borrow videotapes to show (because they'd never made their own) to illustrate what they were talking about, but without passing on any of their fee.

While our experience was clearly an extreme one, ask anybody who's done the grant scene and they'll tell you they feel they've been ripped off. In fact, the larger foundations like Ford have enormous appetites and people there see themselves as running a kind of alternate Department of Health, Education, and Welfare, which just makes them an alternate bureaucracy (but without the restraint of being a public institution).

The point is that without a power base of your own you're always going to be a pawn in someone else's context. But in an information environment like Media-America that power source can be

information, if you don't blow it.

The last thing you want to do is get a lot of publicity every which way. Abbie Hoffman thinks he's getting his message across by going on the Dick Cavett show, but as somebody (John Brockman actually) once said: "The revolution ended when Abbie Hoffman shut up for the first commercial."

And Bucky Fuller freaks think that the more the old man gets exposure, the better. I once met one who was ecstatic because **Life** was going to do a story on him. Yeah. What they'll do (remember I used to work there) is run a lot of pictures beneath a caption like: "Aging Visionary Has Plan to Re-Design World," and put it next to a dog food ad.

The Black Panthers (they actually number about a thousand) were created by TV because the image they put out is fantastic: strong, young black cats with guns. Some news shows even got to flashing a drawing of a charging black panther (the animal) behind the newscaster when he read his story. You can't do that with the N.A.A.C.P. But just as the media created the Panthers, they can destroy them, because the Panthers have no ultimate control over their own information.

No alternate cultural vision is going to succeed in Media-America unless it has its own alternate information structures, not just alternate content pumped across the existing ones. And that's what videotape, with cable-TV and videocassettes, is ultimately all about. Not Polaroid movies.

Context is crucial to the amplification of an idea to prevent co-option. It's rear-view mirror thinking to expect an old context successfully to convey a plan for social re-structuring. Even Nixon is out hyping his actions as "revolutionary."

The successful creation of a context is a process of cultural amplification. Sometimes it can be one man as an image, like Gandhi or Martin Luther King in their time, if the social space is right.

The social space primes itself. Nonetheless some scientists were amazed, for example, that computers came along when they did because they were so sorely needed due to an overload of information. That's naive. Computers happened because of the overload. Cause and effect feed each other.

Similarly, some people are more amazed that the astronauts send back television from the moon than the fact that men are on the moon. In other words, they can't see that the states-of-the-art of technologies feed each other's sophistication.

Amplifying an idea is easy when the social space is ready for it, impossible when it's not. Last year, when we were still naive, we knew we were on to something with this videotape stuff and we'd talk to anyone about it, for free. Now we turn some people down and charge those who can pay. And somebody gave me an advance to write this book.

What's important in putting across a context is that you know its temporal velocity and where it can best be amplified. Often no publicity is better than exposure in even relatively decent publications.* Or if you're trying to organize a movement,

going on the Johnny Carson show won't exactly enhance your credibility. And so on.

Contexts have to be nurtured to be successfully amplified. In Media-America that means not mistaking information process for public relations. Movements and personalities burn themselves out very quickly when they're devoured by publicity. Remember ecology?

*"Mass Media" connotes homogeneity. But most crucial ideas cannot and should not appeal to everyone. Scientists know for example, that a nascent breakthrough is communicated not through formal journals, but through informal networks like letters and word-of-mouth.

DEATH OF POLITICS
14

Most politicians don't understand information systems. Radicals are hardware freaks who think a computer is just another thing to blow up. The only time a straight politician will use an information tool is when he has a poll taken to help get re-elected.

But software or the bias of technology is the real shaping power in an information culture. Misdesign like the InterState highway system, the Army Corps of Engineers and the way they upset our ecological balance or the technological limitations of communications systems in general have more impact on the structure of our culture than the bias of ideology.

It's the bias of technology that calls a politician's bluff. Poor people know that if we can go to the moon then we can do anything we want once we make the decision. Thus, if we don't help them it's because we lack the will, not the way. The real demand is that money being spent on one technology be re-cycled into another. In that context, politics becomes a means, not an end.

Probably the most sophisticated radical politician in Media-America is Ralph Nader. His attacks are solely on the software or design level. He's able to enlist support on the basis of technology (bureaucracies are technologies as much as automobiles), not ideology, because armed with information he makes it easy for people to see how their self-interest is being fucked over.

Your average radical politician, on the other hand, is a counter-evolutionary. He thinks technology is some sort of trick, rather than an embodiment of mind. This leads to political heroes like Fidel Castro or Ho Chi Minh whose countries have no sophisticated technology, and therefore absolutely no parallel to Media-America.

One cop with a walkie-talkie feeding into a computer net has the power of at least ten snipers, who have no information support system. But information systems are not about channeling destruction.

Most radicals misunderstand the bias of information systems. They think all you have to do is substitute your message for the ones going across. But the actual result would be that instead of being frustrated by a one-way system which hypes a plastic product-America, as people now are, they'd be equally frustrated by a radical political message which also gives them no chance to feed back. True cybernetic guerrilla warfare means re-structuring communications channels, not capturing existing ones.

Another major problem with radical politics is that it has to create an artificial base of repression, rather than feed off an indigenous support center as in classic guerrilla warfare.

True, blacks are really repressed, but if you're white and middle-class, as most radicals are, then trying to get in on the heat coming down on the blacks for your own self-definition is parasitic.

A more genuine radical strategy for middle-America would be to build a base at the actual level of repression, which for whites is mostly psychic, not physical. This means developing a base of indigenous information to work from. It might include tactics like going out to the suburbs with video cameras and taping commuters. The playback could be in people's homes through their normal TV sets. The result might be that businessmen would see how wasted they look from buying the suburban myth.

Similarly, it's possible to sensitize the police rather than alienate them, as is now the case. Neither the police nor the middle classes are getting the feedback they need from regular TV. With video, it's possible to organize a community around cable television and begin to enhance all kinds of behavior, not just put over some long-haired, dope-smoking fantasy which if everyone did it would be as fascist a culture as ever was. Respecting diversity, not minimizing it, is the real potential of information tools.

In an information economy like Media-America, real power lies with information centers. An alternate culture should be setting up alternate information systems like video networks and computer data banks. Once you become a source of survival information you don't need political rhetoric, which is what the **Whole Earth Catalog** is partly about.

If freaks don't get into becoming really skilled at working with sophisticated technology, that doesn't mean it's going to go away. And into the vacuum as managers will come the vocationally disenfranchised children of the lower middle class to run things all by themselves.

But a culture like Media-America which survives on free-flow of data can't really suppress centers of creative information. Mass repression, which radical rhetoric considers practically the revolution itself, just isn't ultimately possible in a regenerative information-based economy.

It's not by chance that Russia, which tolerates practically no dissent, has a very crude computer technology compared with ours.

Even fascists like George Wallace are in a bind because without some of the "experts" his supporters so despise, the machinery of America just won't run.

The original American system is as elegant as any ever designed. It's just politicians who don't understand process and technology who fuck things up. The state-of-the-art of government is way behind that of information technology. We could be voting by cable-TV and legislators could use computer retrieval systems to research government programs.

The lack of on-line process models means that social spending by government is always product-oriented. Politicians want programs which are infinitely repeatable. Instead of acknowledging failure as a learning mode, as with scientific funding, the politicians cut off money to "unsuccessful" social programs.

When the first heart transplant patients died doctors were nonetheless calling the operations a success. Similarly, social spending just can't be an all-or-nothing thing. The models have to be flexible enough to enhance the successes while getting enough new funding to cut out the failures, not the whole program.

As government does become more oriented toward information systems, the way information is modeled becomes more crucial. In other words, to key a spending program off a computer analysis means that the questions which go into the data gathering become the real level of decision-making. If the right questions or the right people aren't asked, then money will be misappropriated time and again. The way poor people and blacks are being ripped off now will seem minor unless they have their own people skilled in computer technology.

In a cybernetic culture, power grows from computer print-outs, not the barrel of a gun.

Moreover, the inherent potential of information technology can restore democracy in America if people will become skilled with information tools. The seniority system of legislature will begin to fall for real with the election of some cybernetic congressmen. And the original government system has the capacity to contain that change. It's not by chance that a senator who calls himself a strict constitutionalist, Sam Ervin of South Carolina, is the one most concerned about information technology, especially as it infringes on people's rights.

THE GENERAL MARKET 15

The technology of Media-America has killed the mass market. What we call marketing is essentially the orchestration of information systems, first in finding out who will buy what, and then in coordinating the logistics of delivery.

Information technology is a general-purpose system. Rather than being hardwired into one use like, say, an electric can-opener, a computer has the flexibility to do a variety of tasks. The cost of any particular computation is minimal once the overall program has been written.

The result is that the service economy, which as process is computer-based, is becoming more and more specialized. Service means catering to individuals and the computer offers the administrative capacity to translate personal desires into fulfillment.

A computerized hotel chain, for example, can guarantee a customer a particular room, on a particular day, with individualized meals, and even a special water-bed, for the same cost as if he'd just walked in off the street and took pot-luck.

Even at the product-level of buying, a general-tuned technology can service individual tastes. That's why the automobile industry, which ironically symbolizes mass production, can supply practically any fetish in a car. The permutations of options available is immense.

Besides embodying economic evolution toward a process level, the general market means that distribution networks will be the great business successes of the first part of the 1970s, because they will be what orchestrates the production of goods and processing of services. The more precise they are, geographically and demographically, the greater will be their value. That's why cable television, which has those characteristics, has become such an enormously good investment.

Besides just passing on cleaner TV pictures, cable television can supply any service which can be transmitted electronically, from computerized shopping to a burglar or fire alarm, as well as individualized TV programming. Moreover, CATV technology is capable of directing signals to specific areas, either geographic or demographic.

And it has the necessary data to do that because each subscriber feeds in information about himself just by paying the monthly service charge.

Only by being generalized can service technologies supply individual taste because it is not economically feasible to create specialized networks. An example is a new form of advertising in paperback books (a general technology) which will sell not only specific books to advertisers so they can pinpoint their market, but will also allow them to insert their messages at particular pages to, in effect, optimize mood manipulation.

Controlling the means of distribution, as a new form of power, can be fueled almost from the information fall-out from the sea of census data which can be purchased, in total, on computer tape which has already been cataloged by a subsidiary of the census bureau. Not to mention the innumerable marketing surveys the advertisers are always doing.

Unless those of us who believe that advertising is not survival-oriented, much less a nuisance, develop our own distribution nets and relate to them as a new medium, information power will pass us by. The orchestration of distribution networks is just too crucial to ignore.

This book, for example, is as much a product of book distributing as of the words inside. First of all, the size is limited by what book-sellers consider within their ability to handle. Then the lag time of a publisher selling a book to a store becomes a factor in the timeliness of the information. Some publishers, for example, have seasonal "lines" which are marketed months in advance. And distributing books to the wrong stores can be like throwing grass seed on cement.

The **Whole Earth Catalog** people, because they understand total systems, spawned their own distributors, a group called Book People, which is now handling other publications of quality that old-line distributors won't deal in.

Similarly, an alternate television network will need its own distribution network for videocassettes if control of the information is to remain with the producers.

Technologies which are not biologically sound threaten our survival as a species. Information technologies, because they condition the way we receive and respond to stimulus, are particularly crucial. You can't expect a culture to function with ecological sanity unless its information structures reflect that bias.

Broadcast television is structurally unsound. The way it is used is the result of its inherent technological characteristics. Those attributes create the political and economic environment which determines the nature of programming, not vice-versa. Reforming broadcast television would be, as Frank Gillette says, "like building a healthy dinosaur."

Healthy systems share the following characteristics:

1. they support a high variety of forms, or diversity rather than uniformity;

2. they are complex, not simple;

3. they minimize redundancy and are thus negentropic;

4. they are symbiotic rather than competitive;

5. they trend toward decentralization and heterogeneity; and,

6. they are stable as a result of the above.

Under those ecological rules, broadcast television becomes beast television.

Beast television supports a low variety of forms, or viewpoints. The forms themselves are highly simplistic and extremely redundant; each "network" does virtually the same talk shows, entertainment, and "situation" comedies. The system is overly-competitive; three news shows each night give virtually the same information and rather than symbiotically cover a live event, each company overlaps the other.

Moreover, the system is fabulously overcentralized and wildly unstable. Most shows endure twenty-six weeks and many are axed at half that time. Good programming becomes an event and is called "special."

Each of the above is a condition of the structure of beast television. Artificial technical standards guarantee overly-centralized hardware which limits access. The overhead on that hardware, along with exaggerated union scales and employment policies,* means that one half-hour of so-called "prime" time costs $55,000 to maintain *before* a program is introduced. This militates against a wide range of financial support which would, in turn, fund a high variety of programming. In fact, only two sources can afford to underwrite TV shows.

One, of course, is advertising, and advertisers will pay only for a common denominator type programming. The other is charity, or foundations, and they too will not support information outside their bias.

Broadcast television is simply not a general system like computers, which have a high diversity of use. Because the technology limits the number of available channels, not only is time commodified and information forced to contour itself to thirty- and sixty-minute "slots" but the beast also has to lust after huge numbers of people per program to stay alive.

A standard of success that demands thirty to fifty million people can only trend toward homogenization. Yet homogeneity is entropic. Information survival demands a diversity of options, and they're just not possible within the broadcast technology, or context. Anyone who thinks that broadcast-TV is capable of reform just doesn't understand media.

In place of beast-TV we need an understanding of video as a general-purpose technology which has specific uses after a variety of ends. It's like the difference between using writing as a complete language of expression, or saying that only plays and novels can be written with it.

A generalized video system requires the decentralization of the means of production as well as those of distribution.

*There is a strong parallel between the relationship of monastics to the first days of the written word and the way in which unions and networks control access to television technology.

When writing first came along the church considered it too powerful a tool to give to "the masses" and it was thus controlled by priests who themselves were limited to one use: copying manuscripts.

Broadcast television is similarly controlled by unions which demand apprenticeship and membership (to do essentially one variety of programming) and actually forbid people to touch studio equipment.

In that context, the network administrators are sort of a high priesthood who will not grant access to their tools unless they can be absolutely assured of how they will be used. All live shows are orchestrated in advance and even those which pass as impromptu behavior, *i.e.,* "talk shows," are actually choreographed in advance through the pre-screening of guests so that the moderators can read briefings before each show.

The notion of live transmission from an open camera in a public space, without pre-determined activity like a sports event or demonstration, would probably render broadcast executives apoplectic.

Portable video systems offer decentralized production while alternate distribution technologies like cable-TV and videocassettes mean that small-scale, non-mass market information flow can be supported directly by the end user.

Because consumers don't support television directly, but do buy books individually (even though very few people read five-and-a-half hours a day, the national television viewing average), the notion of information as a product is re-inforced. **The New York Times,** for example, has a weekly book review section which is a quasi-religious (it appears on Sunday) re-affirmation of the pantheon of print. Video information, on the other hand, is relegated to one page in a section called "Arts and Leisure."

The concept of information as a product, inherent in beast television, is antithetical to media-ecology. A lot of that has to do not with the bias of video but of the men in charge of programming.

There has been absolutely no exploration of the grammar of television by the men who run it, because their imprinting was in radio. Thus, they still use television as some sort of "radio-with-a-screen." The really indigenous innovations, like instant replay or slow-motion, are relegated to sports shows because it's somehow felt that to use them in news reporting would be "subjective."

Beast-TV suffers from the radio-men's bias of objectivity. Because a Walter Cronkite *tells* us the news impartially, it's considered value-free. But television is a *visual* medium. The fact that announcers not only use a particular dialect, but also are white and middle-class, and are well-dressed and groomed, implies a very heavy value system through which to filter the news; especially when they sit between you and the real news which is flashed on a screen behind them for "explanation," like an audio-visual slide show.

Because radio-men have been unable to model a visual language, only abnormal modes of behavior are considered news. Far from being an unbiased observer, a television crew at an event creates it through its criteria of coverage. Moreover, that extraordinary events are considered information is inherent in a structure where time is at a premium.

The radio-men have no respect for natural information contours. Because of their radio orientation, newsmen covering an event demand a "spokesman." This is often fatal to community groups because it creates artificial ego jealousies.

Then the "announcer" sticks a microphone in the "spokesman's" face while the real action goes on in the background. Or more often, the newsman does the explaining himself and homogenizes everything by using information to feed *his* context.

A lack of a true video grammar (nearly all television information is compiled on film) also means that the actual experience of being at an event can't be communicated and therefore isn't considered news. At a mass event the announcer usually stands on a platform above the crowd, not in it, and he turns the opinions he solicits into statements rather than dialogue. The very process demands pulling someone out of a crowd or choreographing crowd movement so as not to "interfere" with the interview. Finally, verité camera work is considered abnormal (partly because the broadcast equipment is so cumbersome) and environmental sound, because it has no "explanation," just isn't considered worthwhile and is edited out.

If you've ever been to, say, a peace demonstration, you know it can be a charged experience of meta-verbal communication, or "vibes," as the kids say. But because broadcast language has no capacity to convey emotions, people who see the demonstrations at home feel threatened.

There is a myth that somehow the "airwaves" are public distribution channels, promulgated because the F.C.C. licenses broadcasters. Yet the inaccessible structure of broadcast technology will permit no one direct access to distribute their own material.

This is a kind of psychic genocide. It insures that all information must be filtered through a select, relatively homogeneous group of people. The result is that rather than have true verité programming, broadcasters have to imitate it. Two recent examples, one from commercial TV and the other from National Educational Television (NET), illustrate just how alienating the medium is.

Both shows essentially shit on the less glamorous minorities like the ethnic and suburban middle classes. Indeed, the only verité life style broadcast-TV is capable of confirming is that of the upper middle-class white, or white-acting, celebrity, most of whom seem no different in person than they do on the "talk" shows.*

*Dr. Albert Scheflen points out that because TV does not show normal income, real people dealing with their own problems, millions of TV viewers come to think that their

In early 1971, CBS premiered a show called "All in the Family." The situation of the show is this: five people live in a classic ethnic row house, duplicated as a set right down to the furniture and lace curtains. The characters are a husband and wife, supposedly representative of a bigoted working-class couple; their daughter, who is a newlywed and runs around in a mini-skirt and teases her hair, her husband, who lives with them, and is a "concerned" young college student (although he looks about thirty) who wears work shirts; and a young, black handyman who is reputedly working his way through school to become an electrician.

The gist of the show is that the old man is a bigot who is continually alienating his son-in-law and ruining Sunday dinners. His daughter screams a lot and his wife is sort of a cross between Lenny

own lives are abnormal and thus become afraid to seek help from their friends and family. The upshot is that instead of communities handling their own problems, social agencies must do it for them.

Nicholas Johnson has also written that television advertisers refuse to sponsor dramas showing non-affluent people enjoying themselves because that would lessen the stimulus for product consumption. The Beverly Hillbillies may have been funny, but they were still millionaires. And Julia might have suffered from being a Negro, but her home furnishings and wardrobe never reflected it.

Most behavior on broadcast TV is exclusively symbolic and has no reference to real life. We reference Dick Cavett through the Dick Cavett show so he makes jokes about his own image (e.g., he does a monologue making fun of the preceeding night's monologue).

Feeding these shows is an assortment of "personalities" who symbolically embody behavioral characteristics and thus become merchandisable products. This is why one city's newscasters are indistinguishable from the next. And why the Al Capps and Zsa Zsa Gabors wander back and forth in this fantasy world which has no relation to anything except its own mythology.

The result is that all talk shows are the same because they use the same people. And the trading-off of celebrities like Wayne Campbell and Phyllis Diller from variety show to variety show, regardless of network, means the line between each is non-existent. TV entertainment is one huge, homogeneous variety show and the term "variety" thus becomes ironic.

We never get information about the process of entertainers' lives except as it pertains to their image, e.g., stories about Jack Benny's age or allusions to Dean Martin's drinking.

But try to imagine Dean Martin taking a shit, Jack Benny picking his nose, or the "Flying Nun" farting.

Ironically, real death is also considered in bad taste as was evidenced when a guest on the Dick Cavett show died during the taping (which goes to show that the media can kill you, literally) and the tape "could not be shown." Yet the movie which followed the Cavett show the night when the tape was to have been broadcast showed several people being violently murdered.

Bruce and Gracie Allen: dumb, but knowing in a kind of morbid, hip way.

What makes the show unusual, CBS feels (they hyped it in their advertising as "real people on television") is that the father is fabulously prejudiced and uses every insulting pronoun he can in his dialogue: words like "Polack" and "Kneegrow" (as he pronounces it), or phrases like "that Jew bastard."

Now the basic idea isn't bad, putting prejudice up for ridicule. But the way it's done is savagely patronizing to the type of people it's supposedly lampooning. In the first show, for example, a sort of perverse "equal time" phenomenon was in effect wherein every possible group that could be insulted was. Moreover, practically every cultural problem of the last decade was mentioned: students, welfare, race riots, you name it. The compaction of information was so heavy as practically to equal the pacing of a commercial. Then to top it off, so as to anaesthetize the whole thing, the entire dialogue was overlaid by completely inane canned-laughter.

As a final manifestation of the producers' insecurity, the one black in the show was allowed to put himself down while everybody else had it done for them. This cast him as the ultimate hero who could puncture the old man's bigotry. His triumphant stage exit was scored with overwhelming pre-recorded applause.

"All in the Family" is psychic genocide. Calling something "realism" when it's prepared by $50,000-a-year writers is decadent. I've seen $5 worth of videotape shot by Ken Marsh and Elliot Glass of the People's Video Theater in New York City which, because it allowed people to express themselves, was more entertaining and sensitive, and revealed more in five minutes than the whole half-hour of "All in the Family."

It's hard to know what's worse about beast-TV: people being denied access, or their having to see themselves in caricature.

Beast television has an irrevocable production mentality about it. And NET, which styles itself as an option, is really no more than its golem. Even though it's not commercially sponsored, charity still gives NET enough to produce a "series" at $100,000 a show. One show, which will run once or twice, costs a hundred thousand dollars! That kind of money could support the People's Video Theater, in a style they're not yet accustomed to, for four or five *years*.

The latest NET hype, which is actually gobbling up about $110,000 a production, is a thing called "The Great American Dream Machine."

The format of the show is an unmoderated mix of selected shorts which are supposedly about American culture. Its style is mostly filmic and at best approximate some good television commercials.

One particular episode from the premiere edition of "The Great American Dream Machine" points up probably the whole problem with NET, which is that it gives the cameras to Liberals, rather than to the people themselves.

In this particular segment, Studs Terkel, a Chicago radio moderator who writes "bestsellers" simply by transcribing people's recorded reminiscences and passing them off as cultural documents, cast himself, just like in his books, as sort of patronizing everyman who both empathizes and maintains critical perspective.

The set was, now get this, a neighborhood bar, actually a TV sound stage with an audience watching. The plot was that Terkel had assembled some common folk to talk things over: a middle-class housewife, a construction worker, a middle-aged black, and a student.

What happened was that when the discussion wasn't manic enough for him, Terkel would start yelling at the construction worker and telling him in Liberalese that he was more or less full-of-shit.

Then when the construction worker got into his rap, Terkel would interrupt and lay down his own. At other times he was the moderator (a moderator at a barroom discussion?) who would ask questions to give everyone a chance to talk.

Terkel repeatedly used a gimmick from the other talk shows, like Dick Cavett's and Johnny Carson's, of almost compulsively torpedoing the cadence of someone's rap because "quips" are a subconscious language which they can't hold back, like diarrhea. The rap is permitted to go on, but only if Carson or Cavett can control its pace.

And that's what Terkel did. Under the guise of a verité, opinionated discussion about American culture, he co-opted the genuine energy of people who really did have something to say.

Beast television is a squandering of Media-America's primary information resource. Not so much because of what broadcast does, but because of how it's done. As long as radio-men are in charge there will be no video language.

Using the medium as a "radio-with-a-screen" is like mistaking sheet music for a long-playing record. One is a dummy; the other is the real thing.

Television is an information medium yet the people who run it have developed no process mode. As long as they continue to communicate their bias, essentially print information, and we're nonetheless conditioned to respond to a visual literacy, there will be no process television.

As a storage and retrieval medium, money is a measure of product, rather than process, value. Money units are modular. An increase is arithmetic, not exponential. And the criteria of dollar model investment trend toward repeating past successes instead of capitalizing new attempts. Because money goes where money has already been made, as a rule, the medium generally supports redundancy or homogeneity rather than diversity.

Information, on the other hand, is pure process. Instead of numerical increase, information expands rhythmically, or synergistically. Whereas a sum of money is precisely the sum of its parts, an increase of information is more than its components.

Also unlike money, information must transform differences, that is, be regenerative, or it's simply not information. An information model which repeats itself doesn't inform anymore because redundancy, or increased probability, is entropic.

The first step toward an information economy doesn't, however, mean doing away with money. What it does mean is that instead of money directing information, as is now the case, information potential will direct the investment of capital.

Not until there is a highly sophisticated accounting and (data) banking system for information will it totally replace money. Information is, however, already becoming a form of capital unto itself wherein information is exchanged for information.

Only in a post-product, or process culture can information have capital value. Because Media-America has ascended to an information environment, learning and research are now the dominant work mode. In that context, centers of new information have money value.

A successful commune, for example, is really a survival center doing research on cultural options. The information generated by the people living in it has general cultural value. Thus, an information rip-off occurs when a medium takes news about a commune for its own end, and gives nothing in return.

It's been suggested that there be an electronic, or video **Whole Earth Catalog**. The idea is that a producer will come in and record various skills and then edit an information package. But producers are people who live outside of information. Only by becoming involved in information processing can survival centers generate relevant, experience-based information about themselves.

The print **Whole Earth Catalog** is just that:

people using a familiar medium (writing) to transfer information *from* their own experience, not *about* that of others. Thus the video analogue will require people living with portable video cameras, feeding themselves back to themselves to develop a sense of video self and video grammar, and meanwhile building up a personal and public access video data bank.

Part of the resulting data bank will probably remain private, as intimate shared experience. Other edited portions will enable the transference of skills, either in exchange for information or money. In both cases, the edited package would probably be of as much value for its overall context as its specific "how-to-do" contents. The best tape about building a dome, for example, wouldn't be about building a dome, *per se.*

Universities used to be survival centers. But because they stayed with print, media evolution passed them by. The only skills you can learn in a university, with the exception of professional schools, are geared toward fulfilling roles in anti-ecological systems.

The new universities are any group of people functioning as a survival center, or who are learning while doing. Thus, the information they generate has value enough to be a base of financial support, whole or partial. Universities should pay the students, not vice-versa. There are a few traditional ones which do, and they are engaged exclusively in research, or the regeneration of knowledge.

As information processing and storage media become more decentralized, with portable video and time-sharing computers, the actual physical plant of a university becomes a burden. True *Education Automation* is happening as a sort of University of the Media.

In it, students engage in survival learning while having access to the experience of others through data banks such as an alternate videotape network. Especially in the pure information centers, or those which are exclusively media-oriented, concentration is on process, or learning how to learn.

Education as a whole becomes a process analagous to the way computers handle information. First there is a data base of necessary basic information and skills like reading, writing and videotaping and computer programming, mathematics, biology, and so on. The second level is learning how to program the data base. Some programs, like mathematics, are prestored and need only be applied. Others must be written from scratch. All are created in a particular context of relevance, rather than in anticipation of application, which is the old university way. (Remember: *uni*versity is not diversity.)

Most of the preceding rap is based on my own experience. And because you bought this book I'll tell you a little bit about it.

In late 1969 we started a group called Raindance. The name has several functions. First, because it signifies no specific product or process, it allows us to do anything. Secondly, a rain dance *is* a form of ecologically valid anticipatory design. And finally, Raindance is a play on R&D, or research and development, from which the Rand Corporation takes its name.

The original purpose and idea for Raindance (which came from Frank Gillette) was to explore the possibilities of portable videotape, which was then less than a year old, and generally to function as a sort of alternate culture think-tank concentrating on media.

Our first dose of money came from a freak who had inherited a lot of it and felt guilty about it. Subsequently, we ran out and had to hassle for some grant money. But during that time, as we began to serve more and more as an information resource, people started to give us money to do things for them.

While Frank and a few others have left, our current configuration includes around a dozen people with sound business help and a more stable collective. Ideally Raindance functions as a support center for everyone's individual or collective projects.

I tell you all this because we are a survival center. And although one reason I wrote this book was that we needed the money (we were all living on savings for a while), we are more and more becoming self-supporting.

Our scan on media, along with that of other groups like Videofreex, People's Video Theater, and the Media Access Center at Portola Institute, has value in an information-based culture.

Because our context is one of feedforward, greater acceptance of our software ideas means that money which once went into old contexts now goes to help create new ones. For example, we used to work with a group of junior high school kids and turn them on to video. We got paid out of an original budget which was for some artsy-craftsy filmmaking class.

If enough groups like ourselves can psych out where the technology is going, then we can create self-sufficient networks. As long as we have to rely on outside support, we're screwed.

But as Media-America comes to rely more and more on sound, new information, then access to information has increasing social currency.

As the **Whole Earth Catalog** demonstrates, access can be a commodity which has both social and money value. The true hope for the success of an alternate culture is if it can become a valid information resource instead of a low-variety parody of what it pretends to oppose.

Genuinely new ideas can be amplified in information space when they have survival value. If they cannot be, then this planet has had it.

The strategies and tactics detailed in the Manual of **Guerrilla Television** are intended to enhance our chances for survival in the information environment. A media-ecology is both prerequisite and concomitant with a natural one. And **Guerrilla Television,** this book, is a first attempt at a guidebook, one which will hopefully expand as alternate networks allow us to access each other's experiencing.

MANUAL

OUTLAW ENERGY VIDEOSPHERE

⎍⎍ -4Vp-p

CONTENTS

MANUAL

OLD STYLE: Heavy Hardware

GEORGE ADAMS

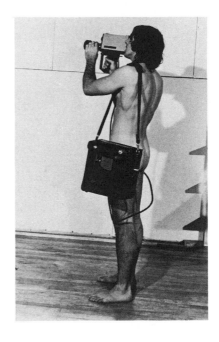

Guerrilla Television

SOME THEORY

In the summer of 1968, Sony, the Japanese electronics manufacturer, began marketing in America a low-cost, fully portable, videotape camera.

Prior to this, videotape equipment was cumbersome, stationary, complex, and expensive, even though it had been used commercially since 1956.

By now it's clear that television has succeeded print as this culture's dominant communications medium. The first videotape equipment embodied its analogue to Gutenberg. Portable video is TV's offset printing, the result of a techno-evolutionary trend toward decentralization and high access; just as developments in printing meant that we could get more than Bibles.

Whereas tens of thousands of dollars were once needed to tool up for videotape, now only $1,495 are required. In place of a machine weighing hundreds of pounds and requiring special power lines, all you need now is standard house current to recharge batteries which will let you use the twenty-one-pound system anywhere, independent of external power. And instead of a mystique of technological expertise clouding the operation of the system, all you have to do is look at a tiny TV screen inside the camera which shows exactly what will be recorded, and then press a button.

Typically, the technology was (and still is) designed and marketed in a rear-view mirror. Treated like Polaroid movie cameras (in other words, "films" which play back right away), they're hyped to industry and government as a low-cost way to train employees or do surveillance.

Sony helps Tinnerman Products in sales, training, production

What started out as an experiment with Sony video tape recording equipment has proved to be such a valuable training and sales tool for Tinnerman Products, Inc., Cleveland, Ohio, that management is weighing more exotic possibilities for its future use.

In application, the VTR system has become a highly practical industrial tool, equally valuable for keeping salesmen in the field abreast of home plant developments and for training other employees in such matters as getting the most out of a computer.

Founded by G. A. Tinnerman, as a hardware and kitchen stove maker in the 19th century, the company today is a subsidiary of Eaton, Yale & Towne, Inc. and engages in the production of fasteners for any kind of metal fabricating. It has annual domestic sales in excess of $20 million and sells in foreign countries through a network of nonaffiliated licensees.

According to William H. Gibbons, director of marketing services, this field, in which Tinnerman enjoys a high reputation, is very competitive. The company's emphasis is on quality, ingenuity, and service and sales engineers who handle direct customer contact and fastener counseling have had intensive training in fastener applications and design.

Tinnerman's first experience with video tape recording came in 1968, when it was bringing all of its field personnel—more than 30 salesmen—back to Cleveland for the annual sales meeting.

"We hold these meetings in other locations most of the time," Gibbons said, "but every third year we like to get the men back into the plant where they can become acquainted with technical advances and operational improvements that are necessary to remain competitive and a leader. In 1968, however, plant tours were out of the question because Tinnerman was in the midst of a major expansion and retooling program. The salesmen needed to be acquainted with this program, but taking all of them around for a first-hand look would have been impossible."

SUBSTITUTE FOR A PLANT TOUR

In cooperation with its advertising agency, Tinnerman arrived at what proved to be an ideal solution: use of a Sony VideoRover, which is a battery-powered portable video tape recording system, backed up by a Sony Videocorder® video tape recorder for tape playback on four TV monitors.

The VideoRover was selected, according to Gibbons, because it provided maximum flexibility: It can be carried and operated by one man and used just about anywhere a man can go. Together with the playback equipment, it could serve to bring the plant to the salesmen assembled at the meetings.

Top executives were taped in their offices, presenting their views on the company's products and its advertising needs.

On the evening before the two-day sales meeting, Tinnerman's cameraman, a member of the advertising department, passed quietly through a social gathering, unobtrusively taping with the VideoRover. Few of the men paid any attention to him.

The next morning, as they strolled into the meeting room, most of the men were busy talking to each other, while four monitors, placed so that everyone in the room could see a picture, were playing the tape recorded the night before.

"A man would be chatting," Gibbons said, "and all of a sudden he'd hear his voice in last night's conversation. He'd blanch, wondering just what he'd said, and then relax when he heard nothing embarrassing. It would be an understatement to say that we captured the men's attention."

Rather than enhance the possibilities inherent in electronics, portable video cameras are still designed like guns with triggers for sighting and "shooting" people.

(Electronics are decentralized in the truest sense of the word. The video signal travels from camera to recording deck through a cable which can be both indefinitely long and unhindered by curving. This means your eye can monitor a TV screen which previews what's being recorded without it having to set in a straight line behind the camera lens, as with film. Instead, a TV camera can even be wirelessly controlled from another planet, as our space program has shown.

(Nonetheless, manufacturers believe that to sell video cameras they must make them look like movie cameras because that's what consumers know, even though the two technologies are radically dissimilar.)

More important, none of the manufacturers, or the educators along with them, seized on the real potential of portable video: that it's the perfect tool for media-children who were raised on TV but never allowed to make their own.

I don't know of any educators who conceive of TV as a tool in the same way they see writing: that every kid must be taught how to do it as a prerequisite skill, even though only a small fraction will become artists in the medium.

The only response of American education to television has been in terms of content. How can we *give* kids better programming?

Out of this mentality has come the juggernaut of "Sesame Street" which teaches other media (reading, writing, counting), but refuses to explore its own medium.

Anything but a radical break with the past, it is the ultimate triumph of the structure it pretends to oppose because it legitimizes the whole broadcast-TV context as acceptable, without question, for children.

"Sesame Street" children are supposed to be consumers who passively sit in front of a one-way TV "receiver" and are bombarded with information at the cadence of advertising messages.

The truly necessary change, one of structure, not content, eludes American education because of its heavy print bias which imagines a schism between actor and audience.

'COMMERCIALS' THAT TEACH — The four scenes above are taken from animated cartoon spots created for the Children's Television Workshop show for preschool children, "Sesame Street." The spots, patterned after television commercials, are designed to be entertaining as well as informative and can be inserted as required during each daily, hour-long show. Clockwise from upper left, the spots help teach numbers (the countdown), the letter "J," the concept of "through," and the letter "m."

. . . .

The first spot utilizes the familiar rocket countdown sequence to familiarize preschool viewers with numbers. The second tells a 60-second story full of words that start with "J," emphasizing the sound as well as the sight of the letter. The third features a know-it-all little girl who prissily promises to demonstrate what "through" means by pouring a bucket of paint through the pipe. (She gets doused when it comes "through" all over her.) The fourth, a 10-second spot, demonstrates the sound and sight of the letter "m."

From: Children's Television Workshop
         1865 Broadway
         New York, N.Y. 10023 phone: 212-757-3545

Neg # CTV-13

SLUG: COMMERCIALS THAT TEACH   5/6/69

Structural change, of course, is contingent upon an available technology. As long as broadcast television is the only means of distribution, its economy prevails.

But there are decentralized distribution technologies within the so-called "state-of-the-art." They are cable television and videocassettes. The decentralized production tools for those channels are portable video systems.

The potential of this technology has coalesced people into a notion of a whole alternate television which doesn't just want alternate programming played across the existing system, but which demands a whole new system.

I have chosen the term "guerrilla" here because it describes how I use and relate to television, and how I see others relating to it.

Guerrilla Television shares strategies and tactics with its counterpart in warfare.

But I do not call it "Guerrilla Warefare Television" because it is not a form of physical warfare or violence, any more than evolution is.

Guerrilla Television is by definition non-violent because violence is a mode of social change which substitutes seizure and destruction of property for a genuine understanding of the difference between Media-America and a product-based culture.

Another function of Guerrilla Television is as counter-technology.

Only the most optimistic liberal can honestly believe that governmental surveillance agencies will not pursue a perverse Parkinson's law of data gathering (information expands so as to fill the space available for its storage) utilizing each new gadget that comes along.

Okay. Then why not a kind of People's Bureau of Investigation where the watched compile open files about their watchers; *e.g.*, videotaping police at events, undercover agents on the street, and so on. (In Pennsylvania, near the FBI office which had its files taken and made public by a clandestine organization, the people in one community became so tired of FBI surveillance and questioning they had an anti FBI street fair where videotapes were shown and you could have your picture taken with J. Edgar Hoover's.)

The purpose, however, shouldn't be counter-tech which mimics what it opposes (and thus becomes what it beholds), but an opening up of what should be public areas.

Thus, counter-surveillance systems will function best as social parody, by taking police intelligence activities and betraying their structure in an alien context.

However, that kind of counter-tech is at best a minor use of a tool which promises a whole system that makes politics irrelevant, both right and left.

Rather, Guerrilla Television is the application of guerrilla techniques in the realm of process.

Guerrilla Television is grassroots television. It works with people, not from up above them. On a simple level, this is no more than "do-it-yourself-TV." But the context for that notion is that survival in an information environment demands information tools.

When a broadcast TV crew goes to an event they stand above the crowd and tell you about it (Sander Vanocur of NBC at an anti-Cambodia demonstration in Washington, D.C.)

When you go to an event with a Porta-Pak you shoot in the crowd and let environmental sound and people speak for themselves (A Raindance videotape of the same event)

SPIRIT OF COMMUNICATION

The structure of Guerrilla Television is biomorphic and decentralized. As opposed to traditional warfare or bureaucracies, where units in the field support a heavy, centralized headquarters (or studio), each component of Guerrilla Television is either self-sustaining or uses more centralized facilities only as its support system.

This is not the way television is done now in America. Camera crews using film go out to the people, "shoot" them, and then bring the film back to a central processing location.

With portable videotape technology, anything recorded on location is ready on location, instantly. Thus, people can control information about themselves rather than surrender that power to outsiders. ABC, CBS, and NBC do not swim like fish among the people. They watch from the beach and thus see just the surface of the water.

Potential in Guerrilla Television is an information infrastructure for Media-America, a grassroots network of indigenous media activity.

In place of a mass consciousness of millions of people all plugged-in to the same "show," is a more flexible collective mind with the option of a high variety of available viewpoints.

I personally don't want everyone to look, act, and feel like me. What I do want is for other viewpoints not to inbreed and degenerate into hatred for my life style. Translated into TV this means many different types of programming made by many different types of people. As only people themselves ultimately know how they feel, they must have access to television tools without mediators.

If there weren't technologies available to accomplish this, **Guerrilla Television** would be a book of theory, not practice. Many of us have an intuitive understanding of these potentials. Others, however, do not. Often they are in positions which retard potential development. They don't need to be politicized, but "media-ized": to understand the conditions of media-ecology as keenly as those of natural ecology.

For the ultimate aim of Guerrilla Television is to embody ecological intention through the design of information structures.

The more options a culture has available to it, the more flexible it is. Media repression trades off short-term control for long-term sterility. But it is less the government which threatens information flow than the bias of the media itself.

I believe that coverage of the government is not fair, that it is subjugated to the biases of a limited number of people with similar views.

The people in broadcast television are just another constituency. (So, however, is the government.) They should have their own channel to express their opinions, but not all the channels; just as the government should get its channel, but not every one.

In other words, given a forty-channel system (already possible under current cable-TV systems), let the networks have one channel, the government a second, and advertisers a third.*

Then open up the other thirty-seven to the people themselves, and set up economic support systems to sustain a high variety of indigenous video production free of any bias but that of people themselves. That is the purpose of Guerrilla Television.

*The response of the broadcasting networks to charges of unfairness made by the Nixon regime has, ironically, helped to substantiate those charges.

In the aftermath of government criticism of the anti-military show called "The Selling of the Pentagon" (done by CBS), Secretary of Defense Laird made a reasonable request to participate in a subsequent show on POW's only if he could appear live. CBS refused, and demanded that he be videotaped in advance without an opportunity to view the show he was to have been a part of.

If CBS really understood the nature of television, they would have produced a show and concluded with a live interview of Secretary Laird feeding back about it. Instead, we must accept the mediated judgment of network newsmen who claim to represent the public, but really only represent themselves and their own select viewpoint.

Subsequent to that incident, Richard W. Jencks, president of the CBS Broadcast Group, was quoted (in the New York Times, June 17, 1971) as saying that demands by various groups for free access to the airwaves threaten to convert the broadcast press into "a common carrier of other people's views with no creative or vigorous voice of its own."

That "vigorous voice" is more of a monopoly than the voice of the government, which is at least subject to electoral referendum from time to time.

TV as a Creative Medium

a personaliz

history

Dear People:

It's not uncommon for two people who don't know each other to have the same idea at the same time because the culture is right for that idea. What I'm writing about Guerilla Television would make no sense if it took me saying it to make other people do it.

Grassroots video is sprouting everywhere across Media-America because it fulfills genuine information needs.

My own experience is being duplicated and bettered by people who could care less about the video scene which has already gone down.

Nonetheless, some people did get to it first. And however brief the chronology of Guerrilla Television, the experience of others can provide useful information. **You can skip this section if you want.**

What follows is written from the first, not the third, person. Thus, the people I've worked with get more prominence, perhaps unfairly. I emphatically don't claim the experiences recounted below are the only way of doing guerrilla television. All I can hope is that my experience verifies yours *

3 Moreover, the historical details pieced to— gether here are from verbal accounts given, out of nostalgia, often when stoned, by the people mentioned. I haven't gone around and interviewed anyone and any and all critical opinions offered are exclusively my own.

In 1968, when Sony introduced the first portable video camera, **Paul Ryan** was doing his term as a conscientious objector from the Army as a research assistant to Marshall McLuhan at Fordham University in New York.

At the same time **Ken Marsh** and **David Cort** were working with one-inch video tape equipment at a museum in Brooklyn into which they'd been initiated by **Eric Siegel**.

Paul claims that he got into videotape to figure out if McLuhan was right, for if he were then **Paul** would be able to decode accurately a medium that McLuhan hadn't touched yet. Thus, he borrowed the new videotape equipment from Fordham for the summer.

*Generally, my brief history concentrates on video groups who have been most preoccupied with structural, not just content, changes in television production and transmission.

Thus, I must gloss over video artists who are nonetheless doing very fine work. Some particular names are: Eric Siegel, Jackie Cassen, and Woody and Steinna Vasulka, working in New York; Nam June Paik at the California Institute of the Arts outside Los Angeles; and Brice Howard and the National Center for Experiments in Television in San Francisco.

I must also mention Andy Mann who, since his fortuitous split with Global Village, has aided many of us in New York with his particular genius. In addition, Andy's collaborator at New York University, Bob Mariano, has shown admirable innovation in helping to establish the student-run Videoteque, along with Red Burns.

Finally, there are Frank Cavestani and Laura Long, pictured in this book as "New Style Video," who until recently have been hindered by lack of resources but who nonetheless have added much to working with video in New York City; as has C.T. Lui of CTL Electronics whose usually generous discounts on equipment have not kept him from worldly rewards: his purple Cadillac Coupe de Ville.

Paul then met **Frank Gillette** on the street on New York's Lower East Side which was, that year, the center of the Eastern hippie renaissance. With borrowed equipment, **Frank** and **Harvey Simons** produced a ten-hour videotape portrait of street life on St. Marks Place, the heart of the heart of Eastern hippiedom.

Meanwhile **Paul** was making tape with a poverty project in Brooklyn which culminated in a documentary made by kids of their experience in Washington, D.C., at Resurrection City, the makeshift village of the Poor Peoples Campaign led by Martin Luther King.

At the same time, **Howie Gutstadt** ran into **Frank** and **Harvey** on the street and told **Ken** and **David** out in Brooklyn about them, and about portable equipment. The upshot was the first video company, **Commediation**, with **Frank, Ken, David, and Howie.**

In the fall of the year **Commediation** produced a videotape documentary of the now-famous school decentralization crisis in New York which centered around the Oceanhill-Brownsville decentralized school district. The taping was sponsored by the Center for Urban Education. Shortly thereafter **Commediation** dissolved.

5

In early 1969, **Ira Schneider**, an "underground" filmmaker, met **Frank** at a party and was turned-on to videotape because he found film too cumbersome to pick up on process. This resulted in an invitation to them to visit Antioch College in Ohio for a month and generally hang out and make tape. **Ira** claims to have paid for most of the expenses himself.

Immediately after they returned, **Howard Wise**, who had a gallery on 57th Street in Manhattan, asked **Frank** to participate in a show he was having entitled "TV as a Creative Medium." **Frank** asked **Ira** to collaborate with him and the result was a piece called **"Wipe Cycle,"** a bank of nine TV monitors playing back live and delayed feed back, broadcast television, and pre-recorded tapes.

Also in the show were **Paul Ryan, Eric Siegel, Nam June Paik,** and others. I heard about the show from **Frank** who was then living with a woman I'd gone to college with. At the time I was working for Time Magazine and I did an article on the show.

6

Out of the show came several new companies. One was called **Televisionary Associates** and included **Ira** and **John Reilly**, a filmmaker he'd met at the **Wise** show. **Ira** and **Frank** and **Paul** and **John** started another company called **Information Structures** and **Frank** & I began to have discussions about **Raindance.**

The idea was that **Televisionary Associates** would concern itself with theatrical/environmental showings of tape; **Information Structures** would design video systems; and finally, **Raindance**, in **Frank's** elegant vision, would function as the counter-culture's analogue to the Rand Corporation — a think tank that would use videotape instead of print. In those days everyone was very taken by the fact that for a few hundred dollars you could form your own corporation and be an officer.

At that point **Information Structures** became embroiled in designing a video matrix, or structure similar to **Wipe Cycle** as subcontractors to a still photographer who made his living doing industrial trade shows.

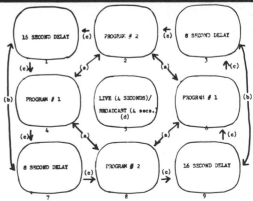

CYCLE (a)   Monitors 2, 4, 6 and 8: Programmed change cycle, Program No. 1 alternating every eight seconds with Program No. 2.

CYCLE (b)   Monitors 1, 3, 7 and 9: Delay change cycle, Nos. 1 and 7 and 3 and 9 alternating (exchanging) every four seconds.

CYCLE (c)   Monitors 1, 2, 3, 4, 6, 7, 8 and 9: Wipe cycle, grey "light" pulse, moving counterclockwise every two seconds.

CYCLE (d)   Monitor 5: Live cycle, four seconds of live feedback alternating with four seconds of broadcast television.

7

The video matrix was to have been used to hype cars for a manufacturer at a trade show. But after copping their design and some rhetoric, the photographer ripped-off **Information Structures**, did the design himself, and kept most of the money for himself. There is a lesson there which is: "**Never trust middlemen when you're the one with the ideas.**"

Meanwhile, **Ira** and **John** were having ad-hoc showings of videotape at various lofts around Manhattan.

Then came Woodstock. **Ira** went with a camera-man named **Carl Goldberg**, while **David Cort** went up with a Porta-Pak by himself; and met **Parry Teasdale** who had carted a stationary camera and deck in the back of his car.

Ira came back and he and John began showing the Woodstock tapes at **Televisionary**. **David** and **Parry** met with several other **people***, and were put in touch with CBS in what became one of the great sagas of Guerrilla Television.

*The Videofreex are: Nelson Becker, Nancy Cain, David Cort, Bart Friedman, Davidson Gigliotti, Chuck Kennedy, Curtis Ratcliff, Allan Scholom, Parry Teasdale, Carol Vontobel, Ann Woodward.

It seems that CBS was, as always, looking for something "new". An assistant to Frank Stanton, the network's president, found the people who quickly formed a group called **Videofreex** to take ad-

vantage of CBS money. The result was a loft with equipment in Lower Manhattan and a mandate to produce a pilot for a show engagingly entitled "Subject to Change."

Over the next few months the **Videofreex** traveled around the country making tape, stopping in Chicago to record a powerful rap by Fred Hampton, the Black Panther who was shot to death in his sleep during a police raid soon afterward; and in California to pick up on some of that alternate education and culture.

The resulting composite was prepared for showing to **Michael Dann** who was then CBS's director of programming, and who now is number-two man at the Children's TV Workshop which does "Sesame Street."

According to the **Videofreex**, Dann and his assistants were so repelled by what they saw that they stumbled out early in a nervous fit. Shortly thereafter CBS demanded all the tape back that the 'Freex had made on the project and even went so far as to charter a plane to track them down in Connecticut.

9

After that, the 'Freex learned how to live out on the street and recently decided to give up their loft to live in a sixteen bedroom house in the country.

While all that was going on **Ira** and **John** teamed up with **Rudi Stern** a light show artist, and set up **Global Village**, a theater/environment on Lower Manhattan which used nine TV screens to show tapes and juxtapose images.

Around that time **Ken Marsh**, **Howie Gutstadt** and **Elliott Glass**, a college Spanish teacher who independently discovered videotape to make street primers to teach language, came together and formed the **Peoples Video Theater**. PVT has worked the most closely of any of the groups in developing community media tactics.

Also around that time **Raindance** formally incorporated with **Frank**; **Me** (I was still at Life); **Louis Jaffe**, a rock musician.; **Fred Vassi**, a friend of Frank's and an erstwhile business manager who shall remain **nameless** because of his ineptitude.

Perhaps the next event of collective significance was an art show put together by **Connor** at the Rose Art Museum of Brandeis Univ. called "**Vision and Television.**"

10

Each of the groups was represented there although **Ira** had split from **Global Village** and was working alone, and **Paul** was also working independently, the companies **Information Structures** and **Televisionary** having fallen by the wayside.

Shortly thereafter **Ira** joined Raindance and **Fred Vassi** changed his name to **Marco Vassi** and began writing pornographic books (quite good, actually) for Olympia Press and thus split, as did our business manager, and ultimately, **Frank**.

Raindance's current configuration includes myself, **Ira**, **Louis**, **Dean** and **Dudley Evenson** who began life in video as the **Fobile Muck Truck**, a traveling video van, **Beryl Korot** who, with **Phyllis Gershuny**, founded **Radical Software**, the printout we do; and we get business advice from two people called **Source Associates**, an investment counseling firm.

All-in-All, I learned more in a year of Raindance than in four years of college and the above permutations of personnel and foundings and dissolvings of companies are probably pretty typical of any field. But if you're going thru it, remember that there's the experience of others to draw on.

Since this was written Megan Williams and Jodie Sibert have joined us.

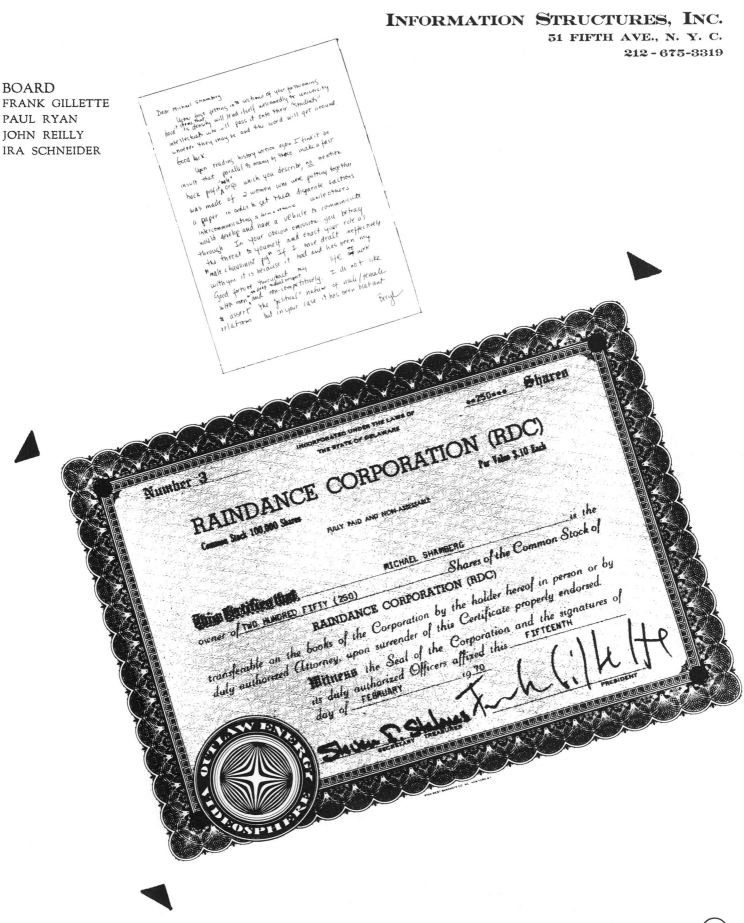

INFORMATION STRUCTURES, INC.
51 FIFTH AVE., N. Y. C.
212 - 675 - 3319

BOARD
FRANK GILLETTE
PAUL RYAN
JOHN REILLY
IRA SCHNEIDER

(13)

BOARD
JOHN L. REILLY
IRA SCHNEIDER

TELEVISIONARY ASSOCIATES INC.
51 FIFTH AVE., N. Y. C.
(212) 675-3319
118 SPRING ST., N. Y. C.
(212) 925-0632

Vision&Television

Done for "Vision & Television" art at Brandeis, 2/70

Ira Schneider "Random Interlace— Content Electronic"

⑭

"Were I de-briefing myself I would remember our incredible infatuation with our own rhetoric in those early days because we knew we were genuinely on to something new. It was then that we'd talk to anyone and even thought publicity was a good thing. Moreover we had a sort of Irish Sweepstakes mentality.✳

The private capital we were initially funded with ran out. Rather than initiate low-key paying projects, we were into high level hundreds of thousands of dollar proposals, directed at people like Warner Brothers and other established film producers and general youth culture exploiters. We were also trying to shag a superstar, a rut I see others getting into all the time.

Essentially it goes like this: You know somebody who knows a rock star or a movie actor, or knows their cousin or something. Rumor has it that Joe Superstar wants to put money into something—and if you can just get to him. . . .

Well, you can't get something for nothing. That's what ecology's all about. And the more you lust after latching onto someone else's trip, the more you lose your own identity. We found that after we'd developed a certain integrity of purpose the people we once wanted to meet either weren't that important anymore, or got in touch with us anyway.

Moreover, we resent having to give something away for nothing. This includes demands by counter-culture people who think you owe them something because you have equipment and they don't.

✳This parallels what I call "the grand scheme." These are super ideas which involve huge amounts of money, publicity, even space, and are expected to consume and give direction to everyone involved.

The original grand scheme, of course, was Woodstock. But it has since been followed by megalomaniacal hippie entrepreneurs who have wanted to stage bigger and better rock festivals culminating in the aborted Earth Peoples Park which was to have been a giant Woodstock that no one would go home from.

Beware of grand schemers. A general rule is: **the bigger their scheme, the less together their shit is.**

Generally they see your equipment going unused and figure they should have access to it without realizing that the reason you're not using it at the moment is because you're hustling to pay the rent and meet your overhead.

When we first set up in our loft we took to loaning out equipment to people for free. Over several months we had one camera stolen by a cat who didn't bring it back, and lots of minor repairs necessitated by people who felt no compulsion to pay for them. (However not everyone ripped us off. Some made good tape which they later let us use.)

The point is that in an alternative economic system you either use straight currency or trust. Straight currency relationships are undertaken with people who obviously can pay, and generally are more in sympathy with making money than with anything else.

Trust relationships are generally backed up by what you know of people and what you've seen of their work. People who come through your door and tell you they want to get into what you're doing, could they hang around, generally aren't too together. If they've already done something, not necessarily in videotape, then it shows. Our rule of thumb is that if someone has a Porta-Pak, no matter how much an ass he might be, we'll talk to him because he's already made an effort. Or if he knows his software and/or has some to show, that too is credibility enough.

RADICAL SOFTWARE

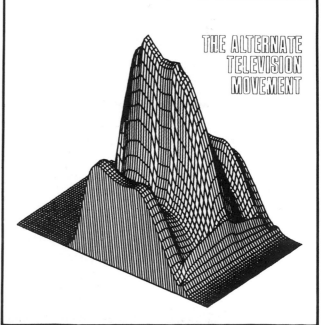

THE ALTERNATE TELEVISION MOVEMENT

NUMBER 1   **1970**

The groups which endure each have found some stable way of self-support and of resisting the above perils. which may just be unique to **Raindance**'s experience.

In terms of financing ourselves, we weathered the initial money lust which came from our first financial advisor who actually wanted to sell stock publically in us although we had nothing to sell but rhetoric (nonetheless we believed him). That was shortly before the stock market bottomed out and you could get away with that sort of talk.

We are living on some grant money for salaries, income from **Radical Software** which meets the publication's material expenses, videotape distribution, gigs at colleges, we hope, and, book royalties. We neither have, nor envision, one set way of sustaining ourselves because we dont want to be locked into repeating the past at the expense of the present and future.

A closer look at some of the people and groups mentioned above gives you a pretty good idea of how far and how fast Guerrilla Television has come since a few people were getting it off making tape on the street. Some of them are:

The Videofreex ↗

Videofreex: The **Freex** are the most production oriented of the video groups. They've developed a high expertise with television hardware which is their strength because they demand respect (even from people put off by their life-style and viewpoint) simply because they know their tools.

On the other hand, **Videofreex** are sometimes too much into hardware at the expense of relating to people and not alienating them. Nonetheless, in terms of finished, cleanly edited, high quality tape which is generally quite entertaining, the Videofreex are clearly the best.

They have also the most collective life style, sharing expenses and space for living. This is in no small part due to the nature of the videotape process and the **Freex** claim to get it off most when they're all plugged in together through an elaborate camera mixing system and taping collectively. They also, of course, make tapes individually using the collective support system.

Peoples Video Theater: PVT has expanded. Besides **Ken, Elliot** and **Howie** there are **Ben Levine** and **Elaine Milosh**. If you want to use the word "pioneers" it applies to them. They have made real break thrus in understanding and developing community media in work they've done with the Young Lords, Panthers, Chicanos, and Indians.

Skilled technoid from videofreex editing videotape. Photo - Louis Jaffe

PEOPLE'S VIDEO THEATRE

544 6th AVE. BETWEEN 14th & 15th STREETS

Making street television

Elliott Glass ↗   Ken Marsh ↗
Photo - Winston Vargas

see mini documentaries

speak back to the news

become part of the news

see yourself

all on two-way television

Theatre Showings Fri. & Sat. at 8 & 10PM

Production & News Coverage Services

Tel. 212-691-3254

They've developed techniques of video mediation which essentially cool people out by taping them and letting them relate to one another through the medium.

If there's a problem with **PVT**, it's that some of their tapes trend toward sociological monologues and propagandize rather than inform.

Global Village: **Global** is the most commercial of the original groups, preferring short-term money and publicity instead of long-term, fundamental media changes.

Their shows consist of multi-monitor images, of rock music and political superstars like Abbie Hoffman or Jerry Rubin. The images change quickly which gives you little time to get into any one. Just as propaganda is entropic because it confirms rather than informs, so is there low information value in **Global Village**, shows.

It's as if they prefer an alternate myth system rather than an alternate reality to the prevailing myth system. This is a trait of other beginning tape makers who think it's a big deal to record a celebrity, even tho' the celebrity may have nothing to say and is generally just providing an audio rap with pictures.

Global Village has also been the quickest to embrace old-style publicity tactics. They're into excerpting quotes from old reviews of their show and running them in ads or on their marquee. Generally the quotes antedate the show by more than a year, and the show has changed very little since, and at last viewing they were, still, incredibly, using Wood-stock footage, even going so far as to dub the sound-track album over their tape because they didn't feel its quality was good enough. And so on ...

Media Access Center: This is a division of Portola Institute, which did the Whole Earth Catalog among other things.

Media Access was started by, and is, four people: **Pat Crowley, Rich Kletter, Allen Rucker** and **Shelley Surpin. Allen** is an old friend of mine from college and he met the others when he was doing graduate work in communications at Stanford. **Media Access** is in Menlo Park, California.

They are heavily into the alternate education scene and, in fact, have developed an unmatched expertise in showing kids how to use videotape.

Media Access has also done community cable television work.

Media
Access
Center

photo:
Fat Crowley

Allen Rucker ↴ Fat Crowley ↴ Shelley Surpin ↴ Rich Kletter

sugar spud

photo — Barbara Miller

Rudi Stern ↓   John Reilly ↓

NT FARM

GLOBAL VILLAGE

john reilly · rudi stern   the electronics of shared experience

global village
454 broome st.
n.y.c. 10012
966-1515

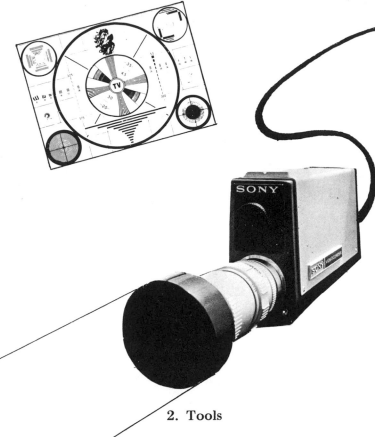

2. Tools

There are four standards of videotape: two-inch, one-inch, half-inch, and quarter-inch.

Two-inch or "high band" videotape is indigenous to broadcasting. The superwide tape holds more electronic information than the narrower standards and also uses a unique mode of laying a signal on the tape called "quadraplex." This means that the scanning signal is laid perpendicular to the edge of the tape. All one, half-, and quarter-inch systems incorporate "helical" scan which lays the signal at an angle to the tape edge.

Typically, clean editing of videotape (*i.e.*, without a visible "roll-over" in the picture between cuts) was once an exclusive function of two-inch machines which are the lowest access possible because of their size and cost.

One-inch videotape recorders are generally used as a cheaper version of quadraplex machines as their size and price range ($3,000 to $10,000) make them ideal for institutions with closed-circuit TV systems which imitate broadcast in technique and operation. Like two-inch, one-inch editing capability is perfect.

There are no one-inch portables. However, all of the half-inch portables (Porta-Paks) can be interfaced with one-inch to provide perfectly edited one-inch masters.

The major problem technically with half-inch systems had been an unstable signal which precluded clean edits and even *intra*system compatibility in some cases. But most of the "technical" objections came from people who had a vested interest in limiting access to television tools.

Indeed, the economics of portable video are subversive to anyone whose authority and security are based on controlling information flow. Thus, the usual argument against Porta-Paks, that they embody inferior "technical standards," is a hype promoted by unions whose jobs are based on scarcity, owners who can't afford both their overhead and "equal time," and educators who build a mystique of expertise and certification.

The bias of self-contained record, storage, and instant playback, punctures the estranging mythology of technology as something to be operated and therefore controlled by an elite.

Moreover, some of the best video we've ever seen was made on the first, relatively crude Porta-Paks which were nonetheless flexible enough to go where people had something to record. Process versus product.*

Many of the initial technical problems in half-inch equipment have been eliminated since Porta-Paks were first introduced in 1968. There is now even a standard of *inter*system compatibility between manufacturers which, like audiotape recorders, allows you added flexibility, especially in networking.

Much of our experience with Guerrilla Television has been grounded in the Sony system, not necessarily because it's the best, but because it has been the easiest to get and get serviced due to Sony's marketing acumen.

---

*All of the strongest video I've seen resulted from the complete opposite of a product mentality. Perhaps the best was done by a student who had no prior experience with a Porta-Pak but just went home and started shooting. While the sound isn't perfect and the camera work is shaky, the information is total process.

The tape is of a group of street kids in a Brooklyn ghetto. While one of them lays down a running audio rap about life in general, some others break into a warehouse in the background. When the commentator sees that, he starts yelling and the kids run in front of the camera, their arms full of stolen clothing. Then the police come. Everyone starts to jive them until the kid announcing discovers they've arrested his brother. "Don't tell them nothing," he yells.

The PortaPak

— The videotape process works through a camera or other transmitter inputing a magnetic impulse onto a coated tape (which is the same as audiotape). Because there is no chemical processing, once the signal is recorded it's immediately ready for replay. Unlike film, videotape may always be handled in open light as the signal is electronic, not photochemical.

Videotape is re-usable. You simply record over it after it's automatically pre-erased electronically by an "erase head" which meets the tape just before it passes the "recording heads."

Depending upon how carefully you handle the tape physically, each reel is good for up to fifty different recordings. The number of playbacks possible on any one recording runs into the thousands.

Videotape also has a soundtrack which is automatically synced to the image and has the same characteristics as regular audiotape recorders.

The cost of half-inch videotape (the kind used in Porta-Paks) runs from $12 to $18 per thirty minutes depending on how friendly you are with your dealer and what kind of price he'll give you.

Finally, you can also do what's called "live feedback" which simply means that a video camera attached to a VTR and feeding into a TV set will give you a real-time image of whatever the camera is pointed at.

— Porta-Paks are fully battery-operated for both record and playback (and also, of course, can work off wall current). Anywhere you can physically carry it and there's enough light, you can make tape.

The batteries are rechargeable and generally last forty-five minutes to an hour (current portables hold up to thirty minutes of videotape). Recharging time is five to eight hours.

You can also adapt movie camera battery belts which give you extra range (up to four hours), or even use a Honda motorcycle battery.

The problem with that, however, is that the motorcycle battery is heavy (nine pounds) although long-lasting. But the Porta-Pak itself is already too heavy (twenty-one pounds including deck and camera) and difficult for women and children to use. You can, however, wear it on a back pack frame.

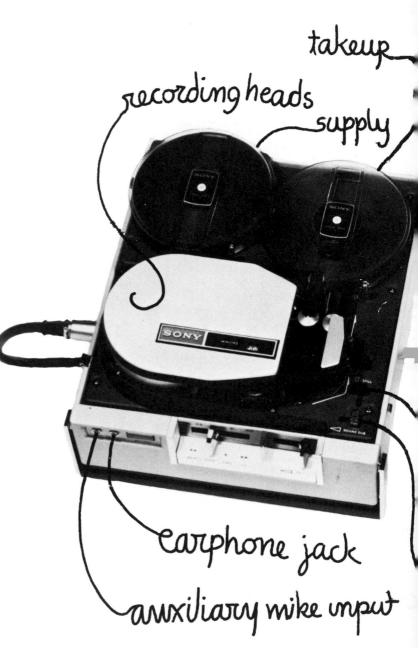

takeup

recording heads

supply

earphone jack

auxiliary mike input

— Portable video cameras either have a built-in microphone or a jack for an auxiliary microphone. This gives automatic sync sound which, like the video signal, is erasable. Some units even have two-track audio allowing for stereo sound (*e.g.*, Ampex Instavideo).

— Porta-Paks also have options built into them to allow you rudimentary control over the tape once it's recorded. The one shown here (Sony AV3400) has a switch for freeze-framing (which simply stops the movement of the tape so that the revolving playback heads keep reading the same field) and a control to allow you to do sound dubbing (*i.e.*, add a separate soundtrack over an already recorded video portion). There's also an outlet for an earphone so you can monitor sound as it's being recorded as well as feed out in playback to either an external sound system like a stereo or an earphone.

— The Porta-Pak camera uses what's called "C-mount" lenses. That refers to the way in which the lens screws into the camera and it's exactly the same for portable video cameras as for 16mm movie cameras. Thus, you have as much variety as with film. In fact, you can also get an adaptor for using Nikon and other 35mm still-camera lenses.

Videofreex especially shoot most of their tape with a wide-angle (12mm) lens instead of the standard zoom lens that comes with the cameras. The wide angle gives you some distortion in close-up but can focus very close (less than twelve inches) to an object or person. At that range the image has an uncanny realism.

You can also use extra fast lenses (*e.g.*, f/.95) for shooting in lower light. Generally the vidicon tube which translates light signals to magnetic ones is equivalent to a film speed of ASA 1000. But there are also infrared vidicons (used by the Army, at present) which will allow you to shoot in total darkness and work is being done to adapt them for Porta-Paks.

About the only thing you can't do with a Porta-Pak is point it directly at a bright light. That's worth repeating because it's the first and only thing you have to tell people when teaching them to use a Porta-Pak: DON'T POINT IT DIRECTLY AT A BRIGHT LIGHT.

If you do, a black spot called a "burn" will become indelibly etched on the face of the vidicon tube and appear in all subsequent taping. Less serious ones, however, will go away over time.

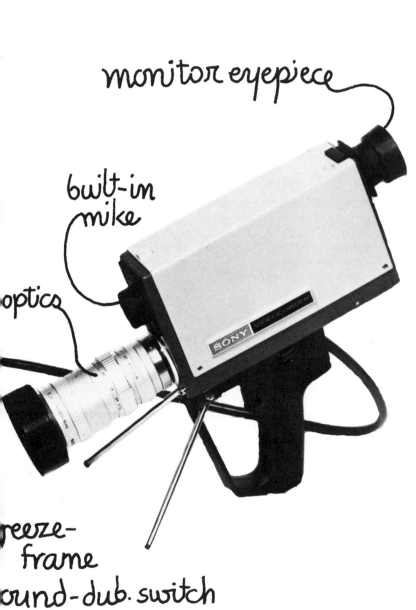

monitor eyepiece

built-in mike

optics

freeze-frame

sound-dub. switch

WHAT TO CONSIDER WHEN BUYING A PORTA-PAK

Generally there are four categories for evaluating a machine:

Technical specifications

They're generally the same for *signal-to-noise ratio* (the strength of the signal in relation to inherent noise); *audio range; tape speed* (the faster it is the more information stored, but the less recording time. Type One, the compatible standard of Porta-Pak, moves at seven-and-a-half inches per second); and *resolution* (most cameras transmit more lines than the tape actually stores so that what the record deck holds is more important than the camera's capacity).

Other system variables to look for are battery life and recharging time. What are the standard microphone and lens like? And does the Porta-Pak itself have playback without your having to transfer the tape to another deck? Some machines are record only (and the signal won't play back through a normal TV set, just a special monitor). Of course, a playback motor means a heavier unit which you may not need.

Design intelligence

Even the best of the systems is an imitation of film technology. Rather than exploit the potentials inherent in electronics, Porta-Paks still have a small TV screen eyepiece between your eye and the lens and you "shoot" people by pulling a camera trigger. Think about what that means.

The lens and eyepiece could be separate. Say a lens extended from your wrist and a monitor on your other hand.

Other design intelligence criteria are how clearly visible is the tape path so you can see if it's screwing up while recording; can you get to the guts easily for repairs; and are the input and output jacks convenient?

On the Sony, for example, you can go in and out only with special Sony connector pins. But with the Ampex system you can use coax jacks which are universally compatible.

Experience

Find somebody who's used the system you're about to buy. Never believe a dealer.

A better way to design a Porta-Pak

Support

Some Porta-Paks are less flexible than others. First, because they have few inherent options (*e.g.*, sound dubbing, still-framing); second, because other units in the manufacturer's line which you'll need for editing aren't that good; and third, because the manufacturer's sales and service network is unreliable or hard to find.

HOW TO BUILD A PORTA-PAK SUPPORT SYSTEM

Here it's important to understand the philosophy of Guerrilla Television.

You should structure your system to maximize access and flexibility. As in guerrilla warfare, your heavy, centralized hardware should help support your most flexible unit, the Porta-Pak, not vice-versa.

If you want heavy hardware (*e.g.*, video mixers, slick editing), design it as a technological support system in service of the portable.

Editing

Electronic editing is done by putting your master (original) tape on one deck and recording a copy onto a second deck in a desired sequence. The edited tape is thus an assembled copy, or "second generation."

Simple sequential editing is called "assembly." Inserting material into already recorded tape is called an "insert" edit.

Insert editing is a function of more expensive machines since it requires a more complex internal mechanism. Assembly editing, on the other hand, can be done whenever you have two VTRs.

The results vary from clean cuts, if the system has an inherent editing function, to mild instability where a simple dubbing (copying) function is made to serve as an editor.

It's also possible to edit tape manually by actually slicing it with a razor blade. However, in electronic editing you preserve the original master and are spared manual labor.

Manual editing is done by chemically developing the top of the tape to find the sync marks and then cutting between them. The edit plays back as a wipe up from the bottom to the top.

Generally, the more sophisticated your editing set-up the less portable it is. Both modes have advantages. On the one hand, it's nice to be able to turn out slick, finished products. On the other, being able to do on-the-scene crude edits means that community groups can have a cheap, quick, self-contained set-up; and also you can go practically anywhere there's simple electrical power and never have to return to civilization.

Thus, a general editing support system breaks down into three basic levels:

Level one: This is the simplest and most flexible editing support system; pure, basic editing.

At this level your actual Porta-Pak deck is used for playing back the master tape. It feeds either into another Porta-Pak (and is thus a complete field system) or the cheapest and lightest table deck.

Going from Porta-Pak to Porta-Pak is essentially a copying system which allows you to leave a copy on-the-scene and take one with you after you've shot tape with two cameras.

However, using a table deck instead of a second Porta-Pak is both cheaper and frees up the portable for more shooting while people inside can watch what's been edited.

A first level editing support system costs approximately $2,195 to $3,000 (list prices) and includes a Porta-Pak.

Level two: At this level your Porta-Pak is not involved and a table deck is used to feed the master

reel into a heavier, more sophisticated deck. (Of course you can use two of the most rudimentary table decks, but generally they minimize signal input control because they're designed mainly for playback only. For just a few hundred dollars more you get a lot of added flexibility.)

This set-up ranges from $1,690 to $2,045, but that doesn't include a Porta-Pak.

Level three: Here you use a half-inch table deck to feed into a one-inch machine. A good one-inch VTR has perfect assembly edits and optional perfect insert editing. Most have two audio channels as well, along with controls over both audio and video modulation. One-inch machines are also upgradable to color with plug-in modular circuit boards.

You should also consider running the incoming signal through a processing amplifier or "proc amp." A proc amp essentially cleans the signal and stabilizes the sync pulse. This practically assures you a perfect, edited master, which is the advantage of a one-inch system.

The disadvantages are that one-inch is exclusively non-portable and much costlier. It ranges in price from $3,000 to $19,000 and that doesn't even include a Porta-Pak.

One-inch tape is also twice as expensive as half-inch, or about $60 an hour.

Finally, there is no intersystem compatibility as in half-inch. Thus, with a one-inch master you've got to find a one-inch machine of the same make.

Special effects

There are many different options beyond simply pointing a camera at a scene and shooting. These include:

Special effects generator: A special effects generator mixes camera signals and produces a composite image of either fades and dissolves (images superimposed) or wipes (one image pushing another off the screen).

Special effects systems will use the Porta-Pak cameras (and even feed them into a portable deck) so if you've got a lot of indoor shooting to do they're a good investment and a completely different way to do video. They also have switches to reverse black-and-white, *i.e.*, create a negative image.

Remember though that for every camera you feed into a mixer you need a separate monitor to see what's coming in. Thus, if you have a four camera set-up you need five monitors, one each for the cameras and one for the composite image. (Most mixers mix two cameras at a time although you can have up to four to choose from.)

A new special effects generator costs about $600. They weigh no more than eight pounds and are about the size of a Manhattan telephone book.

Gen-lock: A Gen-lock system allows you to mix a live and a tape signal. Mixing two pre-recorded signals, however, is not within the state-of-the-art of half-inch technology yet, although you can simulate that optically by playing back two tapes on separate monitors and shooting off the screens through a special effects generator.

A Gen-lock works by syncing up the tape signal with one from a live camera. The tape signal provides the sync pulse for the live one and "drives" the system. The simplest use of Gen-locks is in titling and cheap ones start at $400.

Colorizer: While there are half-inch table VTRs with color capability (price around $1,000) there is not yet a fully portable color camera or color deck. Moreover, tripod-mounted color cameras are at the moment prohibitively expensive (more than $6,000).

What you can do is use a colorizer which adds electronic color information to the black-and-white signal. The effects range from almost natural tones to wild, solarized colors. The box itself is about the size of a lunch pail and has simple knobs to modulate the color.

It's used either on a tape signal or live feed and you can modulate it in real-time.

Color synthesizer: This is the video analogue of an audio synthesizer. It creates its own visual imagery independent of any external camera signal input.

Eric Siegel has built his own and he designed it like a video keyboard which you can sit down and compose on.

Tape delay: A delay set-up can be enormously effective and is pure video.

What you do is position two decks next to each other, one on record with a camera feeding into it, the other on playback. The tape thus records an image and plays it back a few seconds later so you see yourself in a time lag (which is a function of the mechanical distance it takes the tape to travel. The longer the distance, the longer the time delay).

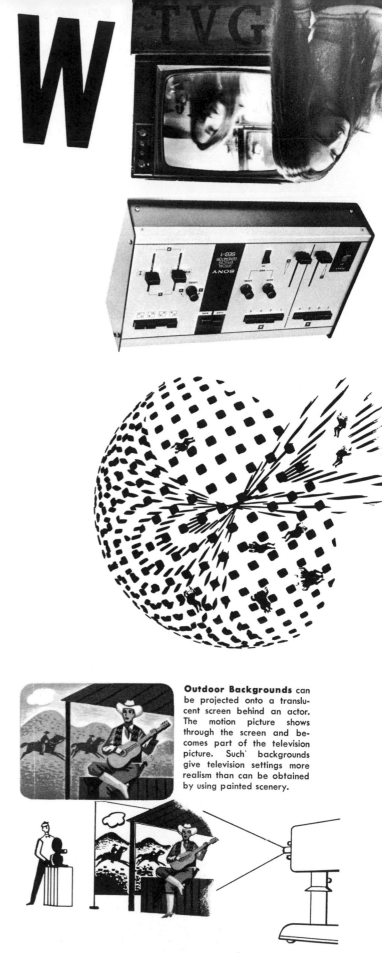

Outdoor Backgrounds can be projected onto a translucent screen behind an actor. The motion picture shows through the screen and becomes part of the television picture. Such backgrounds give television settings more realism than can be obtained by using painted scenery.

Video Output   Vertical Drive Input

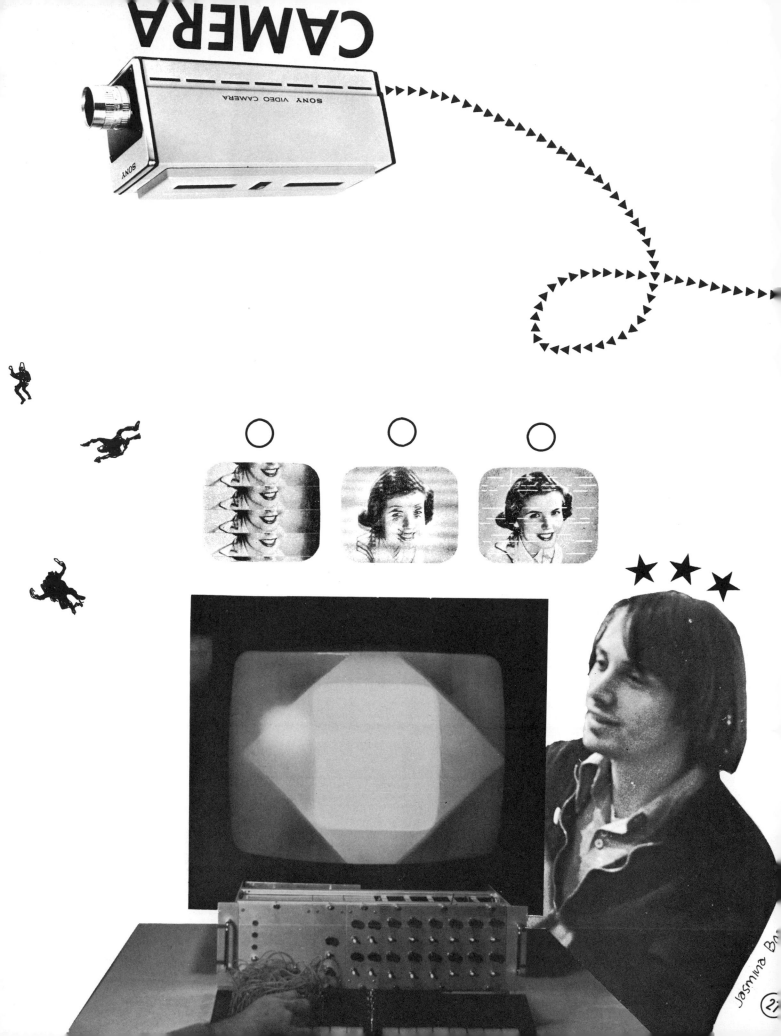

CAMERA

SONY VIDEO CAMERA

Jasmina Bo...

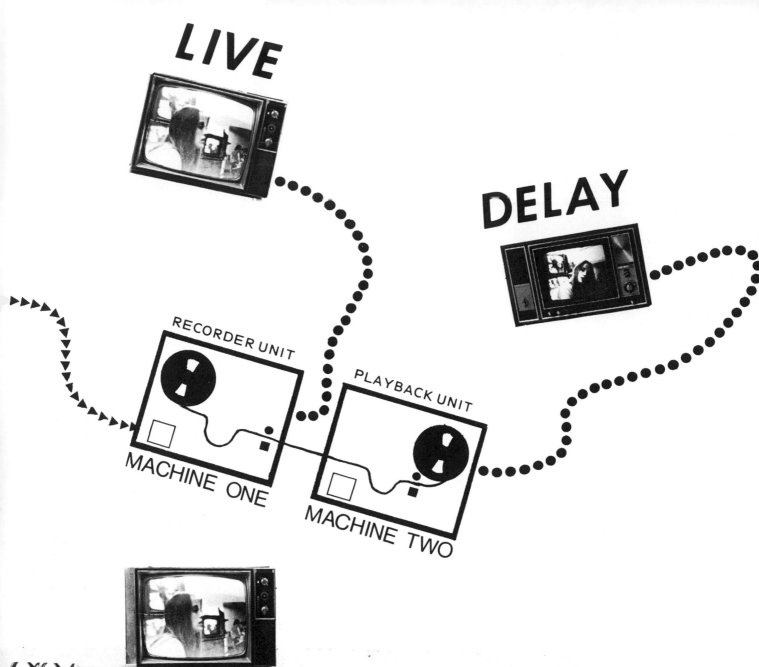

LIVE

DELAY

RECORDER UNIT

PLAYBACK UNIT

MACHINE ONE

MACHINE TWO

VIDEOTAPE VERSUS FILM

Videotape won't kill film any more than television has killed print. But it will supplant it, just as TV supplanted reading.

Many people misunderstand McLuhan when he says that print is dead. Generally they're book-men whose bias makes them impervious to the effects of the medium. They see more and more books being sold and conclude that, despite television, print is still very much alive. This is true.

But, as a psychological environment, print is dead. In other words, although print is still around, future generations imprinted by television will no longer relate to the world through a print-grid or print mentality.

Rather, electronic reality is what's shaping print. Books manifest this in both internal style and form. Staccato anthologies and random access books, especially magazines, are the central print forms, not ponderous and linear developmental novels.

Moreover, you can probably argue that people are reading more because of TV, not despite it. After all, speed-of-light information flow hooks us on data. To feed our habits we need an accelerated information input which print, because of its low cost and high variety and access, can provide.

Similarly, the videotape experience will subsume that of film. To understand this it's necessary to look first at the software or effects of videotape, then to examine the mechanical differences between videotape and film.

Psychological differences between videotape and film

The first one, especially if you're interested in social change, is that 150 million Americans don't sit in movie theaters five-and-a-half hours a day — the national TV viewing average.

In other words, the experience of seeing television and videotape (although VT is not TV, as Paul Ryan says) is more natural than film. Filmmakers are generally concerned just with images, not environment. But to see a movie at home you have to re-arrange your furniture or more often leave your house and travel to a separate building (*i.e.*, a movie theater).

Inside a movie theater the film commands all of everyone's attention and people talking are usually an irritation. Moreover, you sit in the dark, next to each other, and face the same way toward an overpowering image.

TV, on the other hand, is environmental. The lights can be on, you can talk, and if you have more than one set not everyone has to stare in a straight line at the same image. It's hard to imagine films left on as part of the environment, yet that's TV's primary function as the national TV viewing average pertains more to sets which are turned on, not necessarily being watched avidly.

There are also differences in the nature of film and videotape images. A film image is made by light passing through a flat surface and thus appears flat on the screen. A true videotape image is made by light emanating from an object (in the form of electrons) which makes it more tactile and volumetric. Generally, there is a radical difference between film on TV and videotape.

Just as a video projector subtracts from a videotape image, so too does film on TV seem washed out and less vivid than true videotape.

Making videotape and relating to its possibilities is also radically different from making film. I have made a film only once and was put off by the delay between shooting and seeing what I'd shot; the attention that had to be paid to details like light readings; and the pressure of cost: that I had to shoot something "good."

Primarily my attitude toward making films (although I love to watch them) was corrupted by the fluidity I'd come to expect of visual information from watching TV as a kid. After all, I had six channels to choose from, simultaneously, and a guidebook to let me do my mixing.

When I wanted to translate that power into recording my own images, I found film estranging. Subsequently, the attitude I see us manifesting toward videotape is antithetical to film.

Ira Schneider claims he got out of film (he made some very good ones) because he was interested in process and he couldn't pick up on it with movie technology.

At Raindance, we have no notion of ownership of videotape footage. When people make tape we file it together in what we call a "data bank." Everyone is free to take from the data bank without asking, for his or her own edits. In fact, it's not uncommon for us to do editing just as a way to get it off, not to show to someone else.

Accessing the Raindance video data bank.

DUDLEY EVENSON

The experience of relating to each other through tape and the effect of a shared data bank I've detailed in the chapter "You Are Information."

What's important here is that the whole videotape experience is indigenous to an electronic culture where we have no defense against media space given one-way technologies like regular TV.

Videotape lets you feed back into the information-environment at a high speed. It allows you to sculpt information-space. That's analagous to writing a letter which you don't plan to send, to someone you're mad at, or perhaps in love with.

Videotape lets you work it out. Live applications and short-term playback are powerful tools for self-analysis. And the economy of videotape (*i.e.*, it's re-usable) militates against a product mentality and for a process application grafted onto your normal life.

In that context, bad videotape is not the same as home movies. In fact, home movies have a lot of value to the people in them. And why should they feel a compulsion to make them polished for showing to others? The drawback, however, is that people feel compelled to do something while a movie camera is on because of the scarcity economics and the directorial power the cameraman feels.

Personal videotape doesn't need to be shown to a lot of people even if you don't erase it. Shirley Clarke, the filmmaker, says the best tape she's made she won't show to anyone.

Finally, I've always felt that a true understanding of videotape, the perfect information tool for Media-America, would make you want to get into computers to tap that information power. (Film is sequential, or linear, in playback. It cannot be rewound or fast-forwarded. To re-access a portion you must let it play through entirely or manually disengage it from the projector. Videotape, on the other hand, can be automatically fast-forwarded or rewound at high speed. Compared to film, this is almost random access.)

As yet, we've just had rudimentary exposure but we have plans to set up a print accessing catalog about our videotape data bank using computer storage and retrieval. We'd really like to use computers to access and index videotape, but that technology doesn't live yet because there is now no way for a computer to analyze the content of a tape without someone telling it, in print, what's happening.

Ideally, we can develop a computer-video accessing language which is interactive. That is, instead of

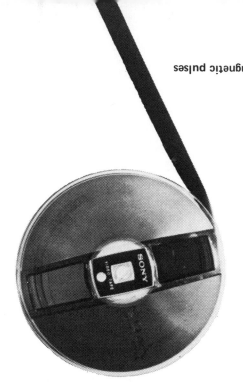

forcing users into pre-determined categories the way a Dewey Decimal System does, you'd be able to feed in what you want to see and mutate the access model.

Gradually, assuming the language were not that of print but some synthesized symbolic form, the accessing model would begin to reflect the terrain and dynamics of the brain's own language.

Right now it's believed that the language of the brain is different from any of man's externalized media. It probably embodies an entirely different logical structure which may even be incomprehensible to itself, internally.

Being out of touch with yourself is essentially a condition of estrangement between the natural biases of mind and the artificial ones of externalized media. Transcendent experiences re-integrate people with themselves by stripping away the binders of culturally acquired ways of knowing.

The natural bias of the brain's structure is toward life-enhancing survival. If we can develop external media forms to embody that sensitivity, then as a culture we will no longer be estranged from ourselves and our environment. Moreover, they would be eco-media, embodying ecological intention so as to keep cultural and natural balance and anticipate disastrous consequences of action, both personal and collective.*

Try to do that with film, Jack.

*Warren Brodey, a founder of Ecology Tool & Toy (E.T.&T), which designs responsive materials and structures (i.e., they relate to you, and the environment independently of you), suggests we design computer decision programs which take into account ecological variables which don't normally intrude into conscious, rational thought.

One example might be attaching sensors to plants so that human interaction alone does not determine decisions of consequence.

In sum, just as techno-evolution has continually provided man with increasingly sophisticated tools to merge with (or mis-use) his physical environment, so is videotape a natural outcome of media evolution, giving us increased control over our psychological environment.*

Physical differences between videotape and film

Essentially the differences between videotape and film in playback and recording have already been laid out in the above section. About the only other things to know are cost and the nature of the recording processes themselves.

Remember first of all that videotape has the inherent option of sound whereas that's an extra feature with movie cameras. On the other hand, color is a possible option with film, but as yet unobtainable using Porta-Paks.

*Many studies of communications technology have ignored their use as personal tools. Instead, they concentrate on how hardware can supplant person-to-person business transactions and thus alleviate transportation and space problems.

But the logical conclusion of these studies, people who stay home to work by videophone and computer net, disregards the social function of people working together in the same physical space.

Instead, we need to teach people how to use communications to enhance their personal lives. The phone company does this, of course, when it encourages you to call long-distance "just to say hello to mom and dad," but it has not yet been realized that using videotape for personal feedback and transaction (e.g., mailing videotapes) is a logical tool to have in an electronic culture.

In other words, unless personal use of communications tools keeps pace with professional use, businessmen are going to be more inclined to work even more feverishly because they will be entranced by their technology, rather than use freed time to re-relate to themselves, their families, etc.

One half-hour of videotape costs, on the average, $13 (and is, of course, re-usable). One half-hour of Super 8, including processing but using an external audiotape recorder for sound, costs $45. Finally, one half-hour of 16mm (black-and-white) film with a magnetic soundtrack on the film itself, costs $110.

What more can I say?

As for the difference in the two processes, here is a description:*

In both film and videotape the moving picture is a series of still images. Actually, the film picture is still because the whole frame is exposed to light in a single flash of the shutter, but in video the different areas of the picture are traced at different times by the tip of a sweeping electron beam. One sweep of the entire picture is called a field.

Sixty fields appear each second (in videotape). Two phosphorescent points continually trace the screen, using the same scanning pattern the reader's eye uses on a page. As one field fades, a second is being drawn. The constantly regenerating image on the screen is an exact reproduction of how motion is scanned electronically in the camera.

Watching sound film, we see twenty-four different pictures a second, interspersed with instants of darkness. In fact, the screen is dark about half the time, but the flicker rate meshes with the retinal image retention of the human eye, and we see a persistent picture. This picture is wall-sized, an optically focused shadow of the image on the film.

The movie image is the light of the projector reflected off the screen, as the TV image is a surface of phosphorescent bits. Greys in the projected film are the light being kept from shining through the film by a barrier of silver grains. The light that does get through projects the pattern of the grain in the film which is the fabric of the image. The brightest part of a projected film image is white light passing through clear film and a lens reflected off the white screen.

Watching television we see a sheet of glass, its far side coated with phosphorus, being swept by the tips of two electron beams. The phosphorescence excited by the passage of the beams in several hundred geometrically exact lines is the television image. Its brightest part is the flash set off by the strongest electronic pulse recorded on the tape. It is an image with brilliance and luminosity which film can't achieve.

*Excerpted from **Videotape Versus Film, Half-Inch, 16mm and Super 8**, by Louis Jaffe. Radical Software #3, Spring 1971.

"GETTING CAUGHT," to a media-guerrilla, means BEING LABELED

3. How to Bankrupt Broadcast Television

In an information-based economy, loss of credibility is the same as bankruptcy. While broadcast is the antithesis of Guerrilla Television, there are still those who think that the medium could be salvaged if only *their* messages could be put across.

Beware. This is untrue. As the Meta-Manual demonstrates, people who believe this don't really understand media. It is the very structure and context of broadcast-TV which are co-opting. Instead of politicizing people with mass-TV, Guerrilla Television seeks to media-ize people against it.

Once you're sensitized to broadcast television it has potential only as entertainment, either intentional or unintentional. The first occurs with some shows which are fun to watch, and there is some live coverage of events done by network television which is superb. But generally the economics of broadcast-TV are such that those shows are labeled "special."

The run-of-the-mill stuff, which comprises better than 90 percent of broadcast-TV time, is crap. It can be entertaining because it's so poorly done, but not everyone has even that awareness.

I know people who lust after exposure on broadcast-TV. The energy I see them wasting is awesome. For perhaps one hour of exposure, once, at a pre-determined time, they will spend months organizing, contacting people, and having meetings.

When I first began working in alternate television I predicted that about a year later we would have a chance to air some of our tape, but only after TV labeled it something like "Crazy Experimental Far-Out Videotape Makers" so that somehow it would set apart from broadcast-TV instead of posing a real challenge to its structure.

Sure enough, eighteen months after I said that, we were asked to contribute tape to a show called "The Television Revolution."

Getting caught, to a media-guerrilla, means being labeled. It's impossible to vary your tactics each time, which is classic guerrilla strategy, if the people you must work with have pigeonholed you in a pre-determined category. The legitimacy you need to build a base of community and economic support may be unattainable if an alien press has already manufactured your image. The moment you surrender control of your media image, you're captured.

This is what happened to the Black Panthers. They got great press as they built up an image of armed reaction to what they deemed a repressive culture. This juiced up people to respond to them *before* they could make their move.

After all, if I am continually bombarded by a threatening image, nine times out of ten I'll move to pre-empt that threat. In other words, I'll strike first.

That's exactly what happened to the Panthers. White America very logically cut them down, both literally and figuratively, because the Panthers lacked the control they needed over media to get the non-belligerent, more constructive part of their message across. (If they had one.)

When Che Guevara went into Bolivia he shaved his beard and traveled incognito. The Panthers did the opposite, practically sending out press releases on where to find them. The media created them and the media destroyed them *because they couldn't control their own image.*

As I write this, the Panthers have broken into a schism between the followers of Eldridge Cleaver and those of Huey Newton. I know about this exclusively from the aboveground press which has used it to replace the Manson trial as the latest media follies.

Perhaps the only hope for the survival of the Panthers comes from portable video. It seems that early in 1971 someone laid a Porta-Pak on Cleaver in Algiers and since then he has been tooling up to make his own tapes and several have filtered back to the United States. But mainly they deal with propaganda. It remains to be seen whether in exile he can send back information which will help his disciples survive in America, or whether he just pumps out empty rhetoric.

BLACK PANTHER PARTY
International Section
B. P. 118 · GRANDE POSTE   ALGER · ALGERIA
TELEPHONE ~~82-14-69~~ 78-21-05

19 March 1971

PEOPLE'S VIDEO THEATRE
544 Ave of Americas
New York , New York
   U.S.A.

Ken March and Eliot Glass:

   We are presently making arrangements to take a delegation representing a cross-section of the Movement on an extended visit to China. You are aware that this will be a historic and unprecedented event. We want to be in a position to guarantee complete documentation of our visit, and we are convinced that video tape provdies the best possible form of documentation for our purposes. Having begun to use video for communication and information purposes, we have discovered the fantastic effectiveness of this medium as a political weapon and we want to develop its potential to a much higher level.

   We need two portable SONY video sets in the American system, complete with all accessories like fuses, cords, battery packs, and so on, with plenty of blank tape. You're in a good position to help us get this equipment through the contacts you have with the video network in Babylon. We'd like you to put the word out that the International Section of the Black Panther Party needs this equipment to video this historic event. The understanding should be that whoever gets together this equipment for us will have full access to all our documentation on China. Perhaps some collective effort could be made by the video network to provide us with the tapes and equipment and then these same sources would be the main outlets for the footage on the delegation's visit to China.

-2-

   Time is running short and you know we are in a tight position due to the contradictions being resolved within our Party. Frankly, we're up tight on all fronts --especially for money. This shit has to be moved on fast, and has to produce some concrete results.

   Let us hear from you soon.

ALL POWER TO THE PEOPLE
DEATH TO THE FASCIST PIGS

Eldridge Cleaver
Minister of Information

P.S.   Another project we need help with is putting together the Revolutionary People's Communication Network throughout Babylon for distributing and reproducing video.

Understanding the terrain of broadcast-TV is essential for Guerrilla Television. There is a reality in the great "message-messenger" debate which must be understood.

That debate goes like this: first the media say something, and then the government criticizes the media for having said it because, they charge, that creates an issue where there was none. In other words, as in ancient Greece when bearers of bad news were put to death, the media are thought to be responsible for creating what they convey.

Well, they do. Anyone who thinks that TV just reports news doesn't understand biological systems. The very fact that a message does get picked up amplifies it tremendously.

Remember that the collective American mind has no physical reality. Rather, it is a process entity of reported opinion, polls about that opinion, and marketing surveys to determine how to act on those polls. That structure is fabulously vulnerable to manipulation, either deliberate or unintentional.

The upshot is that the media amplify all sorts of messages. It's not by chance that social disorder comes in epidemics. Demonstrations on the West Coast are complemented by ones on the East Coast. Airplane hijacking sprang up like Asian flu. One bombing catalyzed hundreds of bomb threats. Many events just wouldn't take place unless TV cameras were there.

However, what the government is asking is to substitute its amplified messages in place of those of its opponents. That's like having your cake and eating it too. The people don't have the machine/money resources of government. All they're left with is the media to keep government honest.

Government is supposed to defend people's interests, so why shouldn't it be on the defensive?

The problem is that the media structure is spastic. The broadcast media just have no control over what they'll respond to.

Ben Bagdikian, in his book **The Information Machines,** points out that advertisers wrap the same old messages in new images to fool people out of their lack of interest. Thus, new movements and ideas are co-opted and made to sell products, like Virginia Slims cigarettes telling women: "you've come a long way baby" which, in effect, renders Women's Lib a merchandising scheme.

The networks themselves, because they must sell to advertisers, are an even more voracious novelty machine, gobbling up any and all new fads, phenomena, and personalities. Decisions to cover political dissent, which Agnew has attacked, are not made by a cabal of newsmen, but are Pavlovian responses by an organism which has surrendered self-conscious control. (No medium critizes itself less than broadcast television. There simply are no TV shows on TV which use the medium for self-analysis. At best people on TV talk about how bad it is, but they never use the videotape technology to show it.)

Perhaps the most decadent media event of the past half-decade was the saga of Michael Brody. Brody was a kid who claimed to have inherited a fortune and said he· was giving it away to the needy. Each day he got more exposure in the press and more and more desperate people tried to get in touch with him. Not one newspaper or TV station checked to see if he was telling the truth.

He wasn't. It turned out he'd probably wasted his mind on drugs and had at best a half-million dollars to play with. When this came out the press actually got mad at him for misleading them, yet he never implored them to cover him. Like a lumbering dinosaur which had to follow its instincts instead of a course of survival, the media gobbled up Michael Brody and then tried to blame him for their own indigestion.

Used by permission

HOW TO BANKRUPT BROADCAST TELEVISION ㉟

★★★★ FINAL

DAILY NEWS
NEW YORK'S PICTURE NEWSPAPER ®

8¢
10¢ OUTSIDE L.I. AND SUBURBS

Vol. 51. No. 178   Copr. 1970 News Syndicate Co. Inc.   New York, N.Y. 10017, Monday, January 19, 1970★   WEATHER: Partly cloudy, windy, **cold.**

BRODY TV SONG:
'I GOT BILLIONS'

NEWS photo by Anthony Casale

Used by permission

Ripe for the Plucking. Strumming a guitar, margarine millionaire Michael J. Brody Jr. makes his singing debut on Ed Sullivan's TVer last night. Brody's bride, Renee, listens. The madcap money man says he wants to give away $100 billion next week. Crowd of 300 waited out side the TV studio. —*Story on page 3; other pictures in centerfold*

Avert Catholic School Strike

Story on Page 2

Well this brings us back to Guerrilla Television. The object isn't to censor what people say about you, or put out propaganda, but to optimize the chances of getting your message across successfully. If you use the broadcast networks, the signal to noise ratio is not favorable.

We once got a videotape from some friends in England, of Jerry Rubin and some of his Yippie buddies "hijacking" the David Frost show in England (on the BBC).

 26

Rubin was an invited guest and he packed the audience with English freaks. After brief dialogue with Frost he invited them all up on stage and they came — with their own Porta-Pak.

 71

Thus the tape we got was a composite of straight off-the-air what the British public saw, and how the Yippies themselves were seeing it from the inside.

It's hard to know who won. On the one hand Frost was revealed as an incredible tight-ass as he demanded, in so many words, that the Yippies conform to his format (in other words, he belittled them when they didn't act like his other guests, docile and verbal); but on the other hand he looked good because the format, despite its straightjacket aspect, has the image of rational dialogue and the Yippies looked like unappealing madmen by not adhering to it.

Generally, Rubin's people had the best point. Plastic television is mental repression and there should be a chance to freak-out on TV. But as long as someone else controlled the cameras, they couldn't get it across.

However, on the tape they made, which the English public didn't see, the point came across very well. Unfortunately, Rubin and his crew have always been more concerned with becoming broadcast celebrities than doing the hard work necessary to set up their own support systems.

Finally, the last group in broadcast-TV to watch out for are the reformers. I've already badmouthed "Sesame Street," but there's lots more where that came from.

LONDON DAILY NEWS. February 9, 1971.

Frost Yippies Show probe

By GEORGE WEBBER and MARTIN JACKSON

THE Home Office has been asked to investigate Saturday night's oath-filled Yippy invasion of the David Frost programme, and the alleged use of cannabis during the show.

And a probe has already been ordered by Lord Aylestone, chairman of the Independent Television Authority. Protests poured in from viewers after the incidents.

NO CUTS

But despite all the objections, a recorded version of the programme went out uncut last night —four-letter words and all—on eight ITV stations from Scotland to the South of England.

These stations always show the programme on a Sunday. It is screened live on Saturdays to viewers of London Weekend, Midland, Channel, and Westward.

The I.T.A. gave the Sunday show stations a free hand in their treatment of the programme. A typical attitude was that of Granada, where an official said: "It was difficult to cut so we decided to put it out uncensored."

But last night's recording *was* preceded—at the request of the I.T.A. —by a warning telling people exactly what to expect.

Frost show shambles: Rubin [standing, far left], followers, and Frost

Used by permission

The difference between regular broadcast-TV, educational-TV, and Guerrilla Television, is this:

The networks are run by people who operate the cameras in their own interest. Educational-TV is where Liberals demand the cameras to operate in the people's interest. And Guerrilla Television gets cameras to the people to let them do it themselves.

This was underscored at a luncheon we went to once for the National Citizen's Committee for Broadcasting, one of those classic Liberal reform groups all the way down to the full-page ads in **The New York Times** soliciting money.

What happened was that each person anted up $15 for lunch in a plastic hotel ballroom and another $5 apiece per panel after lunch to listen to people talk to them.

an open letter to the presidents of ABC, NBC and CBS

and the public:

The first National Conference on Citizens Rights in Broadcasting Monday, October 26, 1970 at the Americana Hotel, offers an unprecedented examination of the role of television in American democratic society. The essential political fact is that the airwaves in the United States belong to the people, yet billions of dollars each year accrue exclusively to the three major networks. By and large it is their interest which finds expression. Our most vital natural resource, our children, will watch 22,000 hours of television before the age of 18 — 50% more than classroom time — and 95% of presently scheduled prime time programs undermines the values responsible parents wish to impart. This fact coupled with the almost total disregard of minority ethnic and intellectual representation poses one of the serious threats to our society.

No total assessment of broadcasting performance has ever been made in the United States. The National Citizens Committee for Broadcasting has undertaken such an assessment. Despite repeated attempts on our part, **NOT ONE MAJOR OFFICIAL OF THE THREE CORPORATE TELEVISION GIANTS HAS ACCEPTED OUR INVITATION TO PARTICIPATE.**

At the luncheon we will honor former FCC COMMISSIONER KENNETH A. COX, long known for his championship of the public rights. Mr. Cox, appointed by President Kennedy, has been denied reappointment by President Nixon. Principal speaker will be SENATOR BIRCH BAYH who will speak on "Television and the Political Process."

Television, the most remarkable communications medium of all time, is needed as never before as an intelligent force in a nation facing the uncertainties of the 1970's. A majority of the American people depend on television for their view of the nation and the world. Yet, television's potential for clarifying social issues, for interpreting the manifold problems besetting this nation, for adding to the quality of our life, lies largely dormant and as a result the medium is ignored by the vast majority of thinking people.

This National Conference will mark the beginning of nation-wide activities by the National Citizens Committee for Broadcasting to ensure that adequate expression of the public's interest is achieved and that the public's concern for the improvement of present policies of the Broadcasting Industry is recognized. To this end, over one hundred organizations representing hundreds of thousands of citizens are sponsoring this Conference.

Six panels will be conducted with such leaders in their fields as: MRS. JOAN GANZ COONEY, Producer of "Sesame Street"; FCC Commissioner NICHOLAS JOHNSON; WARD B. CHAMBERLIN, JR., Executive Vice-President of Educational Television Corporation; Actor OSSIE DAVIS; RAMSEY CLARK, former Attorney General; JOE McGUINNISS, author of "The Selling of the President"; CHARLES BENTON, President of Films, Inc.; Congressman ROBERT O. TIERNAN; JOHN de J. PEMBERTON, JR., Executive Director of the American Civil Liberties Union; REVEREND JESSE JACKSON; DR. W. WALTER MENNINGER; ROBERT LEWIS SHAYON and EDWARD P. MORGAN.

Panel topics will include: 1) *Minority Inclusion and Programming Diversity;* 2) *Children's Television;* 3) *Politics and Television;* 4) *Concentration of Control;* 5) *The Needs of American Society in the Development of CATV;* 6) *How to Effect Positive Change.*

For all our sakes in the years to come, Messrs. Goldenson, Sarnoff and Stanton, I urge you to join in this Conference, so that the leadership of ABC, NBC and CBS will have ample opportunity to express its views.

Sincerely,

Thomas P. F. Hoving
Chairman, National Conference on Citizens Rights in Broadcasting

---

MR. THOMAS P. F. HOVING
Chairman

NATIONAL CONFERENCE ON CITIZENS RIGHTS IN BROADCASTING
95 Madison Avenue, New York, N.Y. 10016   Telephone: 889-2244

_____I will attend the National Conference on Citizens Rights in Broadcasting in New York City and wish to have_____ticket(s) for the luncheon at $15.00 each. (The price for each luncheon ticket includes one morning and one afternoon panel ticket).

_____I will attend only the panel sessions at $5.00 for one morning and one afternoon panel ticket (State panels in order of preference).

_____I will not attend the National Conference on Citizens Rights in Broadcasting on October 26th, but wish to contribute $_____to NCCB in support of the cause of better broadcasting. (All Contributions are tax deductible).

NAME_____
(please print)

ADDRESS_____

CITY_____STATE_____ZIP_____TELEPHONE_____

Morning: Panel 1)_____   Afternoon: Panel 4)_____

Panel 2)_____   Panel 5)_____

Panel 3)_____   Panel 6)_____

Instead of that, as Ken Marsh pointed out, they could have skipped the whole affair and contributed the money to buy thirty or forty Porta-Paks to set up grassroots video projects.

Here then are some tactics for media-izing yourself and others against the psychic straight-jacket of braodcast-TV. Generally, what's below is just fun and shouldn't be mistaken for a particularly heavy or important use of Guerrilla Television.

TACTICS

Essentially the tactics revolve around this fact: with videotape you can record right off the air just as you can pick-up radio with audiotape. Like cutting up old magazines, this means that you can manipulate their myth system, instead of vice-versa.

Anti-ads

Try dubbing the soundtrack from a TV ad over your own video footage. Say one of those fatuous super auto ads and video of an actual traffic jam in your home town.

27   28

Or mix their audio and video, like a Band-Aid ad over visuals of Vietnam; or a catfood ad and something like kids starving in Biafra.

The irony is that this happens all the time. A favorite of mine was a documentary on Red China which concluded one section with pictures of little Chinese kids drilling with rifles as some sort of belligerent threat juxtaposed to an ad for underarm deodorant showing a gleaming white couple just after they'd finished playing tennis.

These jarring juxtapositions go by unnoticed because we've become so inured to the context of broadcast-TV. Even though the ads border on social obscenity, not even newsmen have control over which ones follow their broadcasts.

Doing your own juxtaposition will seem forced and you can't do too much of it because the idea is often more powerful than the execution. But when people object to the staginess of it, ask them why and then get them to try to penetrate their own biases.

An extension of this tactic might be a fully developed anti-ad service where consumers receive videotapes of TV ads with full supporting or non-supporting data. Or teachers might begin assigning ad research to students using VTRs. (Never once in my own grade school experience, however, did a teacher bring a TV set into class and use that as the content of a discussion.)

Screen-within-a-screen

Tape a broadcast-TV show so you see a screen-within-a-screen playing to no one. This has the effect of making an object out of broadcast-TV and reveals an alien absurdity.

Information collages

Make information collages which juxtapose interviews of real people with the phony characterizations in soap operas and ads.

Still-frame and slow-motion

Use still-frame and slow-motion in playback of tapes of talk show hosts or the President. Add canned laughter to the President's speeches.

One effective thing we did was to excerpt a phrase from a Nixon press conference and edit it into demonstration footage. (The phrase was this: "When the action is hot, keep the rhetoric cool." Nixon said it in response to a question from Nancy Dickerson about whether or not he was going to ask Vice-President Agnew to tone down his speeches. The time was shortly after the Cambodia invasion and Kent State. We went to Washington to videotape the subsequent demonstration and inserted that phrase into scenes of passionate, shouting students.)

Another tactic is to edit in a phrase two or three times in succession. To do this you just repeat a word or line for emphasis. ("A generation of peace. A generation of peace. A generation of peace.")

PLAY WITH POLITICAL ADS

It's interesting to contrast what the Republicans think is honest TV versus what the Democrats think it is.

GOP politicians sit calmly with a coat-and-tie on and talk straight at you, sort of like a parental monologue. Democrats, on the other hand, prefer shots of themselves in shirtsleeves walking among

the people. (That's what Lindsay does and that's why they want him to be a Democrat.)

Both attitudes, of course, are pure hype. On-the-scene footage is usually edited from one minute out of hundreds shot; speaking directly into the camera to simulate dialogue is ironic because the politician is actually talking to no one at the same time he's talking to everyone.

Nixon's style of TV is a throwback to the days of radio and consequently his success on the medium is only with pre-Media-Americans. The more natural TV is to you, the more plastic he seems, almost like one of those mechanical Walt Disney historical figures.

This isn't to make a character judgment *per se*: just because someone comes across poorly on TV doesn't mean that he's dishonest or venal.

But what Nixon does is eliminate (if he has it) any apperceptive sense of self. In other words, instead of the usual attitudes — Nixon being himself, Nixon knowing he's on TV, Nixon relating to audience, he eliminates the middle step and goes directly from being himself to relating to audience.

That's why he comes across as a product — because he doesn't acknowledge any process. As a result, he always seems out-of-sync, as if his body movements lag a split second behind what he's saying because he's trying so hard to be natural.

The more important the thing he's saying, the more intent and the less believable he becomes. I mean, who could keep a straight face when he told us he was invading Laos so we would have "a generation of peace." Such schizophrenia between content and intent is strictly a print bias.

Because many old modes of political advertising on TV have been exhausted, there'll probably be a radical escalation. It's already foreshadowed by regular product advertising which gives acknowledgment to the video process itself.

In other words, advertisers have realized that people are so oblivious to the ads themselves that the next thing to do is let on that they're aware that they're ads; the ads then become ads about ads. (It's sort of having your cake and eating it too. On the one hand you tell consumers that they're not so dumb they'd actually believe the ad, while on the other you try to sell it to them anyway.)

A particular case in point is a spot for Doral cigarettes which is so absurd as to make me question the mental age of the men who did it (in fact, most ads are amazing when you consider that *grown men* think them up for a living).

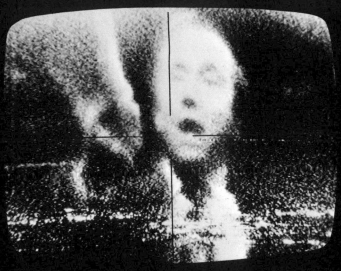

71. The "rational" David Frost as seen by viewers of the BBC

26. David Frost loses his cool as seen from Yippies own video camera

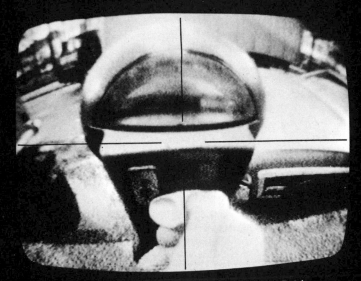

31. An "honest" Republican talking straight to a TV cameraman while pretending he's talking to you

28. Anti-Ad (recorded with a Porta-Pak)

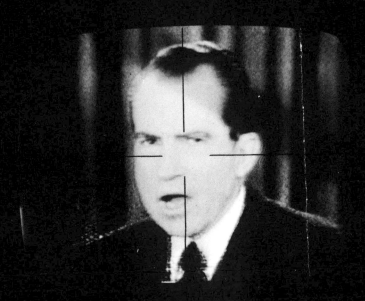

27. Ad (recorded from broadcast TV)

The first round was ads showing Doral cigarette packages dancing around and singing "Taste me, taste me." After that got patently absurd, Doral began to lampoon itself by having the characters in its ads wonder aloud why the package of Doral they'd just bought wasn't singing and dancing like the ones they saw on TV.

Similarly, the next presidential campaign will see politicians making ads about politicians making ads. It might work with an officeseeker coming out and telling you how *he* won't try to manipulate his image. Or maybe it will be one politician attacking the media image of his opponent; not the substance, but the image.

Probably this will be done verbally because to do it visually, with stop-framing or slow-motion or repeating phrases, would seem somehow immoral to print people who've learned to detach criticism from action.

If Nixon catches on to the fact that he can't be resold as a candidate (especially to eighteen-year-old voters) after his over-exposure as President, then his campaign strategists might decide to limit his image in ads for him. At that point, the Democrats might start putting him in their ads. In other words, one party will pay to show you their opponent.

The perception of perception through media is akin to the epistemology of dope wherein you become aware of yourself, and then aware that you are aware of yourself, and so on.

The fact that political advertising employs so much media manipulation seems immoral mainly to print-based people. Once you've media-ized yourself against broadcast-TV and assimilated TV as a tool, you can spot what is survival information and what is bullshit.

The reason we become more incensed over patent lies in print is that we have a working print grammar. When we have a similar affinity for video grammar, ads will become more honest, just as consumerism has fostered great changes in other product advertising.

So what you can do with political ads is make your own. On election night in 1970 we went to Buckley for Senator headquarters in New York and shot some very fine tape (Andy Mann and myself) of his supporters, most of whom we found to be courteous and open and eager to talk about the straight media. Later we edited our interviews with Buckley TV ads which gave a good picture of the man and his supporters.

Granted, this is not high-powered stuff. But ads are the weeds of the information environment, and everyone should have their own non-lethal pesticide.

DEBUNK THE MYTH OF PRIME TIME

When you've recorded a show off the air you can stop it, rewind, and fast-forward so that you, not a distant control room, control the pace at which you watch.

The only place they do this now is in football games where they budget time between commercials. They could do it lots of other places, especially on the talk shows which are videotaped, but they don't because time costs them too much money. You are thus a slave to their economic liabilities.

A thing we've done to point up the artificiality of time scarcity is edit an arbitrary amount of footage of the sea, just rolling in and out, in the time slot reserved for sixty-second commercials. Sometimes we dub audio over it.

BUILD UP A PUBLIC AFFAIRS ARCHIVE

That type of access used to be the prerogative of the rich and royalty when media like sculpture and painting were dominant and it was fabulously expensive to duplicate them.

Now everyone can have their own archive, especially a personal one. (All the Instamatic pictures locked up in closets will boggle the minds of future historians.)

Anything you want off TV is fair game. And all public event shows like presidential press conferences have no copyright on them.

The notion of a personal public affairs data bank is an extension of information power. Having your own record of what people, especially politicians, have said, lets you use their behavior to keep them honest. We have Nixon talking about Kent State, Laos, and Cambodia, and then throwing an incredible party for the astronauts, and that gives us enormous flexibility in relating to current events. (In fact, if you have the right tape you can show up the whole space program as a TV marketing gimmick from Hostess Twinkies ads about little astronauts who need "space food," to astronaut Scott Carpenter hyping gasoline.)

ELECTRONICALLY DISTORT THE VIDEO IMAGE

Eric Siegel, an electronics genius who's built his own video synthesizer (a TV analogue of audio synthesizers, it generates pure, abstract video images), complains that standard TV sets minimize the visual control you have over them.

They're similar to automobiles. The cheaper the car, the less dials and gadgets. About all you get are idiot lights which tell you there's trouble but give no forewarning.

Similarly, about all you can do with a regular TV set is make rudimentary adjustments in the way of brightness and contrast, horizontal and vertical. With more sophisticated monitors you can do all kinds of distortions and image shading.

Eric's idea is that everyone should have as many controls as possible to permutate the size, shape, and color of what they're watching. Of course you can do this to a degree with normal controls, but generally they're offered to "adjust" a picture which is thought to be abnormal, rather than to create your own electronic kaleidoscope.

However, one thing you can do is draw a magnet across the face of the picture tube. This messes with the magnetic field on the picture tube and distorts the image (without damaging the set) at your control.

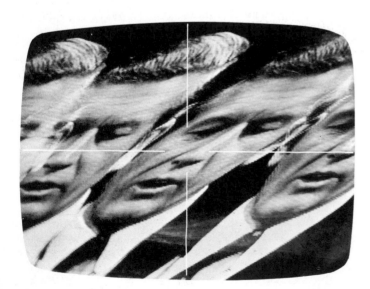

YOU are Information

④

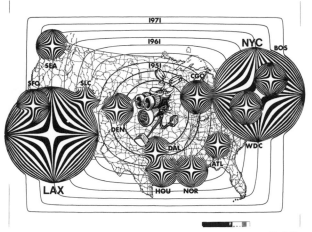

Ant Farm

4. You Are Information

In Media-America, we are extended in an information-space which is as real psychologically as geographical terrain is physically. In other words, TV cannot be understood as a representation of physical reality. Nor is it an extension of anything. It is its own reality. (Would you behave in your own home like a Dick Cavett show?)

Television is also a natural resource. Not only does it physically use publicly held space (*i.e.*, airwaves and cables), but the psychological space it inhabits is our collective intelligence.

Most people feel they suffer from information overload, which is analagous to pollution. Bombarded with electronic stimuli, they feel there's too much to know, too little time to know it in.

Added to that is the immense psychological manipulation of accepted behavior by models which are for the most part images generated by advertising.

There are no tools to fight back if you accept only one-way information technology. There is no way to assert your own value as information, no way to be as much information as, say Walter Cronkite.

For there is a unique cybernetics of self indigenous to an electronic culture. It has been little explored by traditional psychology. In fact, when psychiatrists use videotape in therapy they do so to re-affirm other analytic structures. About all they've concluded is that videotape lets you extrapolate behavior for more sensitive analysis. None have suggested that videotape may be a therapeutic tool which is uniquely applicable in an electronic culture.

If you understand mind not as a self-contained unit independent of external stimuli, but rather as an entity which has definition only with those stimuli, they are then no longer external. Inside and outside become inseparable and, as anyone who's ever been stoned knows, also interchangeable.

Paul Ryan offers the most understanding description of that experience. He calls it "infolding information."

In other words, we have various mental sets or programs through which we filter and select input. "Self-image" and "family ties" are examples of that kind of software.

But not only do we relate to ourselves or our families, but we also relate to our images of them, which Paul calls referencing systems. When we take experience and feed it back on itself, *i.e.*, infold it, we are self-referencing.

Videotape is a tool to externalize and enhance that process. As the tape becomes internalized (*i.e.*, remembered) it is thus infolded and acts as a lever to enhance cybernetic experience. Paul calls this "self-processing" (See page 00).

A standard malaise of ghetto children is that their sense of self-value is denigrated by the constant bombardment they receive from broadcast-TV of people and behavior which are alien to them, but nonetheless desirable. Street behavior especially (and especially on "Sesame Street") is given absolutely no verification. Yet street behavior is often the richest and most imaginative of all.

Making videotape with and about yourself and your friends is first of all just plain fun. But it's also a tool for knowing who you are and combating the superstar behavioral patterns of the media. With tape, being yourself has value in itself. (Which may cause a revolution in fashion and cosmetics when video feedback is widely available.)

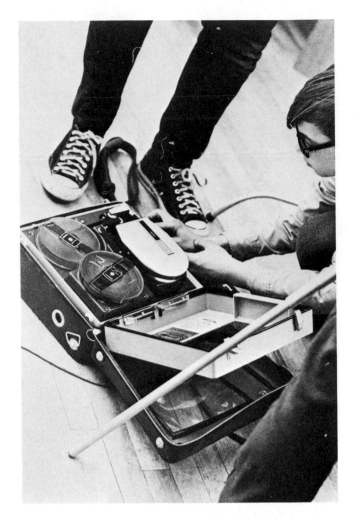

KIDS MAKING THEIR OWN TV

There's been a lot of studies made (exclusively in print!) of the effect of television on children, but none have used videotape (*i.e.*, the medium itself) to survey the effects of TV.

Nor is there much information around about how kids can make their own TV. The only guidance available comes from misguided teachers who think it's cute to have their students imitate the behavorial straitjackets of broadcast-TV (*i.e.*, do "news shows" under adult supervision) instead of setting them loose to enhance their own spontaneous behavior.

What follows is experience of our own (Raindance) with a group of a dozen junior high school kids from New York City. They came to our loft one afternoon a week for twenty weeks from the Clinton Project, an experimental school within a public school based on the Parkway Program in Philadelphia.

Essentially each kid gets to choose what he or she wants to do so that if he came to learn about videotape it was because he wanted to.

I have also drawn on the experience of the Media Access Center who, as far as I know, have done the most with kids and videotape. They recommend that you begin with these assumptions:*

1. Videotape is not film. You needn't script what you shoot nor edit the results into a final product. The tape is erasable and its capacity for immediate playback permits uses impossible with film. Record and playback and erase and record again what seems useful and interesting at the time. Shoot first and ask questions later.

2. Videotape is not television. Don't make record sessions into studio exercises or playback sessions into passive engagements with the tube. Arrange the equipment to fit in naturally with what's going on — *i.e.*, have plenty of extension cords around and avoid cumbersome studio accessories like lights — and freely intersperse recording, monitoring, responding, sequentially or simultaneously. The sooner you break students of standard TV roles (MC, cameraman, audience, etc.) and mindsets about programming, the sooner they'll enthusiastically enter the process of discovering what can be learned via videotape.

3. Videotape is a means of perceptual discovery and interaction; it demands uses more creative than the consumption of instructional knowledge. Students must become active agents in initiating and participating in video projects, with real control over the information generated and its use. The moment kids see themselves as subjects or targets for educational TV, they'll tune out. Teachers must make

*Reprinted from **Big Rock Candy Mountain** (an education access and resource catalog), Winter 1970, p. 53. Portola Institute, Menlo Park, California.

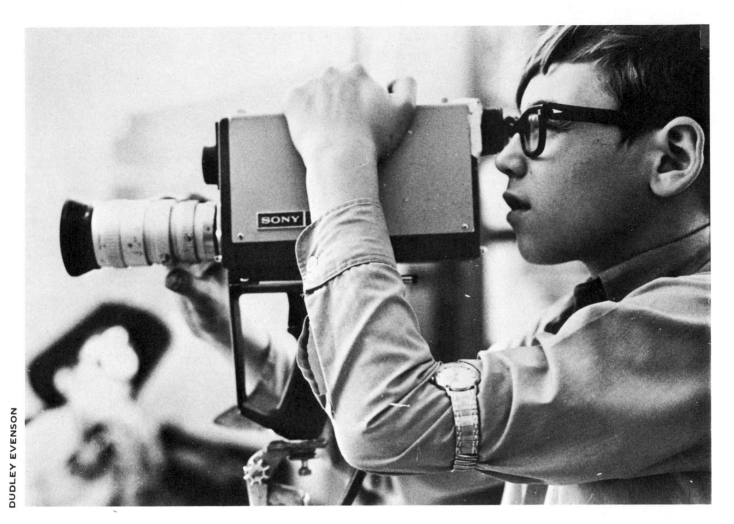

themselves equally vulnerable to exposure on video-tape and be open and honest about the discoveries *they* make.

Our experience with kids at Raindance began through Phil Yenawine of the high school education department at the Metropolitan Museum of Art in New York.

He planned to underwrite a program for the Clinton School Project and wanted to use video-tape to teach film. He called us to ask if he could use our equipment.

Of course we said no, film and video are two different things, and why didn't he just underwrite a videotape course. Which he very generously did. (We were getting $40 an hour, or $120 an afternoon. That broke down to $30 for use of the space and equipment, the other $10 an hour for personnel. Generally one or two of us from Raindance aided two or three teachers.)

The first few weeks of the program the kids went out on the streets and taped interviews with people they'd stop.

When the weather turned cold they stayed inside and acted out scripts they themselves had written or sketched out. They also took to bringing their own props. None of that was suggested by us. All of it was at their own initiative, as we tried to discourage theatrical type productions.

A few of the kids really got into making demands on the equipment's capability. They'd even ask to come on the weekends, when school was out, to keep trying out more ideas.

They also learned editing and we considered it our major failure that none of them wanted to, or did, put together a finished piece at the end of the course.

Of course, that may be our bias, just as our being disappointed by our inability to get the kids to feed back verbally on their experience was more a reflection of our way of doing video than theirs.

What we can pass on from our experience is this:

If there's not enough equipment to go around, especially portables, it's hard to keep interest high. You can usually send out a crew of three kids per Porta-Pak (cameraman, sound man, and someone to hold the recording deck) and thus each one will have something to do. In other words, there has to be some piece of equipment for each one to hold so he feels part of something.

Inside, the group usually broke down into kids who wanted to work the equipment, those who wanted to perform, and hangers on. Some kids are timid about being taped and you shouldn't force them on camera. We found that even the kids who wanted to be taped most often became very reserved upon seeing their self-image in playback.

Don't build up a hardware mystique. The first day of classes one kid asked us how much a Porta-Pak costs ($1,495) and then was awed at the price. He asked: "How come you're letting us kids use it?" We just handed it to him and let him start shooting. No questions asked. You've got to find a healthy balance between having a kid respect the equipment and not be awed by its cost.

Also try to minimize the difficulty of using hardware, mainly because it's very easy to use. Instead of demanding that kids circle around the equipment and get checked out on it as if it were an airplane or something, let them at it right away. They usually want to know how it works to solve a problem, not to anticipate one. And that's a learning mode.

Finally, as Media Access says, don't lay a broadcast-TV trip on them. Most of what you and they see on TV is behavior artificially conditioned by studio and money biases. While our kids often imitated what they saw on TV (*e.g.*, a news show), they quickly broke through its context with their own spontaneity.

Moreover, a Porta-Pak can go anywhere so that copying studio behavior is superfluous. If you don't have Porta-Paks you can still work with kids, but then try to avoid imposing adult control on the equipment.

As for where to get equipment, there's lots of it locked up in school closets because teachers don't know what to do with it. Liberate it!

SELF-PROCESSING

One of the first things to do when you get a portable video camera is take it home and live with it. Tape everyday ordinary events: eating, walking, sleeping, talking, making love.

You should feel absolutely no compulsion to show these tapes to others, or even save them. This is inherent in the economy of videotape because it's erasable.

It differs from film, and home movies especially, because as a product medium film costs money and time and compels people to "do something" when the camera's on. Thus home movies pick up on what is essentially abnormal or forced behavior.

With videotape the commonplace becomes information and the camera is open to everyone. This is antithetical to most modes of self-analysis which are done by people who control your own image.

Paul Ryan, who studied four years for the priesthood before abandoning that idea, once set up his own videotape confessional booth which he called *"Ego Me Absolve* (I absolve myself)." You went in, taped yourself, and then played it back under your own control as a purgative, rather than surrender that power to an authority figure who gains his sustenance from your debilitation.

From taping my own self I have assimilated the confidence that my value as information is as significant as anything I see on broadcast-TV.

I have extended this experience to my family who genuinely enjoyed seeing themselves cast in the role of information.

First we taped ourselves having Sunday coldcut dinner: my brother, his wife, my mother and grandfather. Generally my brother and I did most of the taping which lasted for twenty minutes. Then we went in the other room and watched it on the family TV set.

My mother immediately commented on how sad she looked (my father had just died six months ago). My grandfather was delighted to see himself. And my brother and sister-in-law immediately picked up on their body language.

— Other variations on relating to your own image are taping yourself talking, playing that back and talking to it (yourself); or try touching your taped image on the TV screen with your real body and trace your movements. Extend that to exploring non-verbal space with your body and the camera.

Especially in school situations, we normally surrender control of sensory awareness, either to a teacher or "supervisor" who demand that we sit in a pre-determined pattern, or to rigified building design and furniture placement. Videotape is very effective in picking up on body language and environment (see section: *TV as an Analytic Tool*).

— Try relating to yourself in a feedback delay system (see details under **The Tools**) where your image comes up once or several times a few seconds after your movement. Tape yourself watching tape of yourself.

— For a sense of controlling purely electronic space, do what are called "feedback loops." They're done by pointing a camera on live feedback into a monitor which is carrying the picture. In other words, you're shooting the camera shooting itself.

What actually happens is that the camera picks up both the image and the light variations on the screen in a composite image. That feeds back adding the same reflections of the light off the screen glass. Any time you move slightly the light input changes and so does the image. Even if you mount the camera on a tripod, normal changes in room light usually keep the pattern changing. It's a sort of electronic kaleidoscope which you can play with for hours.

Another variation is positioning the camera so you see TV screens within TV screens, or people within TV screens within TV screens within TV screens. This is similar to an infinity of mirrors except you don't have to be in a straight line to get the effect.

— Finally, ego trip with a camera. It's an incredibly powerful feeling to arm yourself with a video camera which shields you from human interaction, especially in a public situation.

I once went to Central Park with a friend who had a field day directing complete strangers we'd pick up just because we had the camera. (There's a game of upsmanship in the park. Everyone brings cameras although the only thing to take pictures of is people with cameras. The better your camera, the more protected you feel. Well, a portable videotape camera is the ultimate in upsmanship.) Now that you've experienced that, imagine how the network newscasters must feel, all the time, and what that must do to their judgment.

COLLECTIVE PROCESSING

Most of our relationships with friends are mediated experiences. We see them less in person than we communicate with them via telephone or the mail. If it weren't for these channels of exchange, relationships would be impossible to sustain.

Videotaping with friends is like having a collective consciousness both for the real-time experience, and the potential of stored (*i.e.*, recorded) experience. Besides videotape, it would take telepathy to internalize that possibility.

Making a tape with friends is similar to a jam session by a rock group. In a sense, it's an information jam session: improvised behavior within the parameters of a certain skill.

Last year we took a trip to California and carried a Porta-Pak wherever we went. Each day we'd tape. Each night we'd play it back. Gradually the trip became both the real-time experience and the shared accumulation of it on videotape. To this day we remember specific lines and situations and use them as collective codes to describe current thoughts.

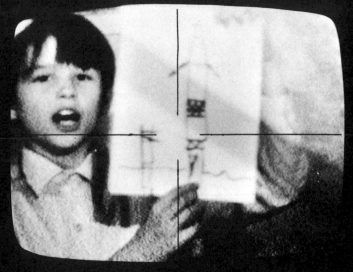

33. A kid's news show

34. An adult's news show

47. An "Editorial Reply"

52. Supermarket

49. How they hype up women to buy supermarket products

50. Interviews by Elaine Tesoro of People's Video Theater asking housewives how they really like shopping

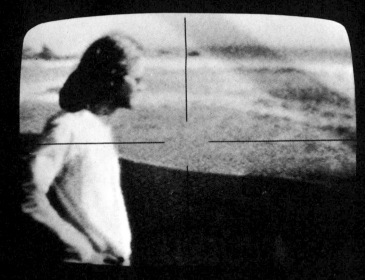

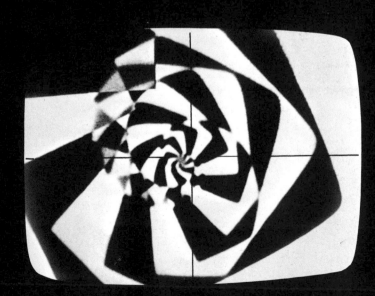

─── FEEDBACK LOOPS ───

We also got into naming our tapes rather than giving them descriptive titles. A particular tape we made called "The Rays" has become almost an archetype to us. Essentially it's just five of us, stoned, on a beach and freaking out. Part of having the experience was making the tape itself which gets its name from video signals from a transmitter near the beach which were interfering with our Porta-Pak and being picked-up on the tape.

 42

Such a stored, shared experience is physically indigenous to the facility of videotape, and psychologically indigenous to Media-America.

The Videofreex have both taped together and lived together communally. It's hard to imagine a similar film collective.

The Freex both make individual tapes using a collective support system, and they make tape together. They claim to be most plugged-in to one another when they're plugged-in to a video mixing system with each person manning a camera and wearing earphones.

They plan to extend their life style to Media Buses (see the chapter "Cybernetic Strategies and Services"), touring from town to town giving video shows and making tape. This is more or less analagous to rock road tours and will probably become self-sustaining when cable-TV opens up: a traveling troupe of video technicians and entertainers being paid to do local gigs at local TV studios or shoot tape in local communities.

Finally, you can always bring videotape into an encounter group.

STREET TELEVISION

There is a whole genre of videotape made simply by people standing on the street with a Porta-Pak and picking-up on what's going down.

If you make yourself visible like this, usually someone will come up and start rapping with you. In fact, I've always maintained that it's impossible to go out on the street with a Porta-Pak and not get some good tape.

Some of the best tape we have was done this way. Most people who live out on the street have something to say and no one to say it to. However, even people not normally predisposed to talking will pick up and give you a monologue.

Some examples from the Raindance data bank:

— A street rap on sex by a Berkeley (California) "street person."

— Three elderly people on New York's Upper West Side telling us how much dirtier and worse the city is now, compared to the old days.

45

— A girl on St. Marks Place giving an honest, rugged account of her experience with STP.

— A monologue by a Cuban drunk interspersed with his pleas for money to buy a drink.

What you have to watch out for is to respect the people you're taping. Legally, you can't use the tape commercially without their permission.

But even for your own use, you have an obligation not to pull an information rip-off by turning someone into street theater and victimizing them.

Generally this means telling them what you're going to do with the tape, who you are, letting them see it in replay (through the camera eyepiece), and then asking if they mind whether or not you keep it. If you don't do this, you're just another media exploiter.

VIDEO ENVIRONMENTS

A good way to familiarize people with both video equipment and the videotape experience is to set up an interactive environment.

There's no one way to do it. What can be done is often limited by resources, *i.e.*, available equipment. What's important is that people be given privacy, if they want, and absolute control over the equipment.

The opposite of that is Cybernetic Fascism: forcing people to have a feedback experience through your biases, not their own. This happened once in a show called "Information" at the Museum of Modern Art in New York.

The environment was set up exactly as you'd expect a museum, especially the Modern, to do it. Essentially it was a neatly constructed room with a chair. You sat inside and responded to audiotape commands like "Sleep, smile," etc. You saw no camera but were being taped from another compartment, not even automatically, but by a technician using one-inch equipment. When your time was up (you were forbidden to bring anyone in with you) the tape was played back next to some live feed monitors on a panel outside the booth. But they wouldn't tell you when.

Well, we went down there with our Porta-Pak and tried to take it inside. A guard came over and said we couldn't and even threw one of us out of the booth while the other was inside. A guard telling you what to do in a cybernetic environment?

There was a similar information rip-off in a piece done by Global Village for the "Vision and Television" show at Brandeis University in February, 1970.

It consisted of a giant box built to look like a TV set. The front was a glass window. Inside you were supposed to look at tapes while they taped you and fed the picture to "spectators" outside. The tapes they showed alternated between political personalities and mild pornography so that people would start to laugh and then find themselves under scrutiny by friends and strangers. That's a kind of bastardized reverse of a straight surveillance system.

Low picture for natural-angle viewing

To involve people you can have cameras on live feedback which they control (*e.g.*, hanging from a ceiling), cubbyholes to retreat into, tape delays (see the chapter "Tools"), and decks where they can select what they want to see by putting it on themselves.

The following "Tentative Design for a Flexible Video Environment"* by Ira Schneider is a full-blown example of some of the things you can do:

The design includes three basic zones: the feedback introduction corridor, the process television interaction space, and a video information center or observation area.

The feedback introduction corridor is designed as a transitional zone between recognitions of where the entrant has been and where he is going. The monitors in the corridor will feed back live television of the entrance to the space itself, the walk up the staircase and/or the elevator exit, and a preview of what the entrant will experience in the process television interaction space and the observation area. (Such a preview helps reduce the initial self-consciousness which people experience upon first seeing themselves "on television," *e.g.*, "Hi mom, I'm on TV.")

Upon turning the corner the entrant finds himself in a more brightly lit space in which he can observe (through a two-way glass pane) others participating in the process TV interaction space. (There is a possibility at this point that the entrant is picked up on a camera held by participants in light pool *C*.)

After this point the entrant can choose to be a participant by entering into the process television interaction space. If one of the cameras which hangs from the ceiling is free then he can become an operator or he can enter the space as an actor. As an operator the participant can interact with other operators or mirrors (one- or two-way) or monitors. If the entrant chooses not to participate he can pass on to the observation area and watch live TV of the antics of the actors and operators and perhaps of the observers, himself included.

He may then choose to become a participant at some level or to remain and observe himself in the private self-observation chamber. The entrant therefore has the choice of being a passive observer or an active participant, either in a social space or in relative privacy. Unlike other museum video pieces (*e.g.*, the "Information" show at the Museum of Modern Art), the participant is given maximum control over his own feedback.

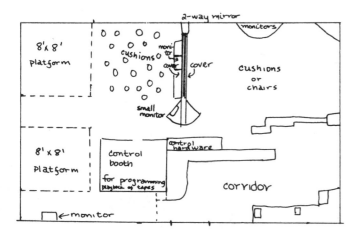

Process Television Environment

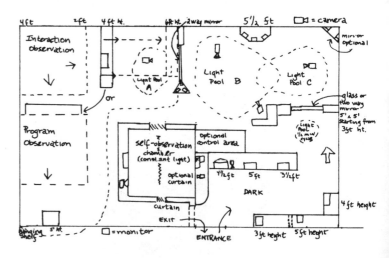

*Reprinted from **Radical Software #3**, Spring 1971. The design was planned for the Jewish Museum in New York City, but never executed.

NOTES:

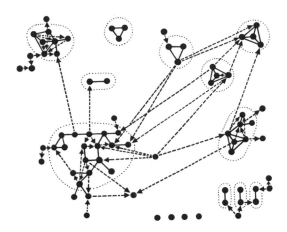

Community Video

Contemporary communities, especially urban ones, have few formal networks for anticipating the intentions of their citizens. Bureaucratic action is generally taken after a "crisis" which has erupted in the form of a physical demonstration over a specific, usually *ad hoc*, cause like highway expansion, police brutality, or an eviction.

As communities have become more complex, the intelligence role of government has not kept pace, except in surveillance. That the police departments in most communities should be entrusted with gathering data about citizens, and that they have the most sophisticated information technologies to do that, is a fundamental flaw in American democracy.

A true community media means an anticipatory intelligence network, not a repressive one. As only people themselves know what they are thinking, such a media structure must be as free of mediators as possible.

This is not now the case. Because local governments have abdicated responsibility for guaranteeing access to the popular media, the ombudsman role has been taken up by "Six O'Clock Newses" all over the country. Traditionally, however, the broadcast structure responds to abnormal behavior and permits feedback only in the form of editorial replies by "responsible spokesmen." The local TV station, of course, determines who they are and generally they must conform to a mode of behavior which is alien to the disenfranchised, *i.e.*, a neatly groomed man or woman sitting behind a desk must deliver a low-key monologue. Never is a community group permitted to present its own response footage shot on location in the community and edited by the people themselves.

Government is just another technology. Right now its state-of-the-art is far behind other bureaucracies because it refuses to embrace the sophisticated technologies which businesses and even its own police departments are using. Information indigency is as real as material poverty. In fact, they go together.

As long as broadcast-TV is the only means of distributing video information, and heavy, cumbersome hardware the only means of production, the function of community television is bound to be controlled by a *de facto* elite.

Guerrilla Television combats that pattern. Even without access to television distribution channels like cable television, or even videocassettes, it's possible to initiate a grassroots television in your community. This chapter, "Community Video," is concerned primarily with indigenous production. A more detailed discussion of how to access the means of distribution is covered in the chapter "Networking: Videocassettes and Cable Television."

There is no one pattern for introducing and using video in a community other than a certain attitude toward the medium which has been laid out in the chapter "You Are Information." There are, however, a variety of options available, some of which will fit your situation.

About the only generalization to be made is that community video will be subversive to any group, bureaucracy, or individual which feels threatened by a coalescing of grassroots consciousness. Because not only does decentralized TV serve as an early warning system, it puts people in touch with one another about common grievances.

My understanding of the community potential of Guerrilla Television comes mainly from two sources: from the People's Video Theater and Raindance.

JAY ITKOWITZ

SET UP A STOREFRONT THEATER

Very few communities have cable-TV yet. If you wait, the franchise in your area will probably be granted to straight money people whose idea of community programming is a stationary camera on the mayor while he talks.

Thus a secondary value of storefront television is that not only do you establish a community information service, but you anticipate the installation of cable by having an indigenous information power base not contingent on the whim of outside owners.

A true community, of course, can be either geographic or demographic. In New York, for example, many of the nascent pressure groups like Gay and Women's Lib draw supporters from all around the city, not a specific neighborhood.

The actual location of a storefront or loft will depend on price and access. You should try to minimize your operating overhead as well as your equipment requirements to remain flexible enough to go into the community rather than demand that it come to you.

Generally, you shouldn't demand that people organize around Guerrilla Television. Rather, it is a tool which can be grafted onto already existing social situations with established social bases. Thus, it was patently disenfranchised and organized groups like the Young Lords and Black Panthers whom PVT chose to work with first.

People's Video Theater is now expanding into Greenwich Village which is affluent, further from the edge of just bare existence struggling. To do this they plan to cultivate existing citizens' groups, coalesce them around prominent issues (*e.g.*, an influx of drug addicts into the neighborhood), and build a programming base to extend into cable-TV.

Another place to begin is in the schools. Most of them are desperate for new ideas, and some even have equipment imprisoned in a closet. Many, however, have no money.

You should also anticipate how subversive your project is going to be. The more uptight the school, the more old-line the teachers and community, generally the more trouble you'll have.

Paul Ryan helped set up a project in Newburgh, New York, in 1969 which used Ford Foundation money to turn local high school kids on to portable video and then let them transmit their programs over the town CATV system.

The fact of kids generating their own knowledge combined with the type of things the kids chose to tape (*e.g.*, they went to Washington, D.C., and taped a peace demonstration including obscene slogans against the government; when the adults objected they replied, in all honesty: "That's what went on. We didn't make it up.") was too much for the right-wing community which forced the program out of the school and into a local theater with an independent administration.

As Paul tells the story, the highlight of the inquisition was a town meeting at which the school gym coach gave a pre-assigned report on new media. He'd read a **Look** magazine piece by Marshall McLuhan on a predicted breakdown in hard-edged definition between male and female dress and concluded with a question/statement to the project's directors: "It says here this guy McClugan (sic) is for free love. Is that true?"

An equally amazing incident took place in a project done by Media Access Center. Out in California they borrowed equipment from Stanford University to give to a group of local black kids who'd just integrated an all-white, suburban high school. The kids went out and taped the school while adding their verbal commentary which was very strong.

The result was that the school principal impounded the tape and told Media Access, which had designed and run the project, that no one could see the programming unless they had a Ph.D. in education, Media Access included!

A filmmaker named Grant Masland reports a similar incident, but one which had a more creative ending.*

A group of students at a California high school taped a teacher reprimanding them for bringing a Portable Video camera into a teachers' lounge. Instead of disciplining them, the assistant principal viewed the tape and then tried to explain what a high school is like from the administrative end.

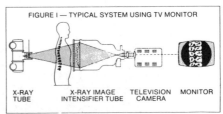

FIGURE I — TYPICAL SYSTEM USING TV MONITOR

X-RAY TUBE   X-RAY IMAGE INTENSIFIER TUBE   TELEVISION CAMERA   MONITOR

*From: "Occasional Papers: A Center Report." Bimonthly publication of The Center for the Study of Democratic Institutions, Santa Barbara, February 1971.

USE THE MASTER ANTENNA IN APARTMENT BUILDINGS

In urban areas, many apartment buildings have a sort of mini-cable system in the form of a master antenna which feeds the sets in the building. It's a simple matter to hook into this system and feed programming over an unused broadcast channel.

If a building is particularly together, not only can the tenants receive programs but they can make them. This is going on at Westbeth, an artists' cooperative building in Manhattan. The tenants wired the building themselves and are working toward their own TV station. Westbeth was an old telephone company laboratory building in Greenwich Village which was converted into 350 artists lofts. Because of the concentrated community, a few of the tenants (Ann Douglas and Allen Katzman) interested in video decided to wire the building.

With help from us and Videofreex for the actual wiring, the system spread through the whole building. Now, nightly, from Ann's apartment she and Allen and others transmit (with a Porta-Pak) live real people (*e.g.*, a look into the refrigerator), tapes they've made and that others bring, and even shoot films from a movie-projected image off the wall, including pornography.

As everyone who gets the channel has made a conscious decision to do so, Westbeth TV is absolved from the frivolous denominators of mass taste which plague broadcast TV. In fact, residents are eagerly putting up fifteen dollars for a year's subscription to the cable for this alternate programming.

Of course, a clandestine variation of this tactic is just to go into apartment buildings and do it anyway. (Another variation, on a grander scale, would be to build a low-cost, short-range transmitter and feed in to broadcast-TV signals.)

Master antennas have enormous potential because many low-income housing projects have them, and many of the people in them have TV sets. Mainly because about the only thing you can do in that kind of poorly designed building is watch TV.

MOBILE SHOWINGS

You can either take a traveling show on the road (see the section "A media bus") or better, in a community context, work with existing hardware set-ups.

We know some people in France who travel around the provinces making and showing tape in people's homes and cafés. Their tape, however, tends to be quite political because that's where the French are at.

The Videofreex giant TV screen inflatable used for outdoor showings (with a video projector)
VIDEOFREEX

PROGRAMS AND PROGRAMMING

As a general-use technology, portable video has no one approach. Guerrilla Television demands applications to fit specific situations.

Nonetheless, there is experience around and some things do seem to work better than others. Generally, all you have to do is make contact with the community and it will begin pouring back its needs to you.

It's better for people to suggest what you can do for them rather than vice-versa. Even if their ideas are the most banal in the world, the fact that they have actually done something for themselves has tremendous value.

Begin by covering local events and people and building up contacts, often by playing back on the spot. Or just hand the camera over to interested spectators and let them begin shooting for themselves. Not everyone will want to, or will even be good at it, but a sorting out happens which draws on the people in the community.

Avoid an onslaught of public relations and hype. Just move in and start shooting. But always, of course, ask permission. To start taping without the consent of the people involved is just a rip-off, like broadcast-TV.

Some tactics you might try are:

Video mediation

This is a mode originated by the People's Video Theater. Essentially it means taping one side in a conflict and showing it to the other. Then taping their response and showing it to the first group. And so on.

PVT first did this in Washington Square Park in New York. The park had been under reconstruction for over a year and a tense situation had developed between park people and local residents.

PVT first made a fifty-minute documentary of the situation in the park by talking to everyone who used it: blacks, students, pensioners, etc. From the tape it became apparent that people were very upset because construction, already past deadline for completion, limited available space.

PVT then made a six-minute tape of the park people talking about the documentary, and a six-minute tape of local residents responding to that feedback. The resulting twelve-minute tape was shown to city officials, local residents, and city planners. They responded to the questions posed and the final tape, documentary with feedback, was then shown in the park.

The New York University Media Co-Op did a similar thing by first taping a meeting of squatters (people who had moved into abandoned buildings because they had no other place to live) and then playing it to objecting neighbors.

There is a similar program in Canada called "Challenge for Change" which works in rural communities to mediate differences. In fact, Canada is way ahead of the United States in decentralized media, much of which is government-sponsored.

Tape a TV crew

When a broadcast-TV crew comes into your neighborhood, videotape them. Demand to interview an announcer. Then organize a local discussion around the announcer's response and the broadcast-TV coverage that appears later (which you can tape right off the air for a community archive).

Two women friends of ours did this with a Women's Liberation demonstration. First they went to an abandoned building that women had seized to convert into a day-care center.

When they got there a CBS cameraman told them that CBS was going downtown to interview the city attorney who had signed an eviction notice. Our friends went down there as participants who had a right to see that media coverage was fair, especially since it involved a public official.

They got there ahead of the network crew which came in demanding that they leave and not tape the network filming an interview. This is a real insight into the whole broadcast mentality.

The local "announcer" was a woman, because it was a Women's Lib "story." Her name was Gloria Rojas and she demanded that the two women leave because she told them: "It's my story. I found it [the idea to interview the city attorney]. Aren't you ashamed of yourself for not being able to think up your own stories?"

In other words, she related to the information as her property, not a process in which others were involved. During her tirade, however, the women kept their Porta-Pak running unbeknownst to Gloria.

Monitor grievances

Instead of approaching bureaucracies with print petitions or alienating demonstrations, ask them to watch a short documentary of people describing and showing the conditions and problems they're protesting. Use videotape as the evidence.

You might try this especially with police behavior and if they threaten you, just leave the camera running. Even if they smash the thing they usually don't understand that, unlike film, videotape isn't ruined by exposure to light.

On the other hand, police are usually as frustrated as everyone else, and often with good reasons. So tape them and let them see themselves on replay. Rather than exacerbate police/community tensions, use videotape to mediate them.

One of the best tapes I've ever seen was done by Media Access who taught local California high school students how to use the equipment. The students then made a tape called "Juvenile Justice."

"Juvenile Justice" is a straight documentary (without the annoying voice-overs of broadcast-TV) made by kids on how the law relates to them. It's particularly concerned with drug laws and interviews kids about why they take drugs, parents about why they think their kids take drugs, and law enforcement officials about why they enforce the law.

The resulting twenty-eight-minute package is a powerful piece of honest information (edited, of course, by the kids themselves) highlighted by the sheriff and judge who claim that the reason they enforce the law is that it's the law, not that it has any particular cogency. Perhaps the punch line is the local judge's plea to them to wait until they're old enough to vote to change the law. In other words, the same culture that's telling kids to assume responsibility renders them powerless until an arbitrary age limit.

Other grievance tapes you might make are local opinions about public services, or lack of them, like garbage pick-up and mass transportation.

Do your own "public service" programming

The best way to build grassroots media support is to appeal to people's self-interest. It's one thing to show them propaganda programming, another to give them useful information.

Depending upon local need, try making a tape about how to get food stamps, service at city hall, or how to get on welfare. Remember these are supposed to be public officials — i.e., your servants — and they should be subject to the scrutiny of being played back in the communities they service.

Work the suburbs

If you're white and middle-class you shouldn't be on a political trip in someone else's neighborhood unless you're prepared not to tell other people how to live. If you think others should listen to you, then go back to the suburbs where you came from. Radicalize your parents.

As the repression they suffer from is psychological, not physical, you need psychological tactics, i.e., Guerrilla Television.

Make tapes of housewives shopping at those sterile shopping centers. Ask them if they really like it. Play back on the spot.

Or videotape commuters waiting in neat rows for those trains they claim they hate. Play back at the station. Or buy a ticket and play back on the train.

Community video can't really happen without indigenous energy and that means indigenous information. People don't want to see films of sugar cane cutters in Cuba when they've got their own problems. With Guerrilla Television you can pick-up on those problems and feed them back right away, under the autonomous control of the people who are experiencing them.

PLAYBACK ENVIRONMENTS

There's no one or two ways to show communities videotapes but there is a general attitude which applies: don't set up a theater, set up an information center.

That means flexibility instead of rigidly scheduled showtimes. If people are going to be late, wait for them. If someone has some tape they'd like to show but you hadn't scheduled it, let them show it. And if people want to stop a show in the middle to talk about what they're seeing, let them — that's one thing that videotape technology is all about.

Also avoid a hard environment where seats are immovable and people have to trip over each other to get around. And, whatever you do, don't turn the lights off.

Some of the pleasantest evenings I've had watching tape were at People's Video Theater where the show was loose and informative and at the end they passed a camera around so people could tape themselves, and people got into talking to each other.

VIDEO FESTIVALS

A good way to bring together video people, let others see what you're up to, and have a good time is to have a special Video Festival.

Everyone can bring tape and equipment and just do what they want. Soft environmental structures like domes and inflatables are good things to have festivals in.

Ant Farm in California once sent out invitations to a "Video Slumber Party." Everyone came with tapes and Ant Farm set up a replica of a 1950s living room with sofas and chairs. A good time was had by all.

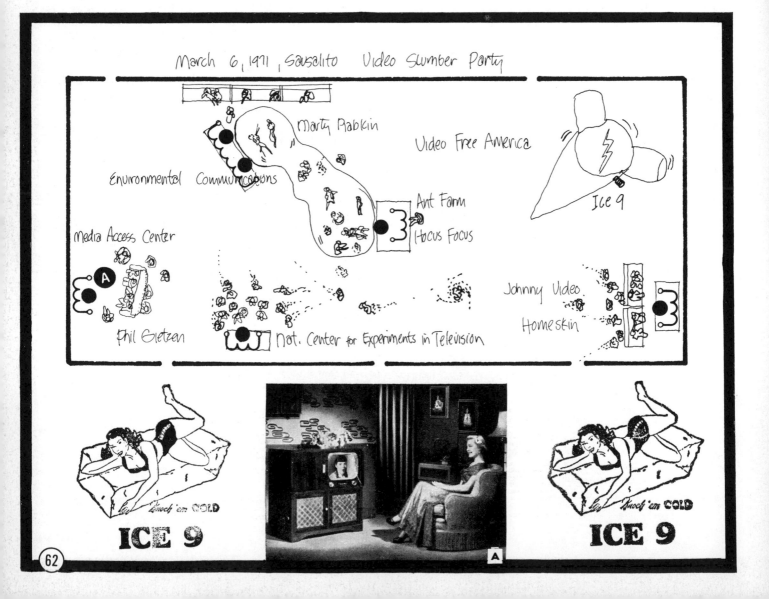

 # VIDEO

SATURDAY MARCH 6 8PM-8AM
SAUSALITO ART CENTER

 INVITATATION
Slumber

 # PARTY

BRING YOUR HARDWARE,
TAPES, EATS, DRINKS, ETC.

NEVADA STREET
GOOD TASTE
MARIN BUSTOP
SHELTER
630 ART CENTER

TO SAUSALITO
WHITE TRASH AREA
BIG "G" SUPER
BRIDGEWAY AV
2 min valley
RED LIGHT

art center is at 630 NEVADA street. for more call (springs) 332-9088

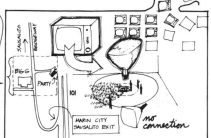

SAUSALITO
BRIDGEWAY
BIGG
PARTY
101
MARIN CITY
SAUSALITO EXIT
no connection

DO NOT *Erase*
EASY ACCESS

ABOUT THIS EVENT: ITS FREE, ITS FOR VIEWING TAPES AND MEETING VIDEO PEOPLE, NO HYPE, NO EXPECTATIONS, BRING YOUR OWN.

GUERRILLA TELEVISION

Videotape As an Analytic Tool

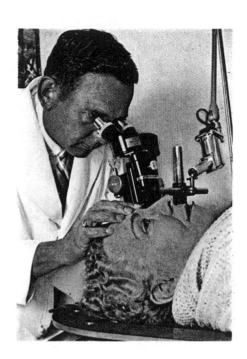

6. Videotape As an Analytic Tool

If print were used exactly as television is now, we'd be allowed to write only novels or plays and news stories, never for ourselves, and always in anticipation of what others were going to say.

But, of course, written language does not have those restrictions. It's a general-purpose medium which applies to an infinity of situations. This is due partly to culture, partly to economics.

The print experience is deeply ingrained in Western Culture. Moreover, print is cheap and accessible enough to be a mass tool.

Until portable video came along this was not true of television. It was limited to just a few, predetermined uses under the control of an elite. Now everyone can use television as a personal tool. Which is just as well because the video experience is now more a part of our culture than that of print.

What follows are specific examples of videotape use. They are absolutely unrelated and needn't be. The point is that video can be used in a high variety of ways, even if it's as simple as doing videotape instead of print reports in schools, government, and industry.

DECODE BUREAUCRATIC STRUCTURES

Some of our best tape was made simply by walking into a public space with a camera. You quickly find that people have all sorts of inane rules about letting you take pictures, even though they think nothing of taking yours.

Probably the quintessential example is a supermarket we went into in Los Angeles. Above our heads we found TV cameras, *i.e.*, a surveillance system, with the lame sign: "Smile. You're on TV. This helps reduce shoplifting and keeps the prices down."

I was taping and immediately Paul started a rap: "This is really sick. They hype you up as a consumer on TV and then to keep you from stealing the things they make you want to buy they have this . . . . It's Big Brother."

52

The next thing we knew the store manager came over and told us we couldn't take pictures "without a permit from the division office." As I tried to tape, he kept putting his hand over the lens.

Finally, we went outside and he followed us, not belligerently but out of curiosity. It seemed he wanted to know what we were up to (nothing really) and began to talk about himself, how he'd worked at Safeway foodstores for six years, and allowed as how he didn't really like his job.

It sure beats reading sociology textbooks.

Another great piece of tape in this genre was done by the Videofreex. They were taping on the street near their loft one day and a policeman came over to ask them if *they* had a permit because, he said, "I'm sure you have to get one, from the mayor or somebody." All the while, of course, the camera was on him ("Video what?" he asked when the Freex told him where they were from). Finally he concluded that they should shoot only on Sundays when there weren't any people around.

It happens every time because Porta-Paks run without noise and can record even when not held at eye-level.

A last variation is to ask to tape your teachers to show your parents, or whoever else pays for your education. When they refuse, tape the ensuing hassle.

MULTI-MONITOR JUXTAPOSITIONS

This is particularly effective for analyzing environmental spaces. Set up, say, three monitors. On one, play a tape of driving through the country. Next to it, play a tape of driving through a city. On the last, either put yourself on live feedback or use street interviews with people rapping about how they like living where they are.

ANALYZE BEHAVIOR

You can use tape to analyze pre-recorded behavior. Dr. Albert Scheflen, a pioneer in the study of kineasics, or body language, has even set up a camera in a Puerto Rican kitchen (the people were paid and soon forgot about its presence) to feed back on and decode ethnic spatial and movement patterns.

We once invited Dr. Scheflen and Vic Gioscia, head of the Center for the Study of Social Change, to watch tapes of broadcast-TV and analyze the behavior of David Brinkley and Walter Cronkite whom they were watching simultaneously on two screens. The third monitor was live feedback and they controlled the camera themselves.

Paul Ryan has an idea for a mail order analysis service. To participate, you take a camera home and tape yourself, family, friends, and physical environment. Then you send the tape off to analysts. They watch it and comment onto the audio track and send it back to you.

At New York University, the Videoteque, a student videotape group started by Bobby Mariano,

Shelly Surpin of Media Access Center taping in a classroom

taped Bucky Fuller lecturing and then taped people watching and commenting for later feedback to Fuller.

I've always wanted to see one of the networks run not just a presidential speech, but people watching one in real-time. Thus you'd see a TV "screen-within-a-screen" and hear the spontaneous comments as they come out. Maybe ABC could have a right-wing family, NBC some middle-of-the-roaders, and CBS a group of freaks.

VIDEO GAMES

One time at the Center for the Study of Social Change we set up a situation wherein we related to each other solely through monitors. (In other words, if I can see you and you can't see me, then I'm in charge, and so on.)

Paul and Vic worked through one situation where they went back over a tape of their conversation and mimicked each other's body movements. Paul played Vic and Vic played Paul.

For example, Vic looked at Paul's hand movements inscribing a tight circle and concluded he was saying: "Yeah, I'll make it nice and small so you'll understand it Vic." The next day Paul claims he woke up feeling like he was in Vic's body.

VIDEOTAPE IN THERAPY

I have no experience with this but it's quite common. Generally, however, shrinks use tape to bolster their psychoanalytic theories rather than to probe a new one configured around the media experience.

In social work, tape is used in family counseling sessions and then played back to the participants. I understand this works very well.

INSTITUTIONAL TAPE

Long before there ever was a Guerrilla Television, industry (especially insurance companies), was using (one-inch) videotape to train employees. Get ahold of some of that tape. Perhaps it's cruel to call it funny, but the insights into American culture to be found in these training tapes are devastating.

And so on. There's more to television than Johnny Carson.

Networking. Videocassettes and Cable Television

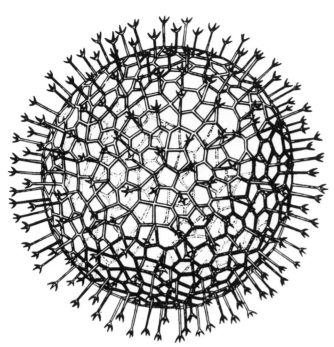

From *On Growth and Form* by D'Arcy Thompson, edited by J. T. Bonner, Cambridge University Press.

7. Networking: Videocassettes and Cable Television

It's no longer the means of television production which are overly-centralized in Media-America as much as those of distribution. With portable video, television technology joins other decentralized media production tools like audiotape recorders, offset printing and Xerox machines, typewriters, and movie and still cameras, in low cost and high access.

But distribution of that information still remains in the hands of a few. Both radio and television transmission power rests with people who own and control heavy hardware licensed by the Federal Communications Commission (F.C.C.), often as part of a media-monopoly. Even print, although it carries less restrictions, is controlled at the point of sale (either newsstand and bookstore, or mail order house) by proprietary distribution networks.

The only true people's network is the mails. Any medium which can be containerized (*i.e.*, recorded and stored), like videotape and audiotape, and, of course, print on paper, can be mailed and received individually.

An ideal network would be a biomorphic balance between centralization and decentralization. On the one hand, it's nice to plug-in to a national grid where the same message is unifying everyone. On the other hand, if that's our only option then totalitarian control is a reality.* (Which it is now under network television. And that power can be pre-empted by government. When the President goes on he demands all three networks for his live speeches, even though each then carries exactly the same picture.)

The government of Sweden is training its citizens in guerrilla warfare so they can defend their country individually, instead of being in a vulnerable, centralized army. In California, experiments are being done with solar-powered batteries which can guarantee a stable electricity supply independent of centralized power lines and black-outs or sabotage (or Con Ed).

To match that capability with electronic media, we'd each need our own transmitters and ideally our own power supplies. Ham radio, of course, is such a mode. But it lives on the periphery of Media-America. A similar form of television, do-it-yourself transmission, is theoretically and economically possible but restricted both by the scarcity of available space in the magnetic spectrum and by law. (The government, of course, controls the airwaves as if they were property.)

But decentralized transmission of information should be dominant, not fugitive. Each citizen of Media-America should be guaranteed as a birthright access to the means of distribution of information. (Perhaps there should even be "information

---

*The notion of a "global village" doesn't mean that everyone responds the same way to the same planetary events, only that everyone has the same information to respond to in a high variety of ways.

As information flow gets more intense it diversifies, and like pure oxygen being fed to a flame it ignites into a variety of responses. Majority (*i.e.* two-party) politics is impossible in a high information environment where every natural viewpoint can feed its information needs. Movement towards plurality and coalition government (*e.g.* third and fourth national parties) will be accelerated by the advent of cable TV and videocassettes.

This means that a counter-political mass movement is becoming less and less likely. Instead of cultural radicals exhorting others to follow their own example, there will be small scale living environments which don't actively proselytize their views as much as they just function quietly and let others pick up on their model.

Moreover, long term adherence to one model is fading as people experiment in different tool environments. Thus, to base a political movement on a highly defined, time stable theme (*e.g.* Marxist bullshit) is impossible.

stamps" for the poor, just like food stamps.) Thus, the mails are a high form of democracy, to the degree to which they are uncensored and economically accessible.

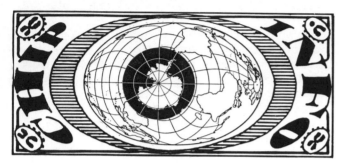

Videocassettes, in conjunction with the mails or any other form of product transportation, are a technology which trends toward highly flexible television distribution. For Guerrilla Television differs from guerrilla warfare in that it is designed as an ongoing mode. Traditionally, and ironically, once governments assume power through guerrilla tactics they degenerate into wildly centralized, totalitarian regimes.

Videocassettes, however, are only half the answer because for every TV set which receives their information, there must be one cassette. Instead, we need channels of decentralized real-time transmission to feed fewer homes than a broadcast channel, but more than one home at a time. Moreover, the economic base of such a system must be able to sustain a high variety of programming. That is the potential of cable television.

VIDEOCASSETTES

The videotape used by portable video cameras and other machines is called "reel-to-reel." This means that a full reel of tape threads through a machine to a take-up reel. The disadvantage of this mode is that it's more cumbersome and time-consuming. Also, to remove a tape from a machine and store it you have to completely rewind it to free the take-up reel and not leave the actual tape physically exposed.

Videocassettes, on the other hand, can be popped into a playback machine and activated by simply pressing a button. They can be removed, intact, without rewinding. Because they have their own casing, they can be stored and passed on or mailed very easily.

The major advantage of videocassettes for Guerrilla Television, and the straight manufacturers, is that they feed into existing hardware systems. In other words, people already have TV sets which generally function as the home information/ entertainment center. Film cassettes would require the expense of a whole new tool-up and restructured furniture for ongoing viewing. Videocassettes can be grafted onto already existing support systems because a player feeds through any TV set.

For Guerrilla Television that means a grassroots base. But more important, videocassettes guarantee total control over the information cycle to software producers. With videocassettes many different tapemakers will be able to do their own copying and distribution from many different decentralized nodes (analagous, in part, to the underground and neighborhood presses).

There has always been that potential in reel-to-reel videotape, but there are too few of those machines available to build a sustaining economic

Reel-to-Reel

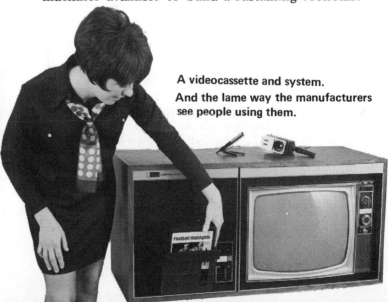

A videocassette and system.
And the lame way the manufacturers
see people using them.

base of small, specialized markets for video programming. Instead of the millions of people now needed to subsidize a type of information, indirectly, through advertising, thousands or fewer will be able to do it directly by paying money for information.

Moreover, videocassettes will enable individuals to distribute tape non-commercially, just one tape at a time if they wish. The notion of a broadcast-TV show made by one person to be shown to just one other person would be considered madness.

Because videocassettes will give total, low-cost control of information to the distributors and thus, unlike the airwaves, fall away from government surveillance, the information they carry will deviate from normal information.

Already, videotape pornography is being stockpiled. To view it will be totally a matter of personal choice as a viewer must personally insert it in a playback machine, and the videotape image (magnetic pulses) has no visual reality unless it is used in a playback machine. It's impossible to see accidentally what's contained on a videotape. Unlike film, it can't be held up to the light. Whether or not the government attempts to censor videocassette traffic will be a true test of individual freedom.

There are some people who think that videocassettes will never make it, that cable television alone or in conjunction with cassettes is the only viable mode of specialized video information. This overlooks simple cost factors.

A videocassette distribution network is simply cheaper and more far-ranging than local cable systems, in installation and maintenance costs. Moreover, ownership and access to CATV is already embroiled in disputes. I even know people who have no hope for cable-TV, not because of technological problems, but because of legal and financial hassles.

My own feeling is that cassettes are a short-cut to decentralized TV. Maybe they will be just an interim stage before full-blown cable television, but that stage could last twenty years and I can't wait. Moreover, they will enable me to do low-volume distribution totally under my control.

The only drawback at the moment is that the people in the videocassette industry are the greediest bunch to hit media since land salesmen went to Florida.

Traditionally, each new information medium has begun with men who had messages they wanted passionately to get across. Except for broadcast-TV, which began solely as a marketing venture, there are individual personalities who stand out in the early days of every new communications medium. Newspapers and magazines were dominated by strong-willed publishers and journalists, book publishing houses began with men (whose names are often still attached to them) who could find no other outlet for what they thought was important, and record companies had their genesis with music producers who often went around to early concerts with hand-held tape recorders.

The videocassette industry is the opposite. Strictly for the money. Because videocassettes have a little in common with each and all of the above media, the people involved are swarming over cassettes trying to figure out where the money is. Many are men who "missed the boat" when broadcast and even cable television came along, but this time they're not going to. So they think.

To confirm their confidence and decide their direction, videocassette "publishers" have taken to doing marketing surveys to determine what people want. Then they commission software. Very few are able to conceive that there are artists or other indigenous videotape makers outside the traditional TV structure who just simply have something *they* want to say that isn't necessarily what they think others want to hear.

There is an incredible degree of paranoia in the nascent videocassette industry. Software or programming houses are signing up any and all old *films* for inclusion in mammoth catalogs designed to appeal to any and all tastes, just to keep all the bases covered, so to speak.

And videocassette executives will attend videocassette conferences at the drop of a brochure for a few hundred dollars apiece per shot.

MARCEL DOT/MR. PEANUT

What happens at these affairs is that men in their late thirties and forties, who generally have little or no idea of what electronic media are about, go to plastic hotel ballrooms and sit next to each other on folding chairs, dressed in coats-and-ties, and then listen to people talk to them.

This is the exact antithesis of what they claim videocassettes will be: kinetic information, what you want, when and where you want it.

Then there are the various hardware systems. As soon as one manufacturer announced work on cassettes, all the others had to get into the act. Some (RCA) even announced systems which they later, and with less publicity, abandoned. That was just to keep the stockholders happy.

Unlike actual portable video systems, none of the videocassette machines are as yet compatible. Some aren't even cassettes, but video discs. At this time discs have the advantage of being cheap, the disadvantage of holding too little information (only twelve minutes), thus requiring a changer and a lag time between changes.

However, the only major difference between machines, besides cost, is whether or not a cassette machine uses videotape and has a record mode. *Can you make your own copies with it?*

There are systems which do not give you that option. They have been designed specifically so that the manufacturer controls the information, just as broadcasters now control information.

Not surprisingly, the machine most vulnerable to these charges is designed and licensed by CBS. It is called EVR (for Electronic Video Recorder, which is not a true description of the EVR process).

EVR is a reactionary technology. Instead of being true videotape it is film which runs through a box that attaches to a TV set and has a tiny TV camera inside. If you think about it, it's awfully silly — a mechanical simulation of what the videotape process does electronically. With EVR, you get all the disadvantages of film and none of the advantages of videotape.

The image itself comes across a TV screen like film, rather than videotape, on TV. Just as a videotape image projected looks washed out, so too does a film image on TV — it doesn't have the impact of true videotape. Videotape on a TV screen is lifelike, volumetric, and tactile. Film on TV is flat (because light comes through a flat frame, whereas in videotape light emanates from the image in the form of electrons) and subject to scratching.

But more important, you can get your software or an EVR cassette only by surrendering your original master (either videotape or film) to their processing plant and then ordering in quantities of at least fifty, which are still more expensive than videotape. Moreover, a color EVR cartridge holds only thirty minutes of information whereas true videotape goes up to ninety minutes.

In other words, you can't do your own processing; you must order in pre-determined quantities; you must let others see your material; and you must wait. It's like sending your film off to the drugstore.

It is irresponsible design which must have been prompted by visions of a mini-CBS in every home. CBS, in fact, is licensing others to manufacture the units and placing no restrictions on potential software, but they are retaining all control over the processing plants.

Primarily, they are hyping EVR to industries where TV is traditionally used as a one-way control system to train employees. The first and largest customer of EVR was the Equitable Life Assurance Society.

But there are also marketeers trying to push EVR into the schools, with pre-determined programming selected by school bureaucracies and teachers, just like books. In fact, EVR seems to have been designed as a video book, which is inherent in sequential film technology. Its one advantage is that as film, it contains single frames that can be highlighted easily by stopping the motor. As one cartridge holds up to twelve thousand different images, that's an enormous storage capacity. EVR's inventor, Peter Goldmark, has even talked of video encyclopedias.

But that's silly too. Trying to make television imitate books, *i.e.*, print that you read off a TV screen, is media sodomy. A book is portable. A TV set is stationary.

With EVR, kids won't be allowed to make their own TV because money that would have gone into videotape equipment first will be tied up for years in amortizing hardware. A complete videotape system, with playback and everything, is only $300

more than the original $900 selling price of EVR. Moreover, there is already planned a high school videotape exchange network (by Media Access Center) which would be impossible with EVR.

(Ironically, it's possible to get around one of the original controls specifically built into EVR to keep people from making copies of pre-recorded material. All you have to do is play an EVR machine through a TV set and hook-up your videotape recorder to the same mode normally used to record off-the-air. Just punch record on the VTR, play on the EVR, and you've got your copy.)

Perhaps the most enlightened cassette machine is manufactured by Ampex. Like audio cassette recorders which accept both blank cartridges for your own recording, and pre-recorded ones, the Ampex (Instavideo) has two modes. One allows you to use the machine as a Porta-Pak. The other flips into extended play for pre-recorded software. Moreover, it's compatible with other Porta-Paks (though not other cassette machines).

The other true videotape cassette recorders are not portable, but do allow you to pull stuff off broadcast-TV. One (Cartrivision) even has a home camera.

Oddly, the manufacturers of cassette machines with a record capability have not thought to encourage people to do their own duplication. The machines are not designed to feed your videotape material (made on a Porta-Pak) into them. As soon as one machine is available to Guerrilla Television, however, plans for plugging-in to a cassette machine will be circulating around the world.

But even if you get into true videotape cassettes, beware of the software people.

The pattern of each new medium is that it's first mistaken for a preceding one. When long-playing records first came along people thought it would encapsulate the concert hall or let you hear railroad sounds in your living room.

Gradually, the LP developed its own indigenous and lucrative form, rock music (which now comprises about 90 percent of all LP sales).

Rock is indigenous to the recording studio, not to the concert hall. Even live performances, like studio ones, are done on twelve- or sixteen-track tape recorders which separately pick-up each instrument for later mixing and remixing.

True to form, videocassette people think that rock music will be the farthest-out thing going in their new medium. Only it'll be music with "psychedelic" visuals. Yet most people listen to music as background for other visual activity.

The inherent fascination of television. Harnessed, finally, to train, inform, communicate and educate for you, by a cassette TV system anyone can operate.

The system: CBS Electronic Video Recording; the *only* cassette TV system actually in production.

EVR displays audiovisual materials more conveniently and less expensively than either videotape or 16mm movie playback devices. And it is used in normal room light. Without screens, projection rooms or trained projectionists. So it *gets* used.

EVR Cassettes can be produced, stored and shipped for less than either videotapes or 16mm movies of comparable running time. And, since the cassettes remain sealed until the EVR Player threads them automatically, the programs inside are never subjected to mishandling or abuse.

To learn more about EVR and how you can convert your audiovisual materials to this low-cost cassette TV system, mail the coupon now.

EVR is here. How will you use it?

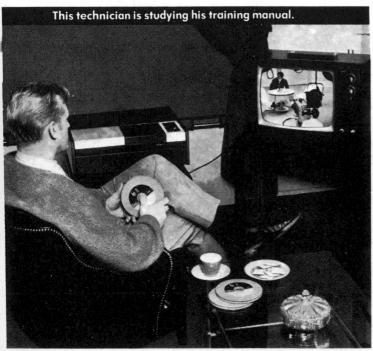

This technician is studying his training manual.

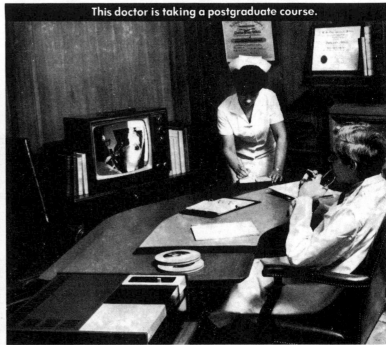

This doctor is taking a postgraduate course.

These reps are attending a sales meeting.

This buyer is examining your latest samples.

CAP'N RIP-OFF By Birbeck

IN A SECRET MEETING
R·O INDUSTRIES TOP
ENGINEERS LEARN OF
R·O NEWEST PLAN—

SOME WEEKS LATER··

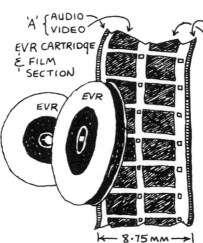

'A' { AUDIO VIDEO } AUDIO } 'B' VIDEO

EVR CARTRIDGE & FILM SECTION

EVR   EVR

|← 8·75MM →|

MEMO; EVR
(Extremely Vile Ripoff)
TO; All departments
FROM; The CAP'N

Well done boys! With
this system and our
control of the supply
of cartridges, we'll
be filthy rich in no
time!

With the tight format
and very fine grain of
the film material it'll
be impossible for any-
body to move in on us.

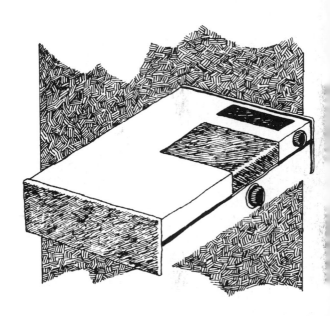

EVR, THE
INCREDIBLE RIP·OFF
IS NOW IN PRODUCTION!

But videocassettes will develop their own indigenous software. And to do that they're going to have to tap the production being done in videotape itself, much of it by Guerrilla Television makers.

There is a group called the Firesign Theater which does parodies of old radio shows by using sound: special effects, loops, delays. Similarly, there will be entertainment groups who live together as a collective with videotape, feed back on their experience, and develop technical expertise. The result will be entertaining software which is pure video in grammar and technique.

Right now, however, the videocassette "industry" doesn't understand that indigenous videotape production is their logical feed. But they're going to find out fairly quickly and then some hard decisions are going to have to be made.

Because if you've got a good piece of tape and sign up with a company that has an enormous catalog of old sports movies and the like, then you pollute the information value of what you've done, and at the same time loan out your legitimacy.

Moreover, unless the economy of cassettes respects the economy of information, the industry will emerge with an inflated value structure which sustains a few things at the top with enormous amounts of money, at the expense of struggling production at the bottom (like rock music).

What *can* happen with cassettes is that for the first time people disenfranchised from television can have their own self-sustaining distribution system.

The programming to feed that structure will grow naturally as process out of native situations, not be produced by outsiders who come in to make a film.

Because the information will be experience-based, it will have high survival value. To appropriate a term from cable-TV, this will be a sort of "local origination" for cassettes, guaranteeing a continuity of information flow (which is important, because one-shot deals have mainly symbolic value).

At Raindance, we have been experimenting with a videotape distribution plan (first reel-to-reel, then cassettes) which is designed to guard against rip-offs and be flexible enough to change itself as people feed back better ways of doing it. Moreover, we wanted a system which would be cooperative rather than competitive. In other words, our way of doing our plan shouldn't be the only one. It should be designed to support other distribution plans.

Essentially, the network paradigm we came up with is this (and you're free to copy it):

The requests we get from people who want to see our videotape break down into three categories: people who just send money for tape, those who send a blank videotape and less money for the information itself, and people who send their software in exchange for ours.

To accommodate this flow we decided to assemble from the tape being sent us a **Video Access Catalog** — *i.e.*, pieces of the tape we'd received compiled into a composite tape which has value in and of itself, and as a sampler of what people are doing.

Then, if the people who receive the **Video Access Catalog** want more of an individual producer's tape, they can go directly to the producer. Thus, the producer keeps his master tape and does all his own distribution which allows him to control where his tape goes and what he thinks is a fair selling price (especially avoiding any one uniform price).

The **Video Access Catalog** itself returns money to its contributors proportionate to how much of their material is used. This serves to maintain an even pricing structure for all material and doesn't inflate the value of one piece of software over another.

Thus, the network is at its most centralized only in the service mode. Actual control of the products, *i.e.*, distribution, is decentralized in totally self-contained nodes. Moreover, any one node can set up its own accessing service so that, in effect, there are many different catalogs, but catalogs which are overlapping and therefore symbiotic, not competitive.

It's still too soon to know how it's going to work out, but the whole idea of a tape exchange and sales network grew out of indigenous information pressure, not a dollar-motivated marketing scheme. People were simply making tapes and they wanted others to see them.

The same network model can also work totally outside any money economy as just straight information exchange. This mode is particularly applicable to informal networks such as communes or artisans' collectives which have no desire to give mass exposure to information about themselves.

A similar schema is immediately possible through a two-way college video network using campus information centers. Each school would produce local programming and trade tapes of

SEE PAGE 93!

more general interest with other campuses. The advantage of working off a college base is the concentration of money and interest.

A variation of this would be for political organizers to circulate both information and propaganda tapes independent of any money profit motive. A Cesar Chavez, for example, could address his union on videotape via battery-powered monitors in pickup trucks. His actual chances of getting on broadcast-TV without moderation or restriction, are probably very slim.

Finally, a Guerrilla Television network via cassettes is a way to beat promoters who try to make products out of alternate culture information. Everyone realizes now that rock festivals à la Woodstock are a rip-off. If you go and they make a movie of it you're actually paying to be an extra for the profit of others.

We had videotapes of both Woodstock and Altamont and they were ready the same day, not a year later in a movie theater. We've also received tapes of a Bob Dylan Concert in England which never received any coverage in the United States. Rather than make modular "albums" out of that material, we gave away copies to friends or used it at shows for our own survival.

Perhaps the greatest electronic counter-rip-off was done by Videofreex. They had rented out their video projector to a franchisee of the first Muhammed Ali/Joe Frazier heavyweight title fight. If you'll remember, the promoters were being incredibly tight about who could see it. Except for closed-circuit TV there was a total black-out even extending to Armed Forces communications networks. So they thought.

When the Videofreex went to operate their projector they brought a Porta-Pak and attached it to the closed-circuit cable bringing the fight. Thus, as soon as the fight was over they had a perfect quality videotape copy.

The next day they gave away copies to anyone who would provide their own tape and sent out duplications all over the country (which protected them from losing the tape). They even went down to the tavern next door to their loft and played it for free on the TV set above the bar.

Let that be a lesson to you about electronics and ownership of information: there isn't any.

There are probably as many *ad hoc* and ongoing alternate network plans as there are tapemakers, and we need to try many of them and build change and feedback into each. The coming together of that flow is a grassroots information infrastructure for Media-America.

Once you have your own means of both production and distribution, Guerrilla Television is a reality. The next step is to formalize (without rigidifying) that option into a legitimate component of American culture. That means cable television.

CABLE TELEVISION

If one "Utility" is owned rent is 4 times amount shown on dice.

If both "Utilities" are owned rent is 10 times amount shown on dice.

Mortgage Value $75.

CABLE TELEVISION

Cable-TV, also known as CATV (Community Antenna Television) promises to be the next public utility.

If you'd been in on the first days of the phone company you'd have a pretty good investment now, right? Or if you got in on the ground floor of broadcast television . . .? Ah yes, if you only knew then what you know now.

Well, CATV has the technological capabilities of telephone and television combined. And the public is just now learning about it even though it's been around for more than twenty years. But the people who know the most are money people, many of whom already control other media (*e.g.*, Time Inc., Triangle Communications which owns **TV Guide**, Foote, Cone and Belding, the advertising agency, and so on). It's a full-blown media gold rush.

Cable-TV originated in the 1940s in rural Pennsylvania. Television reception was so bad in some of the valleys that appliance dealers couldn't sell TV sets. So they went out to the highest hill, built an antenna, and offered to hook up homes to it (via a cable) for free if people bought a TV set.

In other words, a cable ran from that master antenna into individual homes. Hence the name: cable-TV. Typically, it began doing the job of an old medium better — in this case, providing cleaner TV signals.

But cable-TV can do more than that. It's also possible to originate programming on a cable. Thus, whereas a community was once limited by the number of channels in the airwaves, it can now have as many (much cheaper) as the cable's capacity.

For the cable is what's called a "coaxial cable." Rather than being single wires in a bunch, one for each channel, a CATV cable is actually a weave of copper wires which carries a magnetic field that duplicates the magnetic spectrum in space. Thus, it's possible to upgrade the capacity of a cable just by amplifying the signals which pass through it — without rewiring. The New York City systems, for example, carry eighteen channels with a potential of forty. Cables carrying a thousand channels are also within the state-of-the-art.

In your home, you plug into a cable through a box with a dial on it with numbers for each cable channel. The cable hook-up feeds into your TV set on an unused regular channel. Because the cable-TV company knows each home it has hooked up, it can "pinpoint" markets.

You pay for cable through an initial installation charge and subsequent monthly service charges. The service you get is perfect broadcast-TV signals, often with access to more channels than you normally get with a home antenna because the cable system can import them from other cities.

A secondary service, but the one that's primary to Guerrilla Television, is what's called "local origination," or simply those programs which are transmitted from the cable "head end," or origination point. Currently that programming consists of quality old movies, sports events like local or professional basketball games, and some pure dada: stock market tickers, a rotating panel of dials with the temperature and other weather data, and one system in Florida used to have a twenty-four-hour picture of a goldfish bowl.

In only a few communities is there indigenous programming made by the people of the community about their community. In some places, this is done with Porta-Paks.

The as yet untapped potential of cable vis-à-vis local programming is that it can be consumer-supported without advertising, or else such specialized advertising can be sold as not to pollute the quality of the software.

This is possible because CATV has a radically different economy of information than broadcast. First of all, because there is no scarcity of channels and time, overhead is reduced and specialized markets can be serviced. Then, because the cable system has a precise record of each subscriber, and mechanical control over channels, it's possible for home viewers to pay, say, $.50 extra a month per household and get an extra channel. This is analogous to subscribing to a magazine.

But that's not all. The cables are two-way. In other words, not only can you receive signals, you can send them. This might range all the way from transmitting your own videotape (thus making

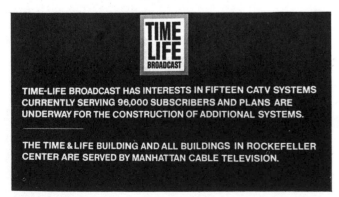

TIME-LIFE BROADCAST HAS INTERESTS IN FIFTEEN CATV SYSTEMS CURRENTLY SERVING 96,000 SUBSCRIBERS AND PLANS ARE UNDERWAY FOR THE CONSTRUCTION OF ADDITIONAL SYSTEMS.

THE TIME & LIFE BUILDING AND ALL BUILDINGS IN ROCKEFELLER CENTER ARE SERVED BY MANHATTAN CABLE TELEVISION.

every home a potential decentralized studio) to simply pressing a button to vote electronically, or shopping by feeding back when you see an item you want delivered. Moreover, the cable is capable of carrying computer data so that the system could automatically keep track of all transactions, or let you have computer services in your home (*e.g.*, a terminal for domestic bookkeeping and business chores).

The nature of the signal which travels a cable can be binary: a simple on-or-off code. Any electronic signal can be broken down into a binary pulse so that the cable can carry all and any electronic information. Besides computer and video services, the cable can act as a burglar or fire alarm, for example. Just as water, electricity, and gas flow into your home from outside as utilities, so too is a cable a pipeline (of information).

Full-blown cable systems are called "a wired city" and it's predicted that by 1980, 85 percent of American homes will have cable. Right now, 15 percent do.

When that happens we'll have a wired nation because it's possible to interconnect cable systems via microwave (short-range airwave transmitters) or satellite. Sophisticated people in the industry don't even call it cable, but "broadband communications," indicating a combined network of communication technologies which will form an information lifeline to homes and offices.

About the only people unhappy about cable-TV are the broadcast networks and the phone company.

The broadcasters are unhappy because CATV will break their hegemony and siphon off advertising dollars to more precise, and therefore more effective, markets. The phone company is upset because it has already wired the nation. The problem, however, is that phone wires do not have a large enough bandwidth to provide what's called "broadband communications." (Even Picture-phones, both audio and video, are not equal to CATV because, forced to send signals over regular phone wires, the images have less information and are inferior, *i.e.*, have fewer lines.)

There are so many interest groups, and such a possibly lucrative pay-off, that the F.C.C. doesn't know quite what to do yet.

The F.C.C. has identified a so-called "Top 100 Markets" (indicating that they too consider communications a marketing system) and restricted the signals that could be imported into them. (This is to stifle competition. New York City, for example, could get Philadelphia's broadcast stations in addition to its own. Then if two CBS affiliates were showing different movies at the same time, CBS would, in effect, be competing with itself — as the networks see it.)

Then the F.C.C. decided that larger systems should be compelled to originate a minimum of programming each week. But later they postponed the deadline for doing that and narrowed the requirements (from systems with thirty-five hundred subscribers to ones with ten thousand). Even that provision was overruled by the courts.

The issue has still not been resolved. And

How one CATV owner conceives of "local origination"

Sterling Manhattan Cable Television (which is owned by Time-Life)

A Porta-Pak local origination crew at a street fair in New York

DUDLEY EVENSON

recently the foundations have moved into the fray by having seminars and issuing print reports. Meanwhile the money interests keep gobbling up cable systems, either buying or building them.

The president of one, Teleprompter (which is owned partly by Howard Hughes, and partly by Jack Kent Cooke, the sports promoter who put a black-out on that Ali-Frazier fight), was forced to resign when the value of the stock kept going down because he and his subordinates kept getting indicted for bribing local city officials to award Teleprompter franchises.

As Guerrilla Television, cable-TV requires two approaches: if your community does not have it yet, how can you guarantee a high access system; or if it already lives where you do, how can you get on?

Who's News

Irving B. Kahn Leaves TelePrompTer Posts Of Chairman, President

Executive, Involved in Two Legal Cases, to Remain a Director; H.J. Schlafly May Become Head

By a WALL STREET JOURNAL Staff Reporter

NEW YORK — TelePrompTer Corp. announced that its embattled chairman and president, Irving B. Kahn, resigned from those two posts but will remain with the company as a director and consultant.

Mr. Kahn currently is involved in two legal proceedings affecting the company, the largest operator of cable television systems in the U.S. He and three city officials of Johnstown, Pa., including the mayor, are under indictment on charges of bribery and conspiracy in connection with the granting of a cable franchise by the city to TelePrompTer. And he was named last week as coconspirator—though not a defendant—in the indictment in Trenton, N.J., of four persons on charges stemming from the award of a city cable-television franchise to TelePrompTer.

In both instances, Mr. Kahn maintained that he and the company were victims of extortion in the granting of the licenses.

TelePrompTer said Mr. Kahn's "agreement in principle" to step down from his top posts with the company will enable him to "expend the time and effort necessary to the defense of himself and the company" against the Johnstown indictment for alleged bribery and conspiracy.

The Johnstown indictment specifically accuses Mr. Kahn of having paid a total of $15,000 to the three city officials in 1966 in order to secure an exclusive cable television franchise for TelePrompTer in the city. A statement issued by Mr. Kahn's attorneys at the time said: "In 1961 TelePrompTer had purchased the existing Johnstown cable system and franchise for approximately $500,000. The clear facts are that in 1966 TelePrompTer was subjected to extortionate demands by corrupt local officials who threatened to destroy TelePrompTer's investment in Johnstown."

The Trenton indictment charged that a former president of the Trenton city council and a member of the council "unlawfully, corruptly and extortively did receive" $50,000 from TelePrompTer in payment for "the power and influence of their . . . offices to induce, procure, and obtain official action" by the council to award the franchise to the company.

Both indictments have been cited as reasons behind the current Federal Communications Commission deliberations into the desirability of giving the states rather than the cities jurisdiction over cable franchises.

A flamboyant personality, Mr. Kahn had served as chairman and president of Tele-PrompTer since its founding 20 years ago. Before that he had been at one time or another publicity manager for the orchestras of Larry Clinton, Les Brown and Van Alexander and special assistant to Spyros P. Skouras, then chairman of Twentieth Century-Fox Film Corp.

First of all, a cable-TV franchise is, by law, granted by individual communities. (However, some state governments are considering appropriating that power for themselves.) Thus, whoever has political power in your community will be closest to awarding the franchise. If your local government is honest, then so too will the process be. If it's not, then money will change hands under some table.

You have two options. One is city ownership of the cable instead of private ownership. The other is setting up a community-owned and -controlled company to vie for the cable franchise.

Right now, the majority of thinking about how to set up and use a cable system is being done by consultants in the form of print reports. This is quite similar to the way America tried to fight the Vietnam War, from above, using the wrong medium.

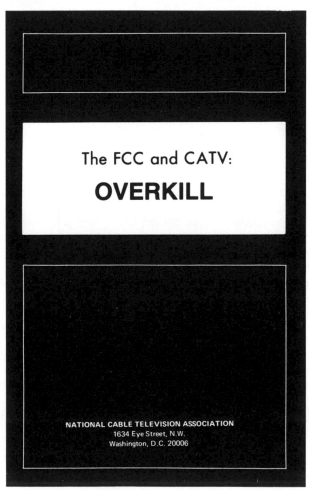

The FCC and CATV:

OVERKILL

NATIONAL CABLE TELEVISION ASSOCIATION
1634 Eye Street, N.W.
Washington, D.C. 20006

An infrastructure of information demands that you organize for cable not just with reports and meetings, but using the medium itself.

This means Portable Video. Out of the strategies suggested in the chapter "Community Video" it's possible to build an information base, feeding back on itself, which knows itself and how to make TV. When a city builds a hospital, it calls on doctors to help in the design. Similarly, if you've got an on-going grassroots TV program, you are the experts in your community. Of course it's going to take all the other political and social organizing tricks normally used on other issues, but a base of video skills is your reserve strength.

You'll especially find that a potential community coalition will be torn by different viewpoints about how to structure access to cable-TV. So that if you are not already into Guerrilla Television when those talks start, initiate video activity at the same time. Don't just *go* to meetings, go with a Porta-Pak. In fact, a documentary of a community just getting into cable would save other areas a lot of hassling.

Now, what to do if a private franchise besides your own group is going to get permission to install cable? Don't let the city give it away unless there are legal guarantees — and go to court, if you have to, to secure them. Particularly, you want open channels, or "common carriers," which are completely independent of any control by the system's owners. And don't ask for channels by number, but by percentage. If you have one of ten channels that's nice, but if the system is upgraded to a hundred and the public access stays the same, that's a rip-off.

I don't pretend that **Guerrilla Television** has all the answers on structuring cable-TV because the medium is more than just programming strategies. The contribution of Guerrilla Television to a developing cable set-up is in an attitude towards assessing and using the technology.

However, don't try to suppose what cable should be without doing your homework in video, and that *is* what Guerrilla Television is about. Right now the foundations especially are thinking about funding cable ownership projects with no thought to what will actually be done with them. Thus, cable may be born in the image of broadcast-TV, only on a different scale.

Specifically, the cable stations which do originate local programming give you high school football games instead of NFL ones, mayoral speeches in place of presidential ones, or local bingo instead of national game shows. In other words, the variety of the programming changes but not the nature of it.

Clearly, there will be no one way to use cable but that's the beauty of it. However, many of the current owners are men who were raised in broadcast-TV or with both eyes on a profit-and-loss sheet. They fall into two categories.

First are the multiple system owners (MSOs) who generally are media companies with publicly held stock. At the local level you can usually find some young guy who may be sympathetic to Guerrilla Television, but too bound into a corporate structure to want to take any chances.

The other kind are single system owners (SSOs). These are men who set up systems, sometimes as a sideline, and then found themselves with a multi-million dollar investment. Basically, they're hardware salesmen.

It doesn't pay to alienate either of the above. In lieu of legally guaranteed access (which will ultimately come, perhaps after a nasty national fight for congressional legislation), they are what you have to work with.

Our experience, and what we've heard from others, is that cable programming directors are usually ignorant of the possibilities of video. Thus, they need to be educated.

Invite them down to your video project. Show them tapes you've made. Back up your proposals with legal and financial expertise so that, in effect, you leave them no choice but to grant you access. Then if they refuse, wail on them: demonstrations, petitions, coverage in local newspapers.

Generally, though, cable technology is in your favor. If it lies fallow it loses money. You can fill it. Probably the most cogent strategy for getting access to an ongoing cable set-up is to bring in new subscribers.

In other words, sign up people who will pledge to subscribe to a cable system only if your group is given access. Or organize people who've already signed up and threaten to discontinue their service.

That's the first level. After a certain point a cable system reaches complete "saturation." In other words they can't increase revenues by increasing subscriptions. Then you have to enlist financial support in the form of extra monthly payments (e.g., $.50 per home) for access to an extra channel.

Or you might consider selling local advertising for access to a local channel. Especially in hip communities, it should be possible to get merchants to support controversial programming.

The following is a model plan for a project which is now under way in Santa Cruz, California:

Programming for cable television

Paul Ryan has suggested that communities set up an information exchange system using both telephone and cable-TV. Essentially it would work by having a twenty-four-hour phone number which people could call and leave a recording of what they'd like to see and how they felt about what they were seeing at the time.

In other words, prior to a physical two-way use of CATV, people could feed back on programming and direct it, rather than vice-versa.

Out of this would come a cultural map or data bank of the variations in a whole community. As the community fed back on itself with video, certain problems would be overcome, others anticipated.

The resulting tape could then be saved and exchanged with other communities facing similar problems. Out of that could come a national knowledge grid or cultural data bank, a video resource of information about shared problems. (Red Burns and George Stoney of New York University are developing a similar process they call "modular programming" which would allow communities to access nationally circulated tapes and edit in local data relevant to whatever problem the tape was about.)

The point is that cable offers the potential of information tools far more sophisticated than one-way, localized programming. About the most radical use of cable suggested up until now has been "town meetings of the air" which would let viewers feed back electronically on certain issues. But as an interactive mode that's restricted essentially to the grammar of meetings, not the plasticity of information space.

Essentially any of the strategies and tactics suggested in this Manual are applicable to cable, especially those listed in the chapter "Community Video."

With Guerrilla Television, you should guard against relating to cable as a high production medium. In other words, innovate with it. Make it a sort of cybernetic happening rather than a conceptual testing ground.

This means, most of all, avoiding the production

techniques and mystique of broadcast-TV. Don't do imitation broadcast-TV shows.

Most important of all, don't limit access by encumbering yourself with heavy, complex video hardware.

Porta-Paks are all you need for basic production. If they are not now compatible with your local cable system it's not an inherent technological flaw, it's because necessary money isn't being spent to make them compatible.

In fact, there is evidence of Porta-Paks being used successfully and directly over cable. Paul Ryan did it in Newburgh, New York. His brother Ken Ryan has done it in Ringwood, New Jersey. Media Access Center has transmitted half-inch tape in San Carlos, California. And New York City stations now have public access channels using Porta-Paks made tape.

Moreover, keep the F.C.C. under scrutiny so that they don't set artificial technical standards, as they've done with broadcast-TV, that limit television hardware to expensive machinery.

Generally people don't mind a little imperfection in their TV pictures if they're getting programming that speaks to their information needs.

Discriminating against a high access technology is plain censorship. Besides some cable owners and especially manufacturers, there may be some unions which object to Porta-Paks being used because they're so easy to operate and thus don't require apprenticeships and artificial job scarcity.

That too may be another battle which has to be fought, but it can be carried on using Guerrilla Television. We were once thrown out of Ottinger's campaign headquarters for using Porta-Paks.

It was the union which objected to our presence. They had, they said, gone to the trouble of setting up lights and we were "featherbedding" on their labor. We offered to let them turn the lights off, but they were adamant in not allowing "mobile equipment on the floor."

The Ottinger people, frightened liberals, supported the union man, who wouldn't quite allow as how he was practicing censorship.

We have tape of it because we kept our camera running.

Not everyone has a sophisticated enough media consciousness to know the consequences of technological decisions like discriminating against Porta-Paks, but it's a struggle which will have to be fought if America is ever to have truly democratic television.

Fortunately, citizens' groups are being formed and an organizational effort is starting. Don't wait for them to come to you, either the organizers or your cable station. Anticipate them with Guerrilla Television.

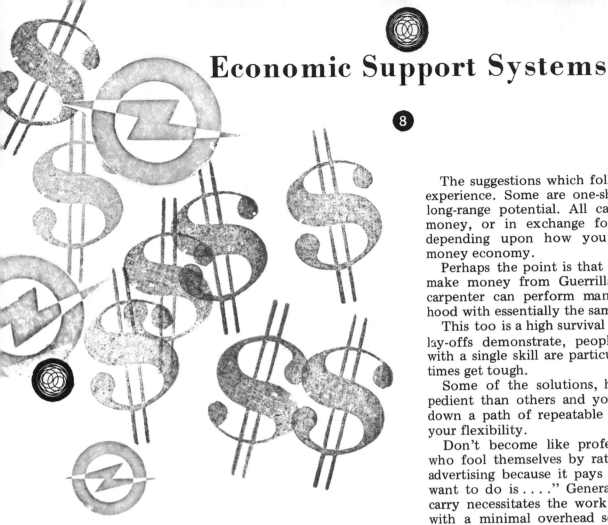

Economic Support Systems

8

The suggestions which follow are from our own experience. Some are one-shot deals, others have long-range potential. All can be done either for money, or in exchange for goods and services, depending upon how you relate to a straight money economy.

Perhaps the point is that there's no one way to make money from Guerrilla Television, just as a carpenter can perform many tasks for his livelihood with essentially the same skills.

This too is a high survival mode for, as industrial lay-offs demonstrate, people too closely aligned with a single skill are particularly vulnerable when times get tough.

Some of the solutions, however, are more expedient than others and you shouldn't be misled down a path of repeatable successes if that limits your flexibility.

Don't become like professional photographers who fool themselves by rationalizing: "I only do advertising because it pays the rent. What I really want to do is . . . ." Generally the overhead they carry necessitates the work they do. Try to work with a minimal overhead so it doesn't become a monkey on your back like the heavy video hardware that the broadcasting networks own.

BERYL KOROT

Too much energy of social change in this country over the past decade has depended on charity with little thought to regenerative sources of income. While most alternate economic schema confront this problem, they do it *in vitro*: they tell us where we are, and where we could be, but not how to get from here to there.

Perhaps the major problem of Guerrilla Television at this point is that it has no permanent economic support system simply because the distribution technologies are not yet widely available. Cable television is but a patchwork across Media-America. Not enough homes have videocassette players.

Film, on the other hand, is established. There are movie theaters for feature-length productions, rental libraries and institutional and home movie projectors for more specialized films. But those distribution media discriminate against a high variety of film production.

The economic support problem of Guerrilla Television, however, isn't to set out a whole alternate support system as an immutable product, but to arrive at one (or many) through process. In other words, try a number of different ways, some *ad hoc*, some continuous. Getting there is all the fun.

In our lean months at Raindance we had to spend most of our time hustling to pay the rent instead of doing videotapes because we were paying more per month than we should have been.

If you don't have a source of regenerative income then you're forced to live and work in monthly time frames on immediate projects rather

Fig. 6-2. A school official addressing the entire student body without requiring them to leave their classrooms.

than extrapolate your energies out into the future.

To do Guerrilla Television you have to worry about two stages: how to tool up, and how to support yourself once you have.

Getting equipment is clearly the first hurdle. Once you've gotten what you need, you require less.

Moreover, most Guerrilla Television tactics are meant to fit into existing social systems, not to create new ones from scratch. Thus, you align yourself with an ongoing support system in some cases rather than require a whole new one. In other words, since you're not going to drop everything you're doing to make tape, you can still depend, in part, on whatever other sources of income you might have had.

On the other hand, that may re-inforce the problem rather than enhance a solution. I certainly wouldn't want to go back to any of my old (newspaper) jobs to keep myself alive to do videotapes. So the best strategy is two-fold: do *ad hoc* video hustles in the context of a developing total support system.

VIDEO TOOL-UP

Schools

The problem with schools, especially universities, is that the best students don't go there anymore, because as total learning situations the social atmosphere is anachronistic. If you're as smart as you think you are, you're into total systems and understand that the university structure is only a partial one.

On the other hand, schools do have hardware and money.

Our experience is that a lot of video hardware is locked up at universities and secondary schools. Sometimes it's just a matter of locating the key because there is no bureaucrat deliberately holding things back, just a bureaucracy which obfuscates resources.

If this is not the case at your school, then make up a specific project. Anything, as long as it's specific. The university is pre-eminently concerned with product. The notion of access to equipment just to experience it as process is generally alien to the university sensibility. But cater to that. Just say you're going to tape a ghetto or something.

Better yet, get some research money. Schools relate to papers and you can usually find a pro-

BROWN UNIVERSITY
PROVIDENCE 12. RHODE ISLAND

October 18, 1957

Mr. Ira J. Schneider
Brown University

Dear Mr. Schneider:

I have just talked with Coach Watmough regarding your swimming test. He tells me that you took a test with fins. Since you attended 39 Elementary Swimming classes last year, you are to attempt the test, without fins, and regardless of the distance you go, your requirement will be considered as passed.

Sincerely,

John M. Heffernan

John M. Heffernan
Director, Physical Education

JMH:H

fessor who wants some research done and can pay for it. Just convince him that video, not print, is the best way.

Finally, remember that you are the customer of the university, not vice-versa. If you went into a department store and they *told* you what you could buy you'd either go to another store or demand what you wanted.

As long as you're the one paying to go to school, access to resources should be your decision, not theirs. If you think money is being mis-budgeted, organize a tuition strike. Find ten or twenty people to coalesce around a project and have them withhold say 10 or 20 percent of their tuition to spend on what you want. But if you can do that, then you don't need the university at all, do you?

A MODEL PROPOSAL

SANTA CRUZ COMMUNITY SERVICE TELEVISION PROJECT

Table of Contents:

-- Introduction - Philosophy

-- Methods of Direct Community Involvement

-- Generalizations of Content

-- Statement of Standards

-- Budget Considerations and Projected Output

GENERAL INTRODUCTION

A non-profit corporation, which will be a legal entity by January 15, 1971, is being created to produce television videotape in Santa Cruz for the purpose of intra-community communication. The impetus for this project is generated by pronouncements by the Federal Communications Commission which have established a policy that compels all community cable systems with over 3,500 subscribers to begin their own programming of local community origination as of April 1, 1971. This programming may be financed by local paid advertising. The goal of the F.C.C. rule and the Santa Cruz Community Service Television Project is to develop a greater awareness by the community of its own potentials and problems.

Most of the larger cable companies, including Pacific Teleprompter (17,000 subscribers,) are building studios in response to the ruling. This is a good development, but unfortunately it leaves a vacuum which S.C.C.S.T.P. hopes to fill. A studio situation is a form well suited to talk shows, news programs and interviews, but because of weight (140 Lb VTR) and equipment complexity problems, it is difficult to get videotape recording equipment out into the community where the action is and action is the essence of the medium.

For instance, it would be rather difficult to protray the dynamic inter-relationship between the land and sea ecologies of the Monterey Bay Area without showing the physical environment that we are talking about. This is where portable equipment pays for itself many times over. A 21-pound video-tape recorder and camera (battery operated) could be taken out in a boat, carried down a narrow cliff, basically go wherever the cameraman does and provide a complete sound and picture record of what he experienced. This porta-pak is small and unobtrusive enough to capture experience not as a performance, but as an occuring reality.

It is becoming increasingly important for us to know not only what we think but also what we do. For instance, a program on what the average family does that pollutes the local environment and what that family can do to reduce its pollution output, would be of enormous value.

The necessary hardware (cameras, videotape recorders, etc.) is being assembled along with a group of Santa Cruz people who possess the necessary technical and creative expertise to produce and teach others to produce quality community programming. A videotape workshop will be set up by these people to educate the community in the techniques and some of the possible beneficial uses of the medium.

Budgetary needs will be met by paid advertising of local businesses during S.C.C.S.T.P. air-time which would be purchased by the corporation from the local cable company. Prior to April 1, 1971, community financial support will be needed to purchase equipment and pay expenses. The money could be paid into a business trust fund from which it could be withdrawn only for certain specified reasons. This money would be paid back once the corporation was financially self-sustaining (refer to Appendix B.) Once the equipment is secured and expenses are being paid, the community can avail itself completely of this service.

PHILOSOPHY

The Santa Cruz Community Service Television Project (S.C.C.S.T.P.) has as its goal the opening up of whole new areas of intra-community communications utilizing the medium of T.V. As the format of T.V. content moves away from network stereotypes of what a program should look like, the humanistic potentiality of T.V. experiences becomes limitless.

Videotape experiences can be designed to rise above the level of stereotyping and rhetoric. A point can be reached where people will dwell on similarities of goals and mutual interests rather than dwelling on differences that lead to polarization and defending points of view. For example, both the left and right of the political spectrum agree on the need for local control of community affairs. This is common ground where differing political philosophies can come together to work for improvement of the community.

Ecological concern cuts across all boundaries. Rather than standing on opposite sides of the street yelling at one another, all people in the community can be unified around ecological activity.

The video productions will communicate the idea that as members of the community we all have to deal with this given situation regardless of our role or status. We all have a stake in community improvement.

Beyond passive participation in viewing community television, the community will be actively involved in the production of the videotapes. The beauty of this medium is that production brings all types of people together - young, old, black, etc. - cooperating in an activity of mutual interest. When people complete the tape, they invariably look back on the communion that developed between themselves during the activity.

When people work toward the goal of communicating a problem or situation to others, they learn more about the positive and negative aspects of the community. In order to communicate the reality, one examines more critically and develops greater awareness.

Community re-appraised by members of the community can be a positive, contructive impetus for social change. The individuals in the community are opened up to what they can do personally and immediately to improve the community.

METHODS OF DIRECT COMMUNITY INVOLVEMENT IN SCCSTP

1) A Media and T.V. Production Workshop will be created by the corporation open to the entire community. The workshop participants will be taught the hardware and software knowledge necessary to create their own videotape production. People from various service organizations, for example, could then produce their own message to be shown on the cable station.

There are many myths about T.V. production that will be overcome in this workshop. To produce a quality tape, one does not require a B.A. in electronics, ten years of production experience, or expensive hardware. We have taught 7th grade public school children in a few hours how to operate the equipment and produce interesting pieces of communication.

2) An equipment access center will be established where anyone can come and rent, for a nominal fee, portable taping equipment to produce a message they wish aired to the community.

3) A tape library and viewing area will be created for the public use possible at the Santa Cruz Public Library. Every tape produced by S.C.C.S.T.P. will be available and indexed. A playback machine will be available to the interested party.

4) Information on the coming week's programming will be published in the local news media. All new tapes will be shown at two different air-times during the week for the viewer's convenience.

GENERALIZATIONS ABOUT PROGRAMMING CONTENT

The videotape productions will as closely as possible approximate the given reality. Network documentaries rely heavily on narration that spoon-feeds pre-digested abstractions of what the viewer should be experiencing in a poorly pedantic manner. We want our viewers to draw from the experience what is most relevant to their own experiential background.

The community tapes will aim towards the alienation of no one. It is our hope that anyone who participates in community television will leave the experience with positive feelings. The viewer will be placed in a situation where he can learn about the social, cultural, political and human aspects of the community of which he is a part.

Content will be no problem because every member of the community has some message, service or expertise that he would like to share with others. In very short order the community will be contacting the production people with ideas and requests.

There are some content ideas, however, that have particular interest to the production team and give insight into what can be done:

a) Ecology - A videotape ecological history of the Monterey Bay Area. The program would visualize changes caused by man altering the bay environment. The bay's present state and projected future would also be demonstrated.

b) The Santa Cruz Migration - New people to the area would be given an opportunity to share their experiences of how they have adjusted. They might wish to relieve their frustrations as a newcomer by voicing them. New people to the community would be immediately involved in a community project. An excellent welcoming device that might shed fresh insights on our community.

c) Tape Weekly Board of Supervisors Meeting - Renew the town meeting concept.

d) A Day in the Life of a Santa Cruz Peace Officer - No editing to package an image - a natural flow with audio being street sounds, car radio, dialogue, etc., employing small battery operated taping unit. The viewer can begin to empathize with the policeman as another human being.

e) Create a Volunteer Community Renovation Service - Advertise with time-lapse visual of a house changing in appearance before your eyes. The Huckelberry Finn "let's all help whitewash the fence" feeling could be created in the community.

f) A Disaster Relief Service - If a fire occurs and a family is on the street, visualize the problem on T.V. and ask for community assistance (e.g., a place to stay overnight.)

g) Community Cultural Notes.

h) Two-Minute Community Service Messages - The spot would be totally visual - showing the service the organization performs and who to contact for further information.

For example, Goodwill Industries Ad (employing the technique of time-lapse photography.) Goodwill people removing an old stove from the garage of a person who has no use for it. Cut to scene of stove being repaired and renewed. And final scene of yound couple on a limited budget happy to fulfill their cooking needs for $25. Visual at end states who to contact if you have items that can be re-cycled.

i) Public School Student Videotape Productions - These can improve community relations between schools and local taxpayers. We already have several secondary schools working on this project under our guidance. The tapes will also provide insight into how the students view their school environment. This approach is better than protest marches and building take-overs.

j) Hundreds of Humanitarian Organizations wanting to inform the rest of the community of their role to gain increased support and serve more people.

k) Re-Cycling - People are becoming more aware of the fact that things can be shared - a communal activity. Visualize church-related junk shops, used book stores, newspaper collections, garage sales, etc., pointing out that much more re-cycling can occur if people know how to go about it.

STATEMENT OF STANDARDS

The Santa Cruz Community Service Television Project will strive to maintain a high level of integrity and honesty. No image or information "packaging" will occur and we will aim at alienating no one.

All people appearing on videotape will be shown the tape on which they appear. If they find it objectionable, their part will be destroyed. Should they view their role with favor, they will be asked to sign a release form.

Hopefully, everyone who participates in S.C.C.S.T.P. willleave the experience with good feelings. Instead of finger-pointing and name-calling, we will get down to the task of improving our community.

Advertisers will be given certain pre-conditions of good taste under which they must operate if they sponsor S.C.C.S.T.P. programming.

Our basic and most important interest is to help the people of the Santa Cruz community.

PRODUCTION BUDGET

The following budget fives a breakdown of the costs involved in producing a programming output of six individual half-hour community videotapes a week. The production crew will also devote one and a half hours per week to the media and T.V. workshop open to people of the community. One recognizes the relative low cost of the production of community input as compared to average local T.V. station cost. The average in-station production is $1,000 per minute of finished tapes.

Weekly Budget:

Production Crew Salaries	$1,000
Expenses (gasoline, etc.)	250
Magnetic Tape (consumed)	160
	$1,410 per week
Cost to create library viewing center (hardware)	$800
Cost to create equipment access center (hardware)	$1,300

Note: Hourly cost of cable television air-time at present unknown.

APPENDIX B-1

22 December, 1970

EQUIPMENT PURCHASE AGREEMENT BETWEEN NATIONAL VIDEO SYSTEMS AND THE SANTA CRUZ COMMUNITY SERVICE TELEVISION PROJECT

The Santa Cruz Community Service Television Project, through its representative Herbert Allan Frederiksen, agrees to purchase the videotaping hardware as listed on the following page of this agreement.

The purchase price to be paid by the Santa Cruz Community Television Project is $2,993.

The terms of payment are 10% down ($299) paid this day, 22 December, 1970.

The balance of the purchase price ($2,694) will be paid within a 60-day period from the date of this agreement.

_____   _____
Herbert Allan Frederiksen,   Authorized agent for National
Representative of S.C.C.S.T.P.   Video Systems, Inc.

_____
WITNESS

APPENDIX B-2

RE: VIDEOTAPE HARDWARE BEING PURCHASED FROM NATIONAL VIDEO SYSTEMS, INC.

(Note: All equipment Panasonic except where specified.)

QUANTITY	MODEL NO.	DESCRIPTION	SERIAL NO.
1	an 69V	19" VTR Monitor	FX 0210059
1	TR 20	13" TV Monitor	68622143
1	WV 350P	Camera	11838E
1	WV 220P	Camera	12489E
1	WV 600P	Special Effects Generator	10667B
1	M 67	Shure Microphone Mixer	
2		Tripods with Heads	
1	Marshal	15-75 mm rear-operated zoom lens	230720
1	NV u75	R.F. Converter	
1	NVB 31	Video Amplifier	
1	WV 7063P	Triple CCTV Monitor Unit	
1	LQM 10A	Colortran 10" mini-lite	B13216
1	NV 3020	½" Video Tape Recorder	

TOTAL PURCHASE PRICE:	$2,850.00	
TAX:	143.00	
	$2,993.00	

ADDITIONAL EQUIPMENT NEEDS NECESSARY TO MEET ALL PRODUCTION REQUIREMENTS OF S.C.C.S.T.P.:

1	940-H I	Monochrome Video Processor	$1,390.00
2	Sony	Portable ½" Video Recorders	2,400.00
		PLUS ABOVE EQUIPMENT	2,993.00
			$6,783.00

Conceived by:

Johnny Videotape and Friends

For further information contact:

Herbert Allan Frederiksen
465 Ninth Ave., Santa Cruz
408 - 476 - 0657

Grants

Be careful here (see the chapter "Context" in the Meta-Manual). To depend on foundations for operating expenses, other than seed money, is always to be less than a total system.

Jerry Kindred, an educational consultant, says that foundation money costs him 30 percent of his time just in the hustling; and Dick Raymond, director of Portola Institute, recommends that you budget one current dollar for every two you'll need to raise in fundraising. Understandably, both men are working to set up alternate economic support systems which will be entirely self-sustaining and regenerative enough to fund long-term research and development.

Foundations are best used for tool-up money, because hardware is something they can see and thus confirm that their money is going for something tangible. The more process-oriented a project, the harder it is to measure or even secure funds for.

So, no matter what you're going to do with the equipment, be very specific when you write a proposal and choose something that is both exotic and obvious, but not threatening.

Generally there will be one person who is your liaison at the foundation and foundation bureaucrats tend to be on ego trips. You need to convince them that what you're doing is different, but not threatening to the foundation board which must approve your proposal.

The more specific your proposal the easier it is for your liaison to present it to his board. Moreover, the foundation can't accuse you of ripping it off when they know in advance specifically what you're going to do. Just keep from limiting your flexibility by not telling them everything.

Sell your car

We know people who've done this just to buy a Porta-Pak.

Or instead of liquidating assets, take out a loan. Not all banks are hip enough to accept a Porta-Pak as its own collateral, however. We once had a bank loan officer refuse us because the equipment was too lightweight and portable for him. He actually told us that he needed heavy, stationary TV cameras to let us use hardware as collateral.

ONGOING SUPPORT

Once you've got equipment there are ways to make money. This means that if you've bought it on credit it's possible to hustle the money for payments, and then some.

We've found that if you get a little exposure (*i.e.*, people actually seeing you with equipment, not "publicity"), especially in a small community, people will start telling you what you can do for them. There are an awful lot of needs out there. Some of them are:

— Equipment rental. Commercial video hardware houses get up to $75 a day for Porta-Paks. Do that twenty times and you've made back your money.

The drawback is that that price includes your maintenance and repairs so that if a machine breaks, it's your liability, not that of the person who rents it.

— School projects. Public schools have a few dollars available for something more exotic than what they normally give the kids. Also, many schools feel they should be getting into videotape. If the school doesn't have the money, but there is either student and/or teacher interest (always work directly with students, whenever possible) then you can use the legitimacy of their interest as a base to approach third party funding sources like merchants, foundations, or cultural institutions. (See "Kids making their own TV" in the chapter "You Are Information.")

Your fee should be no less than a teacher's salary, *per diem*, and probably more. Also get expenses.

— Consultancies. Any time you talk to people they should pay you money because your information is your currency. If you consult a doctor, for example, it costs you, so why should *you* give it away for nothing?

On the other hand, one purpose of consultancies is to subsidize free gigs for the people who really need your skills. So be flexible, not charitable.

As for credentials, you'll find that just having equipment makes you an expert.

But beware of publicity. Unless you think you can in some way benefit by exposure, tell the press to fuck off.

The reason is you're both in the information business. When I worked at **Time** magazine we expected everyone to talk to us for free. Yet I was

on salary and the magazine was using stories to sell advertising and make money. In other words, unless the exposure had definite value to the subjects of our stories, we were getting something for nothing.

But ultimately, you can't get something for nothing. That's what ecology is all about.

— A video theater (see the chapter "Community Video"). A theater can be a source of steady, if not absolutely lucrative, income. It's also a good way to handle people who want to take up your time.

We get people who come by, unannounced, and want to talk. We just tell them to come back on Saturday night when we're having our show. Then for a simple admission charge (usually $2) they get to see tape and we'll talk to them after the show. When people have something real to exchange, both you and they will know it.

Remember, though, that a theater is an ambitious venture. You've got to look out for plant and equipment maintenance, advertising your shows, getting tapes, collecting money, and

customer liability. But it's an excellent base of your own to work from.

— Show your tapes at benefits, in homes, at parties, etc., anywhere people will pay money to have you provide information for their benefit.

— Run encounter groups.

— Do mini-documentaries for groups that want to hustle money themselves and figure that a videotape is a better hustle than a print plea.

— Make pornographic tapes. You'll find a market.

— Videotape weddings and bar mitzvahs. Then get permission to sell copies as entertainment.

— Make survival tapes of whatever skills you or your group have. Then sell the tapes or exchange them (see the chapter "Networking: Videocassettes and Cable Television").

■ Alternate television is not, as you picture it, a strident confrontation of life-styles, but an attempt to guarantee exposure to all views and especially to avoid inaccuracies in conventional media by letting people generate information about themselves independent of unseen controls.

The picture you label as illustrative of our concept of information is not of us, not our studio, nor representative of any of the material we videotape.

Raindance Corp.
MICHAEL SHAMBERG
IRA SCHNEIDER
New York City

· √ NEWSWEEK *regrets the mistake.*

— Cater to narcissism. Rich businessmen and entertainers will pay for private documentaries of themselves.

— Networking strategies. The two support technologies which can provide a long-term, relatively modular source of return are cable television and videocassettes.

With videocassettes you will have fewer options than with cable because the cassette network structure will trend toward being national. With cable you can negotiate local options.

While this is all covered in "Networking," remember that CATV is the natural outlet for what you're doing.

VIDEO FREE AMERICA

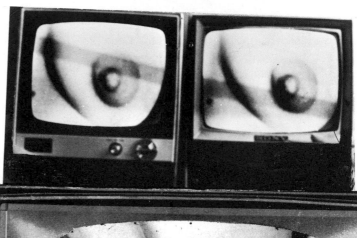

NATURAL TELEVISION

Verité Videotapes
by People's Video Theatre
Raindance, Videofreex
& others
SAT. FEB. 6th
8 & 10 PM $2.
24 E. 22nd St.   982-5566

ALTERNATE TELEVISION

Process Videotapes
by People's Video Theatre
Raindance, Videofreex
& others
SAT. JAN. 23rd
8 & 10 PM $2.
24 E. 22nd St.   982-5566

NO LIE TELEVISION

NATURAL Videotapes
by People's Video Theatre
Raindance, Videofreex
& others
SAT. FEB. 13th
8 & 10 PM $2.
24 E. 22nd St.   982-5566

PROCESS TELEVISION

Everchanging Videotapes
by Peoples Video Theater,
Raindance, VideoFreex,
& others
SAT JAN 16th
8 & 10 PM $2.
24 E 22 St.   982-5566

the Butler did it

A wild and complete
expose of 5 lovely, lonely
girls who turn the Butler
over and on!!!
Send 25¢ for brochure

Cybernetic Strategies and Services

9. Cybernetic Strategies and Services

Survival isn't just a real-time thing. Species which regenerate and succeed through evolution keep options open which may have no immediate application.

Sociologist Philip Slater suggests that the reason we don't completely off the Black Panthers, or ship hippies to concentration camps, is because there's an ecohomeostatic balance in cultures which keeps around seemingly "excess baggage" just in case.

Gregory Bateson calls this "a budget of flexibility." He defines flexibility as "uncommitted potentiality for change."* When a culture's flexibility is totally eaten up, then it has no options for the future.

Industry calls this process "R&D" (for research and development). Generally, when times are tough there's less money available for R&D, although that's when it's needed most.

In an information-based culture like our own, survival options manifest themselves as a potential for regenerative knowledge, not as fallow land and unused machinery.

*From **Restructuring the Ecology of a Great City**, by Gregory Bateson, **Radical Software #3**, Spring 1971.

Any structures which facilitate the regeneration of-knowledge are survival-oriented. Those which stifle it threaten us as a species.

Currently, both the straight media and formal schools are low-option systems. Rather than create new knowledge, they trend toward re-confirming the past. The media do this through continually tracking after the same type of information. Universities manifest entropy by relegating all knowledge to their social context, mistaking it for a high-variety system when it is but *one* of many. Only now are universities abandoning behavioral codes (*e.g.*, dormitory "hours," rules against students cohabitating) but the very design and placement of the buildings works against any true change. The best students have already moved away, to communes or city collectives.

As I've said in the Meta-Manual, the quest for alternate life styles and involvement isn't a philosophical difference with America's sanctioned institutions, it's a biological one. Most of this country's formal structures have very little flexibility.

The whole context of Guerrilla Television means enhancing flexibility. On a personal level it can be used as a system of strategies for (information) environmental survival. At the cultural level, it's a way to re-direct resources and energy.

Essentially the Guerrilla Television model is a cybernetic one. It incorporates change and mutates itself as ongoing process rather than being a quest for a repeatable product.

True cybernetic strategies are ways to extrapolate that bias to the cultural level, to embody them in the fabric of America life. If, for example, money which once went into funding the past (via outworn models) can be re-channeled in cybernetic projects, then that is a social decision to operate in one mode at the expense of the other, a palpable change.

In America, even when times are tough, there is usually some money available for social experimentation. I call this "survival money."

Generally survival money lives at the edge of knowledge-based institutions: process-oriented businesses, some schools, and certain departments of government, not to mention foundations.

The problem with accessing that money is legitimacy. Two years ago nobody knew about us, yet we were into our most original and creative period. Most of the ideas in this book are that old. Thus, we're being paid to live in our past just like a rock

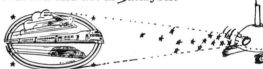

group which can't play new stuff because audiences want to hear past hits.

The true practitioners of Guerrilla Television or whatever the next mode is I probably don't even know about. Thus, they probably lack the resources they need to really get it off. (However, that may also be the reason for their creativity.)

We need a system which allows creative energy to access survival money without sacrificing its dynamics. Right now school districts are experimenting with a so-called "voucher system."

Under this plan parents get vouchers to pay for their kids' education and can spend them not just in the schools, but also on private educational firms. The problem, however, is that of legitimacy. Vouchers are good only at pre-determined places so that if a kid wanted to hang out on a commune or apprentice himself to a craftsman he would have no support.

At Raindance, for example, energetic but undirected students periodically come up to see us. We have to ask them to leave after a while because we have work to do to pay the rent. But if they could pay us as a survival center, then we could both profit. A kid could hang around and help and learn. We could pay our rent.

Of course, we have none of the certified legitimacy of schools. But we don't want it. We don't want to be defined by others.

Thus the question is how do we support survival centers? How can they support themselves?

Probably the **Whole Earth Catalog** and Truck Store has been most successful at solving this problem and funding itself. It supposedly generated over $400,000 in profits to be applied to another experiment (the catalog discontinued itself at the height of its success so as not to eat up its budget of flexibility).

Portola Institute, the non-profit umbrella for **Whole Earth,** is working through strategies for regenerative financing outside of foundations and straight venture capital.

My expertise is in information, not money, economics. Toward that end I would like to see a system using what I call "information stamps."

Essentially they would be purchased with the survival money now being wasted on schools. They would be given directly to the students who would have absolute control over how they're spent. (An interim stage, to guarantee the acquisition of data base skills like reading, math, writing, etc. might be to withhold some of that money from autonomous control and funnel it into more formal teaching situations. But even then the choice of which mandatory institution would be up to the individual.)

Thus, if a kid wanted to become a heroin addict by trading his information stamps for junk, that's his choice. If he wanted to lay out in Mexico on a beach, that's also a possibility. It's just that the information stamps wouldn't last forever. At an explicit point students would know they have to earn their own. That would encourage them to acquire skills, and enter into an apprenticeship system where alternate cultural experiments like communes and media collectives could then receive underwriting.

So that's a plan. But that system is not imminent. There are, however, *ad hoc* cybernetic strategies which are immediately possible.

Their purpose is two-fold. First, they provide financial support for people generating survival knowledge. Secondly they allow people to avail themselves of alternate services, cybernetic ones which enhance feedback and act as catalysts.

A MEDIA BUS

This is an ideal cybernetic service. You go out to communities and do videotaping; they pay you to come. Ideally you plug-in to existing hardware and show people how to use what they already have.

In smaller communities especially, people are hungry for novelty. With a media bus you can entertain them while you're there, and then turn them on enough for them to want to set up their own media system after you've left.

The Videofreex are doing this in New York State. They have several vans and VW micro-buses outfitted for sleeping and taping. Inside, besides a bed, is a full-blown video system for live-mixing and later editing. Thus, they can tape a community and leave an edited copy behind. (The underwriting, however, is coming from a grant from the New York State Council on the Arts. The true test of the efficacy of media buses will be when and if the grant money runs out.)

Ant Farm in California makes it a habit to go on the road for a while every year. (At other times they operate what they call a "truck stop" to service other nomads and support themselves.) They either try to line up gigs in advance, or hustle them on the road.

In each location these cybernetic nomads set up and live in their own inflatables. Thus, the true university is no longer anchored to one place, but free to move in all directions to enhance indigenous cybernetic activity. ➤➤ ➤ ➤ ➤

S VIDEO PRINT
DE-LINEATOR

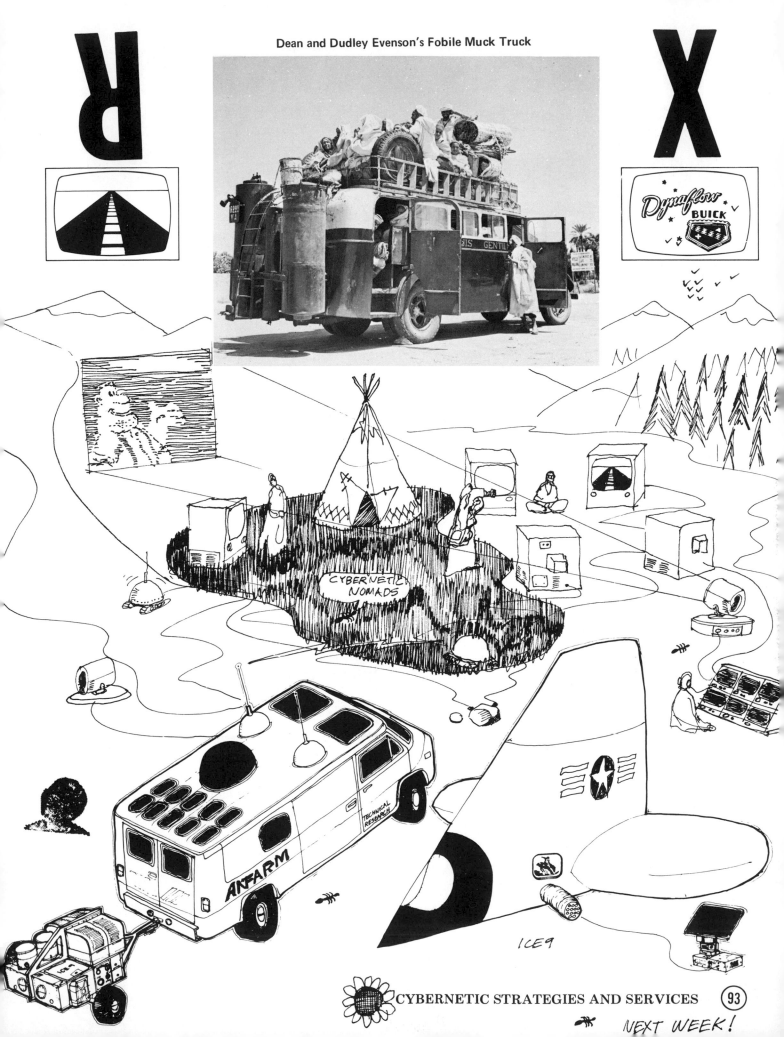

Dean and Dudley Evenson's Fobile Muck Truck

CYBERNETIC NOMADS

NEXT WEEK!

TRUCKIN' UNIVERSITY

EDUCATIONAL DIVISION OF SOUTHCOAST, INC.   A FULLY ACCREDITED LIFESTYLE INSTITUTION

Mr. Goodbar sez:
(HE'S NOT SHITTIN' AROUND!)

Get A Good AMERICAN EDUCATION

WHILE YOU STILL GOT A CHANCE!!

BEN HOLMES

—GET SET FOR THE FUTURE!!
—STEP UP TO GOOD PAY!!

NO.	INPUT/TOOLS	PROCESS	OUTPUT
27	SCHOOL BUS MODIFIED FOR MOBILE EDUCATIONAL STIMULI AND LIFE SUPPORT VEHICLE FOR THE FACILITATORS/CREW.	 SEE CAPABILITY OBJECTIVE AND KEEP READING.	
14 41	STAGE III MEDIA VAN WITH LATEST HIGH OUTPUT ACCESSORIES AND LIFE SUPPORT FACILITIES FOR CREW.	AIN'T YOU NEVER HEARD ABOUT THE SOUTHCOAST MYTH OR HOTFOOT OR ANYTHING? KEEP READING.	
5	PORTABLE VIDEOTAPE CAMERA AND PORTABLE TAPE TRAP UNIT.	SPECIAL EFFECTS DECK FOR EDITING, ALTERING, OR MONITERING VIDEO INPUT. VEHICLE 1.	VIDEO BLOWUP PROJECTOR FOR LARGE SCALE DISPLAYS AND ENVIRONMENTAL SPECIAL EFFECTS.
10 01	SUPER 8 AND 16 MM FILM CAMERAS FOR RESPONSE DOCUMENTATION.	FACTORY FILM PROCESSING. EDITING AND SPLICING FACILITIES. VEHICLE 1.	PROJECTORS AND VARIOUS SURFACES FOR PROJECTION... PLASTIC, PARACHUTES, BUILDINGS.
3	35 MM STILL CAMERAS WITH COMPLETE SET OF LENS, FILTERS, AND ACCESSORIES.	FACTORY COLOR FILM PROCESSING. MOBILE DARKROOM FACILITIES IN VEHICLE 1.	SLIDE PROJECTORS MAY BE MODIFIED FOR HANDHELD PORTABILITY AND MAY BE PROJECTED ON A VARIETY OF SURFACES.
18 81	LINEAR MEDIA MACHINES SUCH AS TYPEWRITERS AND DRAWING EQUIPMENT PLUS CREDIT CARD FOR LOCAL REPRODUCTION FACILITIES.	ACCUMULATION AND ORGANIZATION OF MATERIAL FOR PRINTING. PUBLICATION PREPARATION FACILITIES TO BE IN VEHICLE 1.	LINEAR MEDIA IS USEFUL AS HISTORICAL TESTIMONY OF A CHANGING REALITY. MAKES GOOD ASS WIPES TOO...TRY THIS ONE.
9 6	PHONOGRAPH, AM/FM TUNER, TAPE RECORDERS, MICROPHONES, AMPLIFIER OUTPUTS FED INTO CENTRAL AUDIO CONTROL PANEL.	CENTRAL AUDIO CONTROL PANEL SELECTS AND MODULATES OUTPUT FROM VARIOUS INPUTS.	ASSORTMENT OF HIGH PERFORMANCE SPEAKER SYSTEMS FOR USE AS ENVIRONMENTAL MODULATORS.
35	COMMUNICATION BETWEEN INDIVIDUALS IN DISRELATED SPECIALTY FIELDS.	ACCESS TO AND USE OF LOCALIZED, NON-MOBILE TECHNOLOGY AND RESOURCES.	PROTOTYPICAL TECHNOLOGICAL AIDS TO ENVIRONMENTAL CONTROL, EDUCATION, CULTURE, ETC.

 THANKS AND A TIP OF THE HAT TO CATFISH!

A CULTURAL DATA BANK

The old university uses books to store its knowledge and demands that you write one (*i.e.*, a thesis) to graduate.

A more viable storage medium in Media-America is videotape. Once you've set up that structure you don't need a centralized location, especially because the best tapes are made *on* location, not in a dormitory room.

Gradually a cultural data bank of these tapes is being built up. Indexes or catalogs (see the chapter "Networking: Videocassettes and Cable Television") are available. Thus, people can begin to support themselves by doing videotape.

The ultimate stage may be a national knowledge grid structure analagous to the electrical power system. When New York, for example, can't meet its electricity demands, it can borrow power from the Mid- or Far West because the lines are interconnected.

Similarly, if we had a national information accessing system via computers, specific requests for skills and data could be serviced without geographical considerations. Feeding into this system would be grassroots television producers.

A specific example of tape for this system is Ira Schneider's idea of a "catalog of life styles." Most students get no real knowledge of what different jobs are like. But they do know that choosing one over another means a choice in life style. There are very few freaks, if any, for example, selling life insurance.

Ira's idea is that we compile a catalog of verité documentaries on as many vocations as possible. Then this catalog is accessible to students debating what they want to study. (Forget about "majoring" in anything. What a term.)

Similarly, middle-class families should have access to documentaries of communes made by the communes themselves. And vice-versa.

This trend is already developing in an intermixture of ways. One is the use of communications technology to sculpt one's own life-style, *i.e.*, the recognition that information tools are a prerequisite for freedom in an electronic culture, which is what this book is about.

Another is fluid networks. Perhaps the major shortcoming of communes is their vulnerability to transience. You just can't keep it together if people are physically moving through or moving out all the time. Yet, that option is more and more in keeping with a cybernetic culture.

Thus, we need a system of floating networks where people can access each other through information media to play-out new self options without being bound to a long-term, geographical commitment. We do this now, of course, with phone calls and letters to different sets of friends. By extending this to the cultural level and sanctioning it as a growth experience, we could orchestrate change for individual life stages.

Only information technology will be able to handle these transactions. Experiments in Art and Technology (EAT) has such a system called Eatex which computerizes artists and their skills and how they'd be willing to help others. People in need of experience can punch into the computer net and come away with names of people who can help them. The free schools movement in California is doing a similar thing with a high school apprenticeship program where students can access professionals and learn their skills.

The worst of this trend is embodied by services like computer dating. We might even see those blown-up to a profit-making "life style service" controlled by a big corporation which will offer to plug people into whole new scenes, tell them how to dress (and sell it to them), what to say, and so on.

The best fluid networks will function organically. They will be seeded by people passionately interested in what they are doing who want to share it with others. These networks will contract and expand through natural cultural contours rather than forced advertising images.

Access to products is gradually being subsumed by access to process. In other words, fewer and fewer people are concerned about having basic amenities like food, clothing, and housing, much less luxuries like automobiles, because we are moving more quickly (but not totally, I agree) into a post-scarcity economy.

As that happens, true flexibility flips into the realm of process. That means access to information and the means to regenerate it yourself. If those two options do not become available, then America will be the first culture to perish from misunderstanding the consequences of media-ecology.

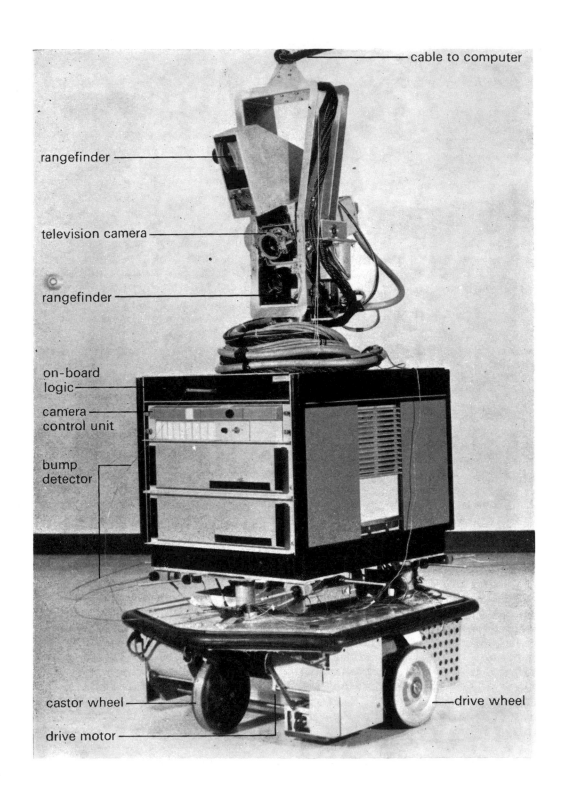

cable to computer

rangefinder

television camera

rangefinder

on-board logic

camera control unit

bump detector

castor wheel

drive motor

drive wheel

Resources

VIDEOTAPE

The following videotapes are representative of the early days of Guerrilla Television (☆ indicates specific reference in this book). However, the lists mention but a fraction of what has been done and are weighted toward tapes we (Raindance) have made because they are the ones with which I am most familiar.

Raindance

☆ ST. MARKS TAPES. Street interviews and scene on New York's Lower East Side made in the summer of 1968.

☆ ANTIOCH TAPES. Pioneering work in natural video living done by Frank Gillette and Ira Schneider in early 1969.

☆ ALTAMONT TAPES. Guerrilla Television takes you to a rock festival.

☆ URBAN ECOLOGY TAPES. Environmental and people scenes recorded in Manhattan.

☆ THE RAYS. Five stoned people on a beach in California.

☆ SUPERMARKET. An American institution revealed. Candid interview with one of its managers.

☆ POST-KENT STATE DEMONSTRATION IN WASHINGTON, D.C. A $168 documentary (including videotape and roundtrip air fare from New York).

☆ THE PARTY THE PRESIDENT THREW FOR THE ASTRONAUTS. A recording made from broadcast television ("off-air," as we say).

☆ CLINTON PROJECT TAPES. Kids make their own TV.

TENDER IS THE TAPE II. A composite edit by Paul Ryan from the Raindance data bank which demonstrates the unique capabilities of videotape.

KNOWLEDGE AND INDUSTRY III. A composite edit by Ira Schneider illustrating the differences between broadcast and Guerrilla Television.

MEDIA PRIMER FIRST DRAFT. A similar composite edit by myself including Buckley Headquarters on election night (☆), Al Scheflen and Vic Gioscia discussing the body language of broadcast-TV announcers (☆), Nicholas Johnson at the Raindance loft, and more.

☆ CUKO. Street theater with a wino. Tends toward exploitation of subject.

SAN FRANCISCO OIL SLICK. What happened when a tanker ran aground.

People's Video Theater

WOMEN'S LIB MARCH. Brilliant edit. Compare this to broadcast-TV.

YOUNG LORDS OCCUPY CHURCH. Protest against jail killing of one of their own.

INDIANS THANKSGIVING. PVT was there when a group of Indians demonstrated at Plymouth Rock (in 1970) and talked with them afterward. Indian consciousness.

HANDS. You'll never see this on broadcast-TV.

SUPERMARKET. Interviews by women of other women about how they like shopping.

Videofreex

☆ SUBJECT TO CHANGE. The videotapes that the Videofreex made for and with CBS money.

☆ FRED HAMPTON INTERVIEW. Powerful interview with the late Black Panther leader.

FERRO CEMENT. A survival tape.

FUCK FLICK. The making of a pornographic movie.

CURTIS' ABORTION. No nonsense information about a recently legalized public service.

☆ MONEY. Freex meet cops while shooting on the street.

Media Access Center

VIDEO POTATOES. A composite of California video.

LIVING SPACE COMPOSITE #3. A look at alternate living structures like domes and inflatables.

☆ JUVENILE JUSTICE. Tape by high school kids about high school kids and the law in California.

Global Village

ABBIE HOFFMAN INTERVIEW. A tape made by John Reilly and Ira Schneider (when he was still with Global Village). Probably the best Abbie has ever come across on TV. A masterpiece of its genre.

JOHN AND SAMANTHA MAKING LOVE. As far as I know the very first exploitation tape.

Ant Farm

WILD SEED. Ant farm media nomads truckin thru the Videosphere.

ADVANCE OF SPRING. Roadside armadillo visits Palo Soleri, R. B. Fuller, & Professor Longhair.

SAM'S CAFE. Documentation of mail art media inversion by Marc Terri & Dave.

PRIME TIME. You are there time capsule journey thru American College Campuses 1971.

WORLD'S LONGEST BRIDGE. 27 mile video crossing of Lake Pontchartrain Causeway in Louisiana.

Addresses: I have deliberately not listed addresses for two reasons. The first is that some of these groups may have moved by the time the book comes out.

But more important, your having to make an effort to locate this information guarantees a more than casual interest and spares the above from fatuous requests.

PRINT

Following are ways to get access to useful print resources.

Books

General bibliographies are less useful than specific ones. However, only a few portions of this book are keyed off specific readings and they are credited. Most of the ideas here are a synergy of what I've read and my own experience. However, just general reading trends toward the university way of acquiring knowledge.

So I'll make you a deal. If you have a specific situation for which you need information (and this book has not answered your questions), or if you want more information on a specific point in **Guerrilla Television,** then write me and I'll feed back what I can.

Publications

Whole Earth Catalog. 558 Santa Cruz, Menlo Park, California 94025. By now (publication of this book) **Whole Earth** has ceased to be, although its mail order service lives on. Moreover, back issues will be useful for years. If you have read this book but are unfamiliar with the **Catalog** I strongly urge you to get a copy.

Radical Software. 8 E 12th Street, New York, N.Y. 10003. This is our own publication which began as a source of alternate television information and is evolving into a resource for technology and information tools in general.

As for other listings, same offer described under **Books** applies here.

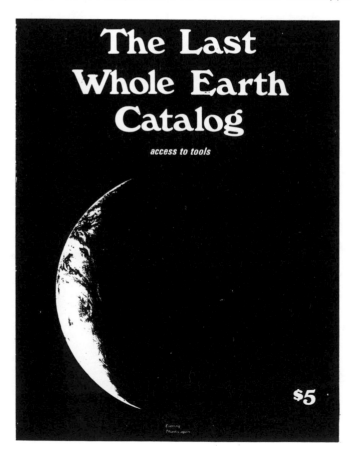

SONY

PANASONIC CONCORD

SHIBADEN APÉCO

SPECS		
model: AV3400 ◄		
tape width: 1/2"		
playback: yes		
viewfinder: CRT (cathode ray tube)		
weight: 6 lbs. plus 19 lbs. equals 25 lbs. (camera plus deck)		
battery life/recharging time: 50 minutes/8 hrs. recording time: 30 mins		
tape speed: 7 1/2 ips (inches per second)		
camera/deck resolution: 400/300 lines		
signal/noise ratio: greater than 40 dB		
interlace: 2:1		
temperature range: 32-104 degrees		
standard lens: 16-64mm zoom f/2 C-mount		
microphone: built-in		
price: $1,495		

SPECS	
NV 3080 (Panasonic) ◄	VTR 450 T (Concord) ◄
1/2"	
no	
CRT	
5.5 lbs. plus 15 lbs. equals 20.5 lbs.	
80 mins/10 hrs. 30 mins	
7 1/2 ips	
525/260 lines	
greater than 40 dB	
?	
40-104 degrees	
15-75mm zoom f/2.1 C-mount	
auxilliary	
$1,250	

SPECS	
SV-707U (Shibaden)	TELE-TAPE BATTERY PAK (Apeco
1/2"	
no	
CRT	
6 lbs. plus 15 lbs. equals 21 lbs.	
?/5 hrs	
20 mins	
7 1/2 ips	
525/300 lines	
40 dB	
2:1	
?	
14-70mm zoom f/2 C-mount	
auxilliary	
$1,395	

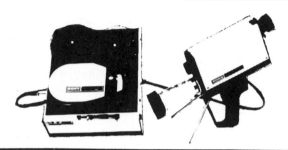
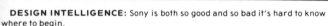

DESIGN INTELLIGENCE: Sony is both so good and so bad it's hard to know where to begin.

In its favor, Sony was the first manufacturer to come out with Porta-Paks (their CV series) and the first to make a quantum leap with a second generation: a toally self-contained system with record and playback (the CV series was record only) through **any** TV set (using an RF converter which changes the output signal to a broadcast one. $39.95 extra). The Sony also has playback through the monitor eyepiece for on-the-scene previewing which can really turn on people you've just taped and help build an instant trust.

On the downside, the Sony camera and deck seem to have been designed by engineers **in vitro,** not for people **in vivo.** The camera is overly heavy and not well-weighted. The pack is very cumbersome and can only be carried in a leather case which obscures visibility to the tape path so you can't run quick checks on whether or not its running right. (see **Experience**)

Sony has its own form of mini-plugs for microphones which are incompatible with other manufacturers'. While the cable from the camera to the deck is a stanard ten-pin, that is the only way to get in and out in video mode. Normal systems accept coax plugs which are universally compatible. In essence, this all means that technological support is not inherent in the system and any options, like editing with a Porta-Pak, require special modifications.

SUPPORT: The rest of the Sony half-inch line (AV series) is pretty good. With a modified cable (see back) you can have editing on a compact table deck (AV3600) for only $650 more. The pack itself has audio dubbing and still-framing.

Next up in the Sony half-inch line is their color deck (AV5000) although cameras are not yet compact or cheap enough, and certainly not portable. The final piece is a full-blown editing deck (AV3650) but they've only been around a month or so and we've not gotten feedback yet. First reports are that it's pretty good except for sound which has the usual two second lag on cuts.

As for dealers, Sony is everywhere. Service will always vary individually, of course, but in terms of getting parts we'd count on Sony everywhere in the U.S.

EXPERIENCE: The Sony Porta-Pak has many, many faults, partly because they rushed it into production which meant that those of us first owners have been doing the necessary field testing. Here are the results:

Mechanically the problems are many. The control levers break off after not much use (they're made of plastic). You'll never see anyone who uses their Porta-Pak a lot who has a camera eyepiece intact. They break off like crazy because of poor hinges which can't take much stress. Finally, it's very easy for the tape to become wrapped around the capstan inside because the reels don't hang onto the spindles. This means that you think you're recording and open the deck up later to find a useless spaghetti of videotape. If you're moving around a lot this can really be a problem.

Electronically, the system could be better overall but there doesn't seem to be any recurring problem.

DESIGN INTELLIGENCE: The configuration of the record deck (more rectangular than Sony) makes for a better weighting and the camera has a detachable microphone instead of a hardwired one. But there is no playback mode on the Porta-Pak itself (tape must be transferred to another deck).

Panasonic actually makes two models of Porta-Pak although they are visually the same. The one not listed here is on their old standard which had a high recording speed (12 ips) and therefore a low recording time (14 mins) and was compatible with only Panasonic decks. Sony, on the other hand, has discontinued its old series (CV) Porta-Paks (which had no play-back) and table recorders.

SUPPORT: Panasonic has a generally good reputation, especially in its half-inch editing. But not all of its current line is Type One (the compatible) standard. As for Concord, its marketing organization is much less solid and hearsay feedback is that it's not very reliable to work with.

EXPERIENCE: Except for encounters with the Panasonic table decks, we've never used the Porta-Pak except demos at trade shows.

DESIGN INTELLIGENCE: The configuration the deck is similar to that of the Panasonic/C cord and likewise the Shibaden/Apeco has no in nal playback. Still not much of an improvemen over the Sony.

SUPPORT: Shibaden has a good reputation, m of their equipment is made for professional (although they've just been bought out by Hitac a Japanese electronics conglomerate), and th just make video hardware. As for Apeco, its an shoot of a Midwestern company whose main p duct is office copying equipment. Neither seems to have a high access marketing and s vicing system.

EXPERIENCE: None.

CRAIG

AMPEX

	SPECS	
	Instavideo ◄	
ut manual rewind	1/2"	
	yes	
	CRT	
lus 15 lbs. equals 21 lbs.	5 lbs. plus 15 lbs. equals 20 lbs.	
	?/?	
s	30 mins	
	7 1/2 ips	
	525/300 lines	
han 40 dB	?	
	2:1	
	?	
m zoom f 1.8 C-mount	4 to 1 zoom, C-mount	
ilt-in, one front, one back	built-in	
	$1,300	

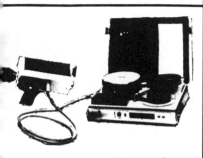

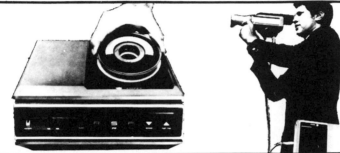

ESIGN INTELLIGENCE: The Craig has one and one sort of nicè thing about it. First, there two microphones, one front, one back. This ns that whoever is taping can also talk into the dtrack. The other thing is that the Craig has back but only with a manual rewind. This offers convenience of a total system without the extra ht that a rewind motor means. Like Sony and ex, it also has playback through the camera iece as well as any TV set.

PPORT: The Craig is not Type One standard ugh there is one model in the support line that ut it's pretty hard to find a dealer.

XPERIENCE: Except for some editing we did from Sony half-inch to Craig one-inch, which ed very well, we have none.

DESIGN INTELLIGENCE: Ah, here it is, the first total system Porta-Pak. Instavideo (it used to be called Instavision but Ampex changed it because someone else had that copyright) has all the options of the Sony and more.

This is because the pack itself sets into a more stationary (weight 6.5 lbs.) service pod. The back of the pod is a regular patchboard with standard coax and audio in-and-out jacks. (Of course, it also interfaces with a regular TV set through the antennae plugs, like the Sony). This means you don't have to hassle modifications to do editing.

The pod is upgradable with modules. Basic price is $800 for a black-and-white playback only system. For $900 you get record too (plus $400 separate for the camera, or $1,300 system total) and another $100 buys a color clip-in circuit board. (Remember that the module, not the pack, has the additional circuitry so color is not a function of the Porta-Pak per se).

The reason for all this is that Ampex (in conjunction with Toshiba, the Japanese company which will do the actual manufacturing) wanted a machine to compete with both cassettes and Porta-Paks. Thus, the tape has two play modes. One is normal recording and playback with a thirty minute tape time. In an extended mode, for prepackaged material, it will play 60 minutes.

Here's some more goodies: The tape has a plastic leader and is self-threading. You don't have to touch the tape path. There is an internal brush activated by a button for head cleaning. And a pulse code button which electronically marks your last stopping place so next time you insert the tape it will do an automatic high speed search.

You can also do electronic editing, still-framing, and slow motion (no other Porta-Pak has that). There are two sound tracks which means the option of stereo, and of course the system subscribes to Type One standard.

Finally, you can adjust tape tension (Sony has only a tracking control on its portable) and both audio and video input levels. The control levers themselves are configured like an autiotape cassettes recorder for easy control and access.

What's wrong with Instavideo? Well, the camera design is awfully hokey, sort of an old movie (or video) camera in drag.

Another major problem is that although tape is compatible with other systems, the physical reel is indigenous only to Ampex. Thus although you have the electronic capability of playing another systems tapes, you are totally restricted mechanically.

SUPPORT: Ampex has a generally bad reputation in its one- and two-inch lines. They have too many mechanical parts and down time is high.

Instavideo is their only half-inch machine and they have done a pure paranoid thing. They keep hyping it as a non-professional machine, but people are going to start producing with it. This means that come editing time to stay with Ampex you've got to go to at least a $6,000 machine (in one-inch format).

Not many people can afford that. As a result Ampex will be used for shooting, its competitors for editing support. So for every Porta-Pak they sell, Ampex will generate business for another company. Control instead of service.

EXPERIENCE: Ha! The only machine we've seen represents three prototypes travelling in America. In that form they're high Technology costing about $75,000 apiece. There simply are no production models available (Ampex claims late summer). They wouldn't even let us touch the thing at a demonstration which consisted of one vacuous model shooting another ratting her hair. They were even too paranoid to let us shoot the scene with our Sony, which they made us keep in a closet.

So, even though the thing shapes up as the next generation of Porta-Pak, a major improvement over the last, stay skeptical until you can actually feel and buy one.

AKAI

SPECS

model: VT-100

tape width: 1/4''

playback: yes

viewfinder: optical

width: 4.1 lbs. + 12.8 lbs. equals 16.9 lbs.
 (camera + deck)

battery life/recharge time: 40 mins/8 hrs
recording time: 20 mins

tape speed: 11 1/4'' ips (inches per second)

camera/deck resolution: 400/200 lines

signal/noise ratio: better than 40dB

interlace: ?

temperature range: ?

microphone: built-in

lens: 10-40 zoom f/1.8

price: $1,295

DESIGN INTELLIGENCE: The Akai has two major differences which set it apart from the other Porta-Paks. One, it uses quarter-inch tape. All the others use half-inch.

The advantage of quarter-inch videotape is that it's fabulously cheap compared to other standards. Quarter-inch is the same size as audio tape (for reel-to-reel machines) and lists for $7.95 for twenty minutes as compared to $14.95 for twenty minutes of Sony videotape. The disadvantage of quarter-inch is that it has less information storage capacity as reflected in the 200 lines resolutions of the system, the lowest of any.

The other unique feature of the Akai is that it has a small detachable monitor which clips onto the recording deck. The camera itself has an optical viewfinder which means reduced weight. Overall this means that Akai is the first system not to place a tiny TV screen between your eye and the lens in imitation of a film camera.

SUPPORT: The Akai is, of course, on its own standard. This means you are limited solely to the Akai line for back-up editing and table deck replay. As we understand it there are only two other decks in the line, one black-and-white, and one (1/4'') color.

The problem is that it's literally impossible to find an Akai dealer, at least here in the East. Roberts Corporation used to be the Akai distributor (and the machine was called Roberts) and we saw it about a year ago at an electronics show in New York.

Since then Roberts got nowhere with distribution and Akai took the rights back. Now they have an office in Los Angeles, but the only east coast representation is one man who lives in Philadelphia and it's impossible to get ahold of him. He doesn't answer his phone. So even though the machine has distinct advantages, you'd probably do best to wait until Akai gets itself together. Meanwhile we can only list it as a ''coming'' Porta-Pak.

EXPERIENCE: None, of course, except for fondling it once at that electronics show. But we have gotten correspondence from Australia and Germany where people said the system worked very well and in one case (Australia) was even broadcast.

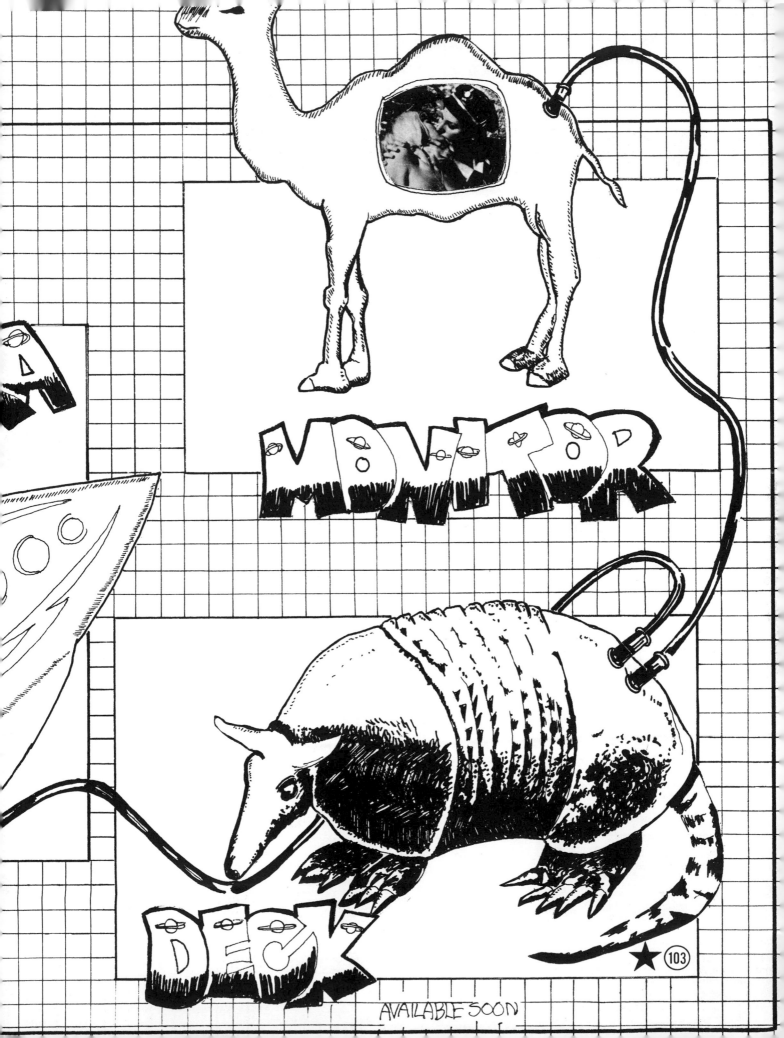

MONITOR

DECK

103

APPENDIX

WASHINGTON UNIVERSITY
ST. LOUIS, MO.

	SHAMBERG,	MICHAEL	AARON	56115
	SURNAME	FIRST NAME	SECOND NAME	NUMBER

ENTERED 9-24-62

HOME ADDRESS 1300 LAKE SHORE DRIVE, CHICAGO, ILLINOIS APT. 12C

PARENT OR GUARDIAN: MR. JACOB SHAMBERG (FATHER)
ADDRESS 1300 LAKE SHORE DRIVE, CHICAGO, ILLINOIS APT. 12C

BIRTH DATE MARCH 22, 1944   BIRTH PLACE CHICAGO, ILLINOIS

DESCRIPTIVE TITLE	DEPT.	COURSE NO.	SEM UNITS	GRADE
LIBERAL ARTS		**FALL 1965**	356-38-3335	
MODERN ART	A&A	360	2	B-
ADV WRITING FICTION	ECMP	321	3	B-
THE AMERICAN NOVEL	ELIT	355	3	C+
FUNCTIONAL FRENCH	FRCH	101	4	C-
FUNCTIONAL SPANISH	SPAN	201	4	A
PHYSICAL EDUCATION	PHED	102	1	B-
CUM.105		94	114	AV.1.0..

DESCRIPTIVE TITLE	DEPT.	COURSE NO.	SEM UNITS	GRADE
LIBERAL ARTS		**SPRING 1965**	56115	
RELIGIOUS THEMES	ELIT	367	3	C+
BOT NATURAL HISTORY	BOT	126	3	C
INTROD TO MUSIC	MUSC	102	3	B
FUNCTIONAL FRENCH	FRCH	101	4	B
PHYSICAL EDUCATION	PHED	102	1	C
CUM. 89		78	85	AV. .96 SEM.13 13 20 AV..1..

LIB ARTS SPR 64   FALL 1964   56115

LIT ENGLISH BIBLE	ELIT	365	3	C
SHAKESPEARE	ELIT	395	3	F
GENERAL BOTANY I	BOT	103	3	D
INTRO TO MUSIC	MUSC	101	3	D
FUNCTIONAL FRENCH	FRCH	101	4	F

LIBERAL ARTS		60 56 62		

LIB ARTS SPR 64   56115

MASTERPIECES OF LIT	FLIT	242	3	C-	3
GEN HISTORY OF ART	A&A	104	3	C-	3
COMP ECON ORGANIZTN	ECON	214	3	R-	6
GENERAL EARTH SCI	FSCI	102	3	R	6
GENERAL PSYCHOLOGY	PSY	206	3	C	3
		15	15		21

LIB ARTS FALL 63   56115

MASTERPIECES OF LIT	ELIT	241	3	C-	3
GEN HISTORY OF ART	A&A	103	3	C	3
GROWTH AMER ECONOMY	ECON	210	3	C+	3
GENERAL EARTH SCI	ESCI	101	3	C	3
GENERAL PSYCHOLOGY	PSY	205	3	C	3
PHYSICAL EDUCATION	PHED	101	1	F	
	45 41 41	15	15		15

ARCH SPR 63   56115

COMP & RHETORIC II	ECMP	102	3	C+	3
WESTERN CIVILIZATN	HIST	102	3	C	3
ANAL GEO&CALCULUS I	MATH	116	4	F	.4
COMPARATVE POLITICS	POLS	102	3	C	3
STUDIO WORKSHOP	ARCH	102	2	C	2
	30 26 26	15	15		15

ARCH FALL 62   56115

COMP & RHETORIC I	ECMP	101	3	C-	3
WESTERN CIVILIZATN	HIST	101	3	C+	3
ANAL GEO&CALCULUS I	MATH	116	4	F	
AMER GOVT & POL I	POLS	101	3	C+	3
INTRO TO ARCH	ARCH	101	2	C	2
	15 11 11	11			11

MITTED FROM NEW TRIER TOWNSHIP HIGH SCHOOL
WINNETKA, ILLINOIS

MITTED BY EXAMINATION   WASHINGTON U. DEGREE

	TRANCE UNITS	ENG	LAT	FR	GER	SP	HST	SOC S	ALG	GEOM	TRIG	BIOL	BOT	G SCI	CHEM	PHYS	MSC
	4½			3	2	2½	1	½	1								

IN RECOGNITION OF OUTSTANDING CONTRIBUTIONS
TO THE VIDEO TAPE RECORDING INDUSTRY, AND
FOR THE INNOVATION OF COMMUNICATION
TECHNIQUES THROUGH THE USE OF SONY® VIDEOCORDERS®

Michael Shamberg

IS HEREBY NAMED

AN INNOVATOR

IN TESTIMONY WHEREOF, WITNESS
MY SIGNATURE THIS 24 DAY OF Aug
19 70.

John J. McDonnell

INNOVATOR CLUB ADMINISTRATOR
SONY CORPORATION OF AMERICA
VIDEO PRODUCTS

(105)

אַרְבֶּה · זְאֵם

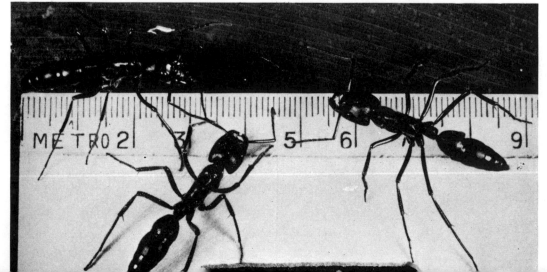

9283